AF270737

What's Next for Mom and Dad's House?

Vol. 1
Essays on the Single-Family Housing
Type and Its Future

Martino Tattara and Federico Zanfi eds.

Spector Books

Contents

INTRODUCTION

IMAGINARIES AND DISCOURSES

CHANGE

INTRODUCTION

Preface

This book was conceived and realized in the context of the joint research program "Investigating the Transformation Potential of the Existing Single-Family Housing Stock," coordinated by Martino Tattara and Federico Zanfi at Politecnico di Milano, Italy, and KU Leuven, Belgium.[1] The goal of this research program is to create a research network where scholars and designers can discuss strategies and projects for retrofitting the extensive, low-density residential territories that were built in the second half of the twentieth century for the middle-class, and update the existing single-family housing stock for the demographic, environmental, economic, and social challenges of today. Within this framework, the international symposium "What Next with Mom's and Dad's House? The Transformation Potential of the Single-Family House," was held at Politecnico di Milano in September 2022. The present volume—which will be followed by a second volume featuring prototypes for the transformation of Italian single-family homes—is the result of this event. Several of the essays collected here were originally presented at the symposium, while others were commissioned specifically for this book, given the expertise of authors and the proximity of their research to its focus.

Taken together, the essays speculate on the transformative potential of the single-family house in different ways, which are represented by the volume's different sections. The introductory essay by Tattara and Zanfi presents a schematic overview of historical projects that have addressed suburbanized residential territories and the single-family housing type as specific objects of redesign, to highlight both critical issues that need to be overcome and opportunities to be explored further.

Essays in the "Imaginaries and Discourses" section explore the varied, multilayered, and influential role played by popular models and institutional discourses in shaping housing preferences during the second half of the twentieth century, which allows us to grasp the distance between those models and discourses and the current evolution of lifestyles, consumption models, and household patterns. In her essay, Hilde Heynen

1. The program was initially funded by the Department of Architecture and Urban Studies at Politecnico di Milano through the 2021 Visiting Research Program, of which Martino Tattara was a recipient between 2021 and 2023.

reconstructs the different historical periods of criticism of the single-family house in Flanders, with concerns ranging between aesthetics and ecology, affordability and welfare. Michela Bassanelli's contribution investigates the Italian *villetta* housing type by studying Italian women's magazines, bringing to light the aspirations that determined the rise of the single-family housing type in Italy from the 1960s. Rebecca Carrai discusses the influence of IKEA, through its catalog images, in promoting and supporting a suburban and single-family housing lifestyle.

The "Change" section contains four contributions centered on case studies from the United States and Europe that describe processes of adapting single-family houses that were triggered by shifting demographic and socio-economic dynamics such as housing insecurity, demographic change, energy policies, and tourism flows. The essays highlight the different impacts of these dynamics on the housing stock and raise design and policy questions at different scales. Through stories of remodeling houses in Portland, Oregon, Kateryna Malaia discusses how single-family houses are transforming—expanding to fit extended families or converting into multiple units for rent—to face housing insecurity in the United States. Lawrence C. Davis investigates how new residents from abroad are increasingly adapting the existing environments in the historically white postwar suburbs of parts of California. Céline Drozd and Daniel Siret describe the struggles faced by the inhabitants of Claire Cité—a residential area built between 1949 and 1954 in Rezé, Nantes, France, according to the principles of the "castor movement"—to adapt their buildings to current energy requirements while preserving their historical values. Ester Gisbert Alemany investigates the transformations of single-family housing in Mediterranean Spain through a series of "house biographies," shedding insight into how people are imagining concrete responses to tourism and economic crises by transforming their living spaces.

The "Perspectives" section presents strategies and perspectives for intervention. In particular, it focuses on re-parceling strategies, the transformation of accessory housing spaces to accommodate new working activities, and micro-interventions to upgrade obsolete housing typologies to present-day standards. Gabriel Cuéllar and Athar Mufreh share some design strategies based on cadastral adjustment and architectural reconfiguration to take on the spatial-legal infrastructure of the minimum size ordinance—a zoning device that governs the lots and buildings of North American single-family suburbs—to construct more affordable and differentiated buildings. Rory Hyde looks into Melbourne's single-family suburban housing, examining how the traditional "slack spaces" adjacent to single-family homes have been crucial in supporting such informal and diverse activities as small businesses, retail, restaurants, childcare, and co-working, and thus has the potential to support new forms of entrepreneurship, care, local energy generation, social services, and multigenerational living. Fabio Lepratto discusses the process of taking over a second-hand home in Northern Italy and making someone else's house one's own by proposing a series of micro-interventions into typical elements such as fences, side buffer spaces, entrance doors, windows, stairways, porches, pitched roofs, and front or back lawns.

Overall, the authors aim to consolidate reuse and adaptation strategies for single-family homes in ways that make this vast and heterogeneous heritage more consistent with social change, more sustainable, and more lasting. In this sense, this book should not be understood as a point of arrival, but on the contrary, as an initial step toward the development of other projects, further moments of discussion and sharing, and new academic, professional, and policymaking networks.

In conclusions, the editors would like to express their gratitude to the Politecnico di Milano and the Faculty of Architecture at KU Leuven for their support of this publication. Special thanks go to Alexander Eisenschmidt, Enrico Formato, and Maja Lorbek for their valuable feedback during the peer-review process. We are also deeply grateful to Massimo Bricocoli and Alberto Geuna for their assistance with the September 2022 conference, Chiara Merlini for her insightful discussions in the early stages of this project, Sandro Armanda and Jana Metzger for their contributions during the editorial phase.

Redesigning the Single-Family House: A Critical Look Back, and a Glance Forward

Martino Tattara and Federico Zanfi

Driven by an agenda that increasingly emphasizes circularity, recycling, and reuse, architectural culture has recently turned its attention to the adaptation and transformation of existing structures, thereby broadening the category of heritage that traditionally defined what was worth preserving or converting and what was not.[1] Following a number of critically acclaimed projects,[2] attention in the field of housing has largely become focused on either the upgrade of the large-scale postwar housing stock,[3] or the transformation of former production and service facilities (such as factories, equipment, office buildings) into living and working spaces.[4] Both illustrate the emergence of "adaptive reuse," a term coined to identify the process of reusing an existing building for a purpose other than that for which it was originally built. Despite this widening scope of adaptive reuse practices, which target a multiplicity of anonymous built structures that would traditionally be considered to lack any explicit heritage value, the transformation of the single-family house remains surprisingly underrepresented in this debate.[5] An urgent and wide cultural, social, and economic issue, the single-family house is the architectural embodiment of specific planning policies, real-estate values, forms of property, and cultural tenets. As such, it seems to represent an ossified object, about which it is difficult to imagine a transformation—despite the urgency to do so.[6]

The single-family house is one of the most ubiquitous and quantitatively most successful residential types ever built. It has also long attracted critical attention, mostly from two perspectives. Firstly, rather than the single architectural object, many observers have criticized the forms of scattered, low-density settlements that this type of housing entails: what has commonly been identified as urban sprawl. Secondly, some

1. Christoph Grafe and Tim Rieniets, "All Buildings Are Beautiful; Stop Building More: The Winding Road Toward a Culture of Conversion," *ARCH+* 252 (2023): pp. 28–37.

2. We are primarily referring to the work of the French office Lacaton & Vassal in collaboration with Frédéric Druot. Their approach to the refurbishment of the French "grands ensembles" was first developed as a broader national project described in the book *Plus* and later tested in a series of projects, including the renovation of the Grand Parc apartment building in Bordeaux. See Frédéric Druot, Anne Lacaton and Jean-Philippe Vassal, *Plus: La vivienda colectiva, Territorio de excepción* (Barcelona: Editorial GG, 2007).

3. See, for instance: Maren Harnack, Natalie Heger, and Matthias Brunne, eds., *Adaptive Re-Use: Strategies for Post-War Modernist Housing* (Berlin: Jovis, 2020); Spartaco Paris and Roberto Bianchi, *Ri-abitare il Moderno: Il Progetto per il Rinnovo dell'housing* (Macerata: Quodlibet, 2018); Elli Mosayebi and Michael Kraus, *The Renewal of Dwelling: European Housing Construction 1945–1975* (Zurich: Triest Verlag, 2023); and Andrea Migotto and Martino Tattara, eds., *Contested Legacies: Critical Perspectives on Postwar Modern Housing* (Leuven: Leuven University Press, 2023).

4. See Hilde T. Remøy and Theo J.M van der Voordt, "A New Life: Conversion of Vacant Office Buildings into Housing," *Facilities* 25, no. 3/4 (2007): 88–103; Hilde T. Remøy and Theo J.M van

der Voordt, "Adaptive Reuse of Office Buildings into Housing: Opportunities and Risks," *Building Research and Information: the International Journal of Research, Development and Demonstration* 42, no. 3 (2014): 381–390; Martina Baum and Kees Christiaanse, eds., *City as Loft: Adaptive Reuse as a Resource for Sustainable Urban Development* (Zurich: gta Verlag, 2012); Bryony Roberts, ed., *Tabula Plena: Forms of Urban Preservation* (Zurich: Lars Müller, 2016).

5. Amongst the few recent research initiatives in the European context focused on the transformation of the single-family housing type, worth mentioning is the work of the research group *Krise und Transformation des Eigenheims* at the Bauhaus-Universität Weimar, accessed September 16, 2024, https://forschungswerkstatt-eigenheim.de/en.

6. Renee Chow, "Ossified Dwelling: Or Why Contemporary Suburban Housing Can't Change," *Places* 17, no. 2 (2005): pp. 54–57.

7. Robert Bruegmann, "Part 2 – The diagnosis: three campaigns against sprawl," in *Sprawl: A Compact History* (Chicago: University of Chicago Press, 2005), pp. 115–66.

8. On this, see the seminal work of John Archer, *Architecture and Suburbia: From English Villa to American Dream House, 1690–2000* (Minneapolis: University of Minnesota Press, 2005).

9. Dolores Hayden, "Home, mom, and apple pie," in *Redesigning the American Dream: The Future of Housing, Work, and Family Life* (1984; New York: Norton, 2002), pp. 63–95.

voices have scrutinized the specific architectural forms, spatial organization, and rigidly defined patterns of housing, work, and family life that such a housing type implies.

Regarding the first critical perspective, American historian Robert Bruegmann has meticulously reconstructed the rise of anti-sprawl arguments. He identifies three main periods: the first, which was directed against the sprawling British cities of the 1920s and 1930s; the second, which responded to postwar suburban developments in the United States; and the third, which started in the 1970s, focused on recent developments at the periphery of American urban areas and became a wider movement that exceeded disciplinary debate.[7] While each of these campaigns is characterized by a specific set of arguments in response to specific historical conditions, they were all generally triggered by a mix of concerns: aesthetic (monotonous and bare urbanization), economic (higher infrastructure costs and loss of agricultural land), social (alienation and social segregation), and environmental (pollution, car dependency, energy consumption).

The second critical perspective has focused more specifically on the single-family house as a normatively defined architectural object, one that is deeply ingrained in notions of private property, privacy, and selfhood.[8] Dolores Hayden has put forward a gender critique, recalling how such a type was designed in the United States for a white nuclear family with a father as breadwinner and mother as housewife, thus demanding a "great deal of unpaid female labor."[9] Hayden stresses how the assumptions underlying such a model soon failed to meet the socio-demographic conditions of a country dominated by the two-earner family, and where the single-parent family represents the fastest-growing type. Although her argument refers to the United States at the turn of the millennium, many of her points are even more relevant today, especially in light of transformed living and working patterns (a trend exacerbated by the recent pandemic), changing demographics, and a gradual shift in housing preferences linked to the awareness of the costs embedded in such housing models.

In recent decades, in order to address some of these aesthetic, economic, environmental, and societal issues, several studies, publications, exhibitions, and projects have addressed suburbanized residential territories and the single-family housing type as specific objects of redesign.[10] Here, we wish to trace a brief genealogy of this little-explored tradition of architectural (and urban) design, delimiting our gaze in two ways. First, we will primarily look at examples from the last five decades, when—starting with the oil crisis of the 1970s—the single-family house and extensive forms of urbanization started to be discussed as a heavily resource-consuming architectural and urban type. Second, we will look specifically at transformation projects developed by designers that have openly tackled existing suburban territories and single-family houses by studying and engaging with their spatial and architectural dimensions.

Each of these projects, which are often unbuilt and exist only on paper as the result of curatorial initiatives, is concerned with a specific site and condition. Although our geographic scope is quite broad—every project that concerns urban sprawl or territories of extensive urbanization is deemed relevant—we are particularly interested in those design schemes that investigate and challenge the main architectural tenets of suburban architecture: the type of the single-family house; the notion of privacy and family living; and the suburban settlement with its labyrinthine and cul-de-sac urban structure. We are also interested in those projects that have focused on one or more of the very finite architectural elements through which suburban living has been architecturally defined (fence, garden, typological organization of the living unit, garage, etc.).

Such an approach is particularly relevant as we consider suburban living today not only as a spatial, environmental, and urban issue, but also as the manifestation—through deeply ingrained architectural forms—of a powerful cultural and political project that has defined the idea of the middle class all over the world.[11] This cultural and political project must be reconsidered both in light of rapidly changing economic, demographic, and social conditions, as well as, more broadly, in light of the emerging agenda of socio-ecological transition. By reflecting on the last five decades of discussion on the single-family house, we have identified five main design "trajectories." In the following, we aim to elucidate the themes, as well as historical, geographic, and cultural frameworks, for each trajectory through a limited number of case studies. The aim of each section is not to offer a complete historical overview, but to discuss the premises,

10. In this respect, one can think of three works by Avi Friedman, who was particularly interested in exploring ways to build houses that could accommodate progressive change over the years: *The Grow Home* (Montreal: McGill-Queen's University Press, 2001); *Planning the New Suburbia: Flexibility by Design* (Vancouver: UBC Press, 2002); and *The Adaptable House: Designing Homes for Change* (New York: McGraw-Hill, 2002).

11. Robert A. Beauregard, *When America Became Suburban* (Minneapolis, MN: University of Minnesota Press, 2006), 123-132. See also Gaia Caramellino and Federico Zanfi, eds., *Post-war Middle-Class Housing. Models, Construction and Change* (Bern: Peter Lang, 2015).

12. For an overview of these efforts, see Giovanna Borasi and Mirko Zardini, eds., *Sorry, Out of Gas: Architecture's Response to the 1973 Oil Crisis* (Montreal: Canadian Centre for Architecture, 2007).

13. Borasi and Zardini, *Sorry, Out of Gas,* pp. 216–19.

14. Richard G. Stein, *Architecture and Energy* (Garden City, NY: Anchor Press, 1977).

ambitions, and limits of each of these design traditions, in order to reflect on their relation to today's condition and the current debate on the single-family house.

Five Design Trajectories

Eco-Renovation and Self-Sufficiency

The first trajectory encompasses projects that respond to the single-family house as a type and its settlement form as particularly energy inefficient. Starting from the 1970s, a series of projects attempted to imagine how to make single-family houses more self-sufficient, anticipating by several decades what today is considered common practice such as coating the building envelope with an insulating layer, placing solar panels on the roof, switching to non-fossil-fuel energy sources for heating and cooling, using electric batteries, and recycling water and waste.[12] However, only a few of these projects directly looked at sprawl as an existing urban condition made of highly energy-demanding and (indirectly) polluting houses that needed to be retrofitted.

Among these was the 1975 Ouroboros project by a group of architecture students at the University of Minnesota working under the direction of Dennis R. Holloway. Their project was developed as two prototypes. The first, Ouroboros South, was a new energy-efficient building whose shape made the best possible use of climate and natural sources of energy. The second, Ouroboros East, proposed to retrofit an existing suburban house in Saint Paul, Minnesota, into a passive house. [Fig. 1] The prototypes revealed how a typical wood-framed house of an American suburb could be transformed into an energy-efficient house by applying solar collectors as well as rethinking the house's waste, recycling, heating, and venting systems while restructuring the interior.[13] The focus of these efforts, however, remained limited to improving energy performance, without proposing alternatives to the urban form of the house or any social and economic reprogramming essential to promote a better and more efficient use of space.

In the last fifteen years, surging environmental and climate crises have sparked a renewed interest in low-carbon architecture and the concept of "grey energy" in buildings, which was originally discussed in the 1970s.[14] While this has resulted in greater awareness of the amount of energy that is embedded in building materials and the need for their reuse, Paola Viganò and her research group have expanded this understanding to the urban scale. She suggests the need for recycling and reusing every built environment, since "infrastructures, buildings, existing cities and territories can be looked at as reservoirs of fossil energy."[15]

From the Boston metropolitan area to the central Veneto region, the implications of such a hypothesis have been tested in a series of design investigations exploring the capacity of diffuse urbanized territories "to adapt to and to integrate the transition towards a sustainable future."[16] Starting from the reinterpretation of both natural and anthropic traces, these proposals reveal the potential of the "Horizontal Metropolis," a term used to indicate territories where metropolitan centers coexist with dispersed settlements in a horizontal relation. [Fig. 2] Contrary to the approach exemplified by the University of Minnesota students, which anticipated what today has become common practice in many European countries, Viganò's approach explicates the difficulties—and, despite these, the urgency—of implementing large-scale plans among traditionally distant fields such as spatial planning, energy and industrial production, transport policies, and water management.

Molecular Densification

The second trajectory includes proposals that respond to the low density of urban sprawl, which results in wasted space, high infrastructural costs per capita, and a general lack of urbanity. These projects have consequently embraced the logics and devised strategies for densifying the urban fabric. They have been developed on different scales and at different levels of governance, ranging from strategic plans and policies to building codes and architecture projects.

Some proposals aim to densify urban fabrics "softly" through the construction of detached or semi-detached accessory housing units—also known as garden suits or granny flats—within original single-family housing lots, thereby extending the livable area of a house and potentially also increasing the number of dwellings. Among these are initiatives developed in cities in the United States that, over the past half century, have developed specific zonings and building codes

15. Paola Viganò, "Elements for a Theory of the City as Renewable Resource: A Design and Research Programme," in *Recycling City: Lifecycles, Embodied Energy, Inclusion*, eds. Lorenzo Fabian, Emanuel Giannotti, and Paola Viganò (Pordenone: Giavedoni, 2012), pp. 15–16.

16. Chiara Cavalieri and Paola Viganò, eds., *The Horizontal Metropolis: A Radical Project* (Zurich: Park Books, 2019), p. 17.

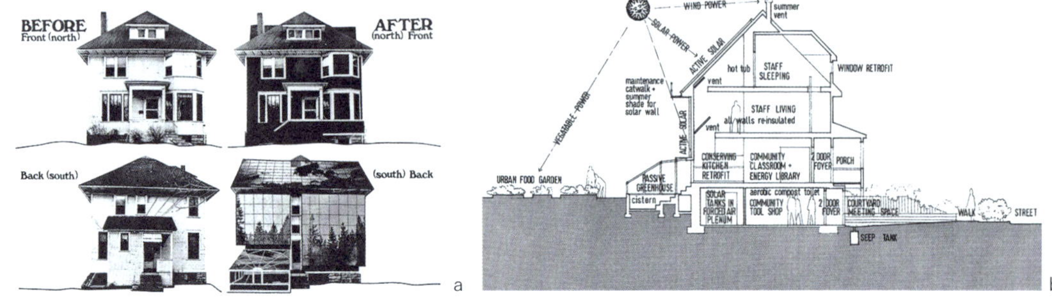

Fig. 1 — Project Ouroboros East, St. Paul, Minnesota, 1975. Project for an energy-retrofitted house in the Upper Midwest developed by a group of students working under the direction of Prof. Dennis R. Holloway at the College of Architecture & Landscape Architecture, University of Minnesota. a. "before and after" photo collage; b. building section; c. scale model.

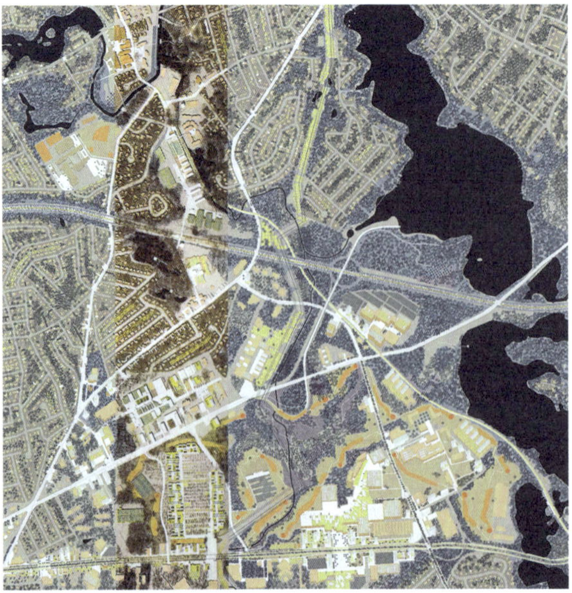

Fig. 2 — Proposal for rethinking low-density residential fabrics and commercial and industrial patterns in the western Boston metropolitan area "middle ground," 2013. Project developed by students working under the guidance of Prof. Paola Viganò and Chiara Cavalieri at the Harvard GSD.

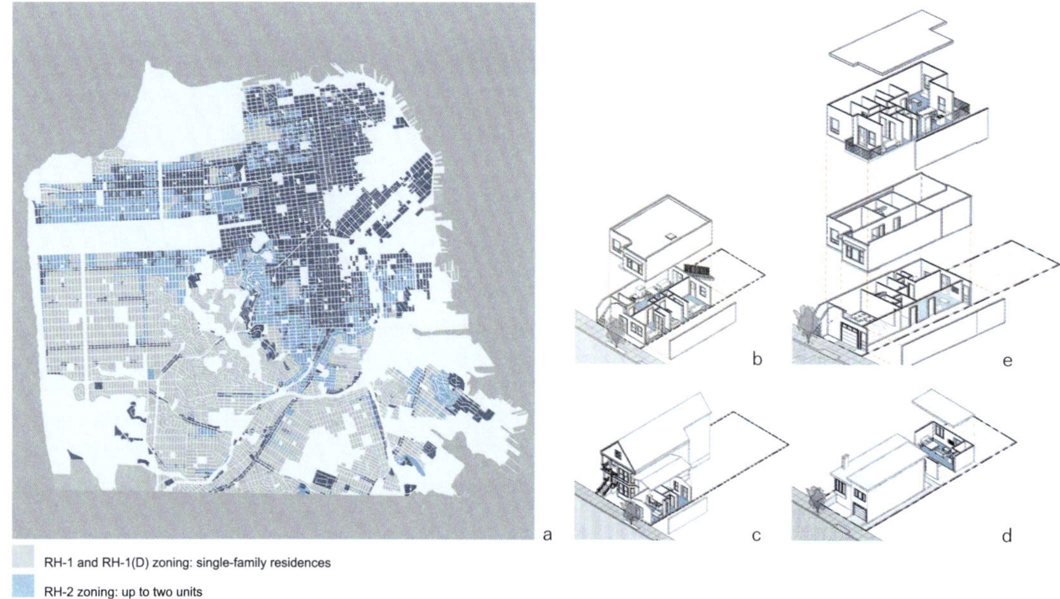

Fig. 3 — Excerpts from the San Francisco Planning Department Accessory Dwelling Unit handbook, 2018. a. residential zoning; b. prototype of a full garage conversion in a single-family house with an open ground floor; c. prototype of a full conversion of a free-standing garage; d. prototype of a new free-standing rear-yard dwelling unit; e. prototype of vertical and horizontal expansion of a single-family house.

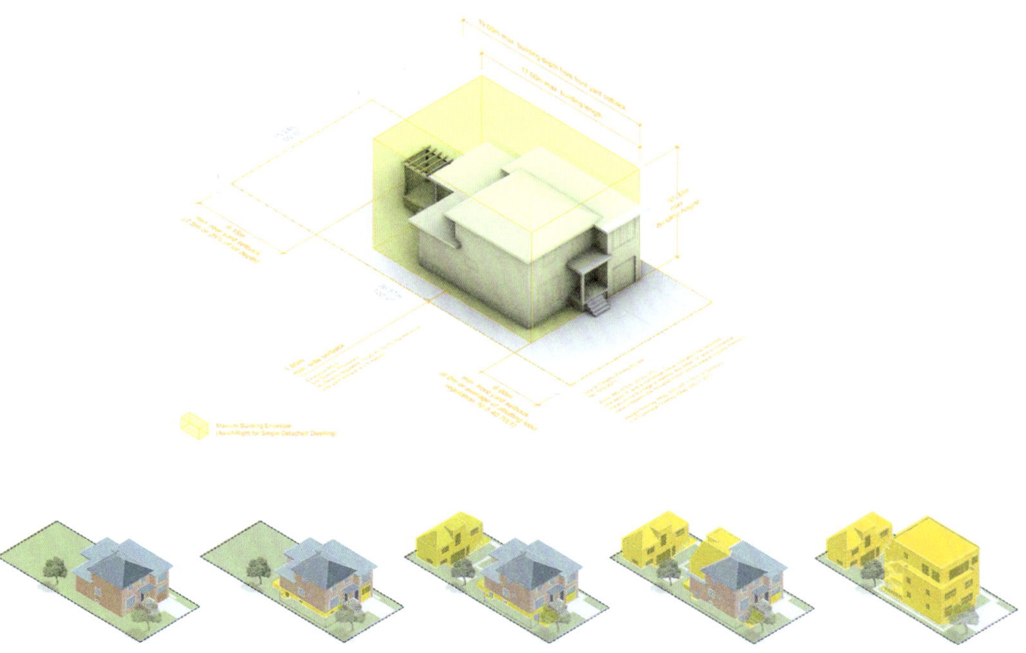

Fig. 4 — Conversion options for a postwar two-story single-family house in the Toronto metropolitan area: from a "low" intensity retrofitting (total floor area 331.6 square meters/3,569.3 square feet) up to the demolition of the existing building and the construction of a new multiplex (total floor area 760 square meters/8,180.5 square feet). Project by the University of Toronto tuf lab and LGA Architectural Partners, 2022.

17. Among the many references, see Martin Gellen, *Accessory Apartments in Single-family Housing* (New Brunswick: Center for Urban Policy Research, 1985); Coralette Hannon and Gerri Madrid-Davis, *Accessory Dwelling Units: Model State Act and Local Ordinance* (American Association of Retired Persons, 2021); Vinit Mukhija, *Remaking the American Dream: The Informal and Formal Transformation of Single-family Housing Cities* (Cambridge: MIT Press, 2022).

18. San Francisco Planning Department and Openscope Studio, *sf-ADU: A Guide for Homeowners, Designers, and Contractors Considering Adding an Accessory Dwelling Unit to an Existing Residence in San Francisco* (San Francisco: San Francisco Planning Department, 2018).

19. Guy Desgrandchamps et al., "Lotir les lotissements: Conditions architecturales, urbanistiques et sociologiques de la densification douce de l'habitat individuel," in *L'Habitat pluriel*, ed. Sabri Bendimérad (Paris: Puca/Certu, 2010); David Miet, "L'architecture du projet de recherche BIMBY," *Les Cahiers de la recherche architecturale et urbaine* 26/27 (2012): pp. 219–24.

20. See "Verkavelingswijken in Transformatie," Flemish Government Architect, accessed August 14, 2024, https://vlaamsbouwmeester.be/nl/instrumenten/pilootprojecten/verkavelingswijken .

21. See "Expanding Housing Options in Neighbourhoods," City of Toronto, accessed August 14, 2024, https://www.toronto.ca/city-government/planning-development/planning-studies-initiatives/expanding-housing-options/.

to overcome the rigidity of exclusionary zoning typical of single-family-home neighborhoods and allow for the self-promoted and controlled construction of Accessory Dwelling Units (ADUs).[17] San Francisco's ADU program, for instance, was launched in 2016.[18] The program identifies urban areas where the construction of ADUs are permitted and defines guidelines and design standards for intervening into single-family houses, the construction of extensions, and new freestanding structures. [Fig. 3]

Similar European initiatives are also worth mentioning, such as the French research program BIMBY ("Build in my backyard") which, since the 2000s, has been developing densification strategies for the peri-urban *pavillonnaire* by re-parceling existing lots and infilling new buildings between existing detached houses.[19] There is also the Subdivision in Transformation initiative promoted by the Flemish Government Architect since 2020, which is aimed at improving quality of life in mature suburban single-family-house neighborhoods.[20] All these cases create processes of molecular densification to address issues such as changes in family and cohabitation patterns, the emerging needs of the aging resident population, and the opportunity for land-use optimization in the face of the affordable housing crisis.

Unlike these projects, which mainly seek to retain the structure of preexisting buildings, other proposals push toward more "intense" densification processes. Through an intervention into zoning and building codes, they allow for the redevelopment of previously existing single-family houses into larger multi-unit housing. Among these is the recent Expanding Housing Options in Neighborhoods (EHON) program by the city of Toronto, which is aimed at incentivizing the creation of multiplexes (residential buildings containing up to four units) across low-rise neighborhoods.[21] Through amendments to the official plan and zoning bylaw, the initiative allows for the construction of more surface area and residential units within the permitted zoning envelope in specific areas of the city and along major streets. The goal is to expand the offer of "middle" housing typologies such as duplexes and low-rise walk-up apartments.

Within this framework, a team of architects and scholars at the University of Toronto recently developed the ReHousing research project to explore possible configurations for the owner-initiated conversion of single-family houses into multi-unit housing while providing good quality design and construction principles.[22] For each of the most common low-rise housing types existing in the city, the research project developed a set of different transformation layouts with increased density and number of housing units according to location, lot size, and land value. [Fig. 4]

Overall, whether soft or intense, these densification strategies are a double-edged sword. On the one hand, there are good arguments to support an intensification of low-rise building fabrics in certain areas that are served by public transport and amenities. In these contexts, densification could encourage a more diverse and more affordable availability of residences. On the other hand, however, these proposals may generate speculative processes—when interventions are driven by real-estate investors, not by longtime homeowners, for instance—and "diversifying" the building landscape of the suburbs in an architecturally incongruous way may lead uncomfortable results for existing residents.

Typological Adaption

The retrofitting of single-family houses is a common task for architectural offices and is traditionally one of the first commissions at the start of an architect's career. In certain cases, such tasks have marked the starting point for incredibly successful practices, as in the case of Frank Gehry, with the famous 1977 retrofit of his residence in Santa Monica. While this type of project might be relevant within an architect's portfolio, the scope of these interventions is often limited in scale: they concern a single house. They do not challenge the socio-economic tenets of the type, as their forms and architecture still represent a solid investment which should not be put at risk.

When architects have been able to challenge the conditions of domestic life engendered by this type, their work has often been relegated to the realm of exhibitions, art installations, research, and publications. One example of this is the work of the artist Gordon Matta-Clark, who trained as an architect. In 1974, Matta-Clark was given permission by the Planning Commission of Niagara Falls, New York, to "saw" the façade of a condemned single-family house into regular parts.

22. See "ReHousing," accessed August 14, 2024, https://rehousing.ca/.

[Fig. 5] The resulting fragments were then freely reassembled in a gallery, which produced a disorienting experience for the visitor. The evidence of the processes of subtraction and destruction challenged conventional domestic attributes typically associated with the idea of home, such as domesticity, comfort, solidness and privacy.[23]

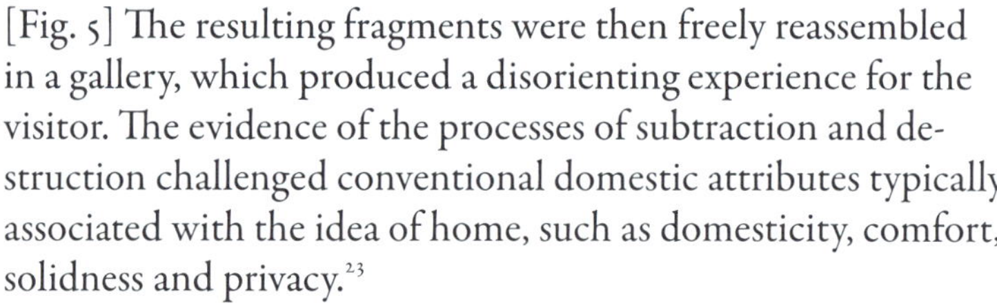

Fig. 5 — Gordon Matta-Clark, *Bingo 3* (Documentation of the action "Bingo" made in 1974 in New York, United States), 1974. Intervention of selective disassembly on the façade of a single-family house in Niagara Falls, NY.

24. Lars Lerup, *Planned Assaults: The Nofamily House, Love/House, Texas Zero* (Cambridge, MA: MIT Press, 1987).

25. See Los Angeles Municipal Art Gallery and Southern California Institute of Architecture, *Re: American Dream: Six Urban Housing Prototypes for Los Angeles* (Princeton: Princeton Architectural Press, 1995). See also Mary-Ann Ray, Roger Sherman, Mirko Zardini, eds., "The Densecity. Dopo la dispersion-After the Sprawl", *Lotus Quaderni Documents* 22 (Milan, Electa, 1999).

26. Mark Robbins, "Building like America: Making Other Plans," *Assemblage* 24 (1994): pp. 8–11.

Another challenge to the typology of the single-family house can be found in Lars Lerup's 1987 book *Planned Assaults*, which contains a series of design explorations that question the accepted social and economic structures at the base of single-family housing in North America.[24] [Fig. 6] Although these proposals were fictional, they can be considered transformative in the way they engage with some of the "real" architectural tropes of the suburban domestic landscape. Similarly, the 1992 exhibition *Re: American Dream* at the Los Angeles Municipal Art Gallery consisted of "realistic" strategies and proposals by a group of Los Angeles-based architects for retrofitting low-rise settlements.[25] And in the 1994 exhibition *House Rules*, held at the Wexner Center for the Arts at Ohio State University, architects were paired with theorists and asked to rethink the architectural conditions of the single-family house in relation to "demographic shifts, programmatic differences, and theories about identity and liberation."[26]

Among all of these proposals, the scheme by studio Guthrie+Buresh for *Re: American Dream* stands out. Instead of starting from an empty plot, which many of these projects did, it engages with the existing conditions of a block in Los

Angeles, with houses set back from the street and garages in the back.[27] Through a gradual process of addition, the architects explored the possibility of hosting multiple buildings within the plot or extending the existing building in relation to the type of street they overlook and the characteristics of the surrounding context. Within their proposal, building and open space blur into a continuous fabric, one that is denser, but not compact. [Fig. 7]

Such a proposal anticipated the construction of a residence/studio for a small family in Los Angeles by the same office a few years later, which realized some of the compositional schemes that questioned typical features of the single-family house such as the lawn, the driveway, and privacy. The project transformed the traditional single-family house into a more "urban" one, producing a new, hybrid model of living, one that maintains some of the original qualities of the single-family house while providing greater density. Projects such as these show how the single-family house has been a source for disciplinary debate and design investigation. However, largely being developed on the occasion of curatorial initiatives, they seem to confirm the inability to break into the conservative housing industry with alternative schemes.[28]

Substitution and Reconfiguration

The fourth trajectory responds to urban sprawl's monofunctional nature, car-oriented design, and segregation between activity districts, mobility corridors, and residential neighborhoods. These projects reconfigure the structure of settlements and substitute portions of existing single-family house fabrics with alternative building typologies and functions. The most significant context for the development of these kinds of proposals has been the New Urbanism movement, which, starting from the 1980s, developed dedicated strategies, guidelines, and master plans for the transformation of many North American suburbs.[29] In these projects, the desire to reestablish an "urban" pattern in the sprawling suburbs has led to proposing denser, more structured, and functionally integrated settlements located in central places with enhanced public accessibility, where mixed-use and multistory building typologies should have originally been put in place. Although the urban areas most frequently subject to redesign proposals of this kind have

27. Los Angeles Municipal Art Gallery and Southern California Institute of Architecture, *Re: American Dream*, p. 68–75.

28. Archer, *Architecture and Suburbia*, pp. 368–69.

29. Peter Katz, *The New Urbanism: Towards an Architecture of Community* (New York: McGraw-Hill, 1994); John A. Dutton, *New American Urbanism: Re-forming the Suburban Metropolis* (Milan: Skira, 2000).

30. Katz, *The New Urbanism*, pp. 134–41.

31. Ellen Dunham-Jones and June Williamson, *Retrofitting Suburbia: Urban Design Solutions for Redesigning Suburbs* (Hoboken: Wiley, 2009); Galina Tachieva, *Sprawl Repair Manual* (Washington: Island Press, 2010); Emily Talen, ed., *Retrofitting Sprawl: Addressing Seventy Years of Failed Urban Form* (Athens: University of Georgia Press, 2015).

32. Berry Bergdoll and Reinhold Martin, eds., *Foreclosed: Rehousing the American Dream* (New York: Museum of Modern Art, 2012). See also https://buellcenter.columbia.edu/projects/foreclosed-rehousing-american-dream.

been commercial strips, shopping centers, and office parks with large parking areas, extensive residential fabrics of single-family houses have also been the object of reconfiguration.

A good example of this type of project is the 1991 proposal for the revitalization of the Riviera Beach district in Florida by Mark Schimmenti Architecture and Town Planning and others.[30] The master plan addresses an area of 1,600 acres (about 650 hectares), including the coastal city's downtown and low-density areas of detached homes that were developed in the postwar decades, and restructures the existing fabric into an integrated system of nine mixed-use neighborhoods. The project develops along a twofold scheme. Firstly, it re-hierarchizes the existing road network, defining a new urban structure with a limited number of main axes converted into urban boulevards and clusters of civic facilities and public spaces. Secondly, a specific zoning and urban code allows for the selective conversion of existing single-family house allotments into denser, more compact building clusters, where mixed-use buildings and public open spaces create "neighborhood cores" for the daily life of the community. [Fig. 8]

Over the last twenty years, similar approaches have been further developed and refined by a series of books aimed at defining general operational strategies to "retrofit" and "repair" urban sprawl.[31] An eloquent example focused on the single-family house type is offered by Galina Tachieva's 2010 *Sprawl Repair Manual*. The author codifies a method to transform typical detached house subdivisions into neighborhood centers. The proposal targets not only the building and property structure by substituting existing single-family housing with denser, more compact, mixed-use buildings through rezoning. It also addresses thoroughfares by redesigning new walkable networks that cross the residential blocks and new open and civic spaces. [Fig. 9]

Different from the above examples (and far removed from the urban models attributable to New Urbanism) but within the same spectrum of replacement and reconfiguration are the reflections developed on the occasion of the 2012 MoMA exhibition, *Foreclosed: Rehousing the American Dream*. Five interdisciplinary groups of designers were invited to envision the transformation of the American suburbs in response to the foreclosure crisis.[32] Projects responded to issues connected with the crisis of the single-family homeownership model by proposing innovative urban forms. These included altering the typical single-family development property divisions, inserting new building typologies into existing interstices or brownfields within existing fabrics, and redefining the external fringe of settlements with new developments. The overarching aim was to densify while creating new living and working typologies, as well as enhancing relations between the built and natural environments.

In the proposal by MOS Architects for Orange, New Jersey, a new mixed-use development fills the street spaces between the existing buildings of a typical suburban fabric. In the proposal by WORKac for Keizer, a suburb of Portland, Oregon, a new housing development on the edge of an existing settlement of single-family houses offers new residential typologies and a stronger relationship with surrounding natural and rural spaces. [Fig. 10]

The relevance of these proposals lies in their capacity to envision alternative and radical urban models to that which is embodied in typical single-family housing developments. Their ability to translate into tangible outcomes, however, is less certain.

New Commons

The fifth and last trajectory describes projects that attempt to move beyond the condition of private property and privacy of suburban settlements by transforming them into more cooperative environments. This follows two parallel types of interventions: the retrofitting of a number of single-family houses to make them fit small groups of people who decide to (at least partially) share their abode; or the development of a series of policies and strategies that try to counter land privatization and forms of tenure typical to suburban single-family housing developments.

As suggested by Silvia Federici, it is in fact women who must reclaim the house as a center for collective life, "one traversed by multiple people and forms of cooperation" and one capable of "providing the foundation for collective forms of reproduction."[33] Inspired by the work of material feminists, the HOMES project by Dolores Hayden proposes a strategy to retrofit suburban homes into a collective housing system equipped

33. Silvia Federici, "Feminism and the Politics of the Commons", in *The Wealth of the Commons: A World Beyond Market & State*, eds. David Bollier and Silke Helfrich (Amherst: Levellers Press, 2012), p. 388.

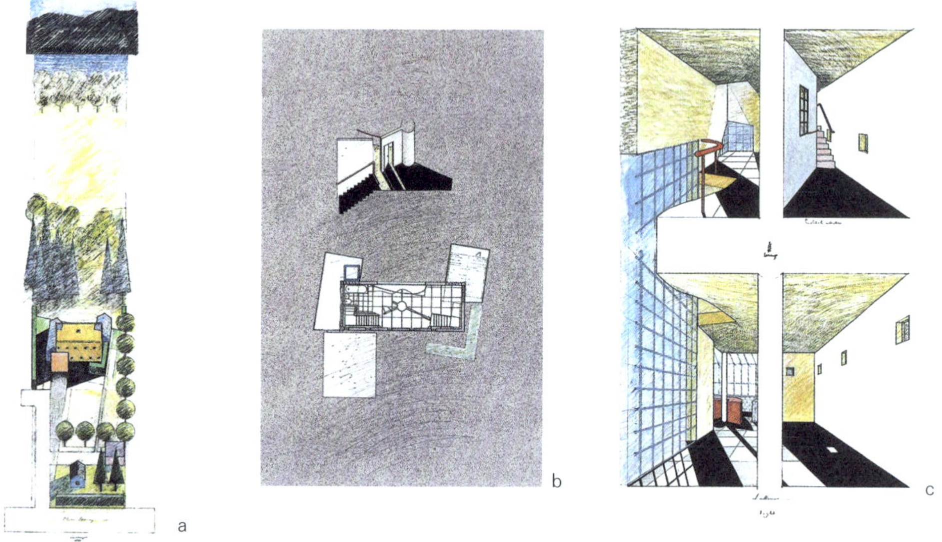

Fig. 6 — Lars Lerup, *Nofamily house*, design explorations of a single-family house, 1987. a. site plan; b. the useless door; c. interior views.

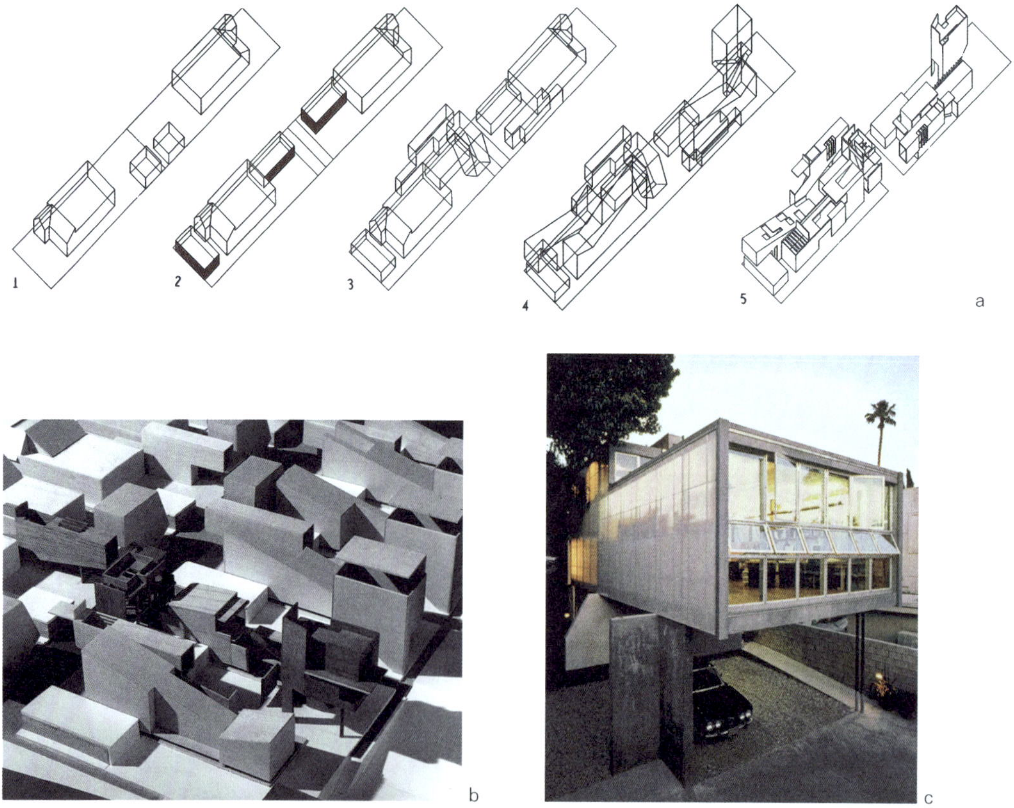

Fig. 7 — Projects by Guthrie + Buresh Architects to transform single-family housing in Los Angeles. a. and b. incremental densification scheme and scale model of a transformed fabric, from the exhibition *Re: American Dream*, 1992; c. residence/studio built in West Hollywood, 1996, photo by Tom Bonner.

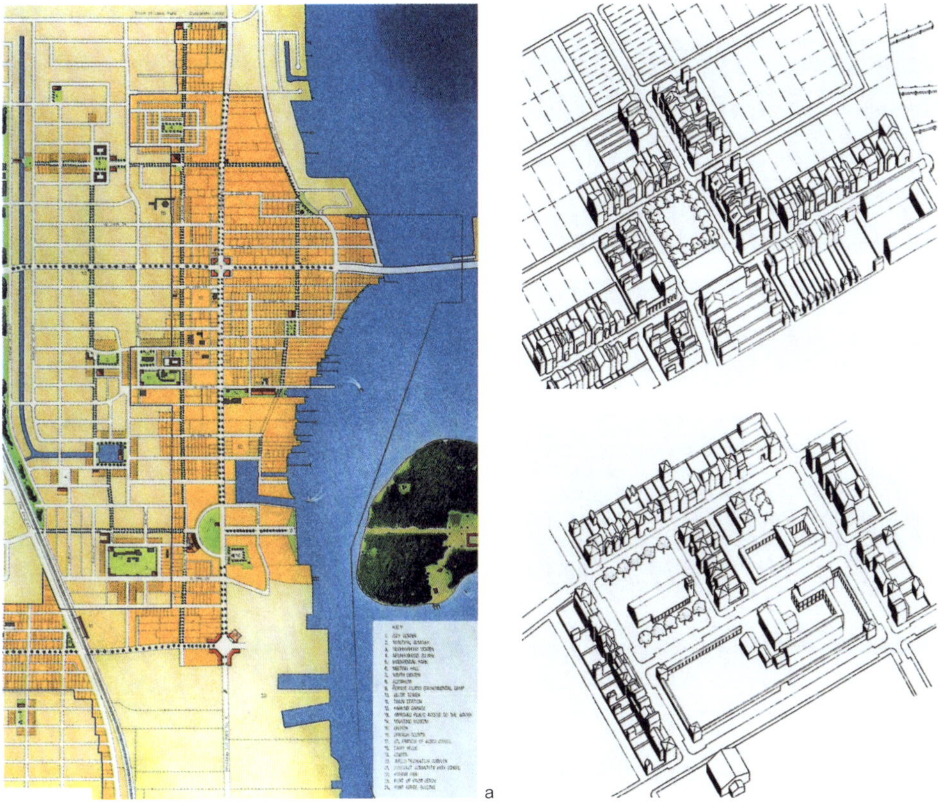

Fig. 8 — Masterplan for the Riviera Beach district, Florida, 1991. Project by Mark Schimmenti Architecture and Town Planning with Dover, Correa, Kohl, Cockshutt, and Valle urban design firm. a. re-hierarchization of the road network and new centers for the existing neighborhoods; b. schemes to re-organize low-density single-family house fabrics into denser neighborhood clusters.

Fig. 9 — Galina Tachieva, diagrams to "repair" single-family house subdivisions, 2010: a. existing single-family subdivision enclave; b. subdivision repaired into a neighborhood center.

34. For a complete overview of the architectural work of material feminists, see Dolores Hayden, *The Grand Domestic Revolution: A History of Feminist Designs for American Homes, Neighborhoods, and Cities* (Cambridge: MIT Press, 1981). For HOMES, see: Dolores Hayden, "What Would a Non-Sexist City Be Like? Speculations on Housing, Urban Design, and Human Work," *Signs* 5, no. 3 (1980): pp. 170–87.

with shared facilities that give special consideration to women's prerogatives, who will benefit the most through the proximity between home and reproductive services.[34] The name stands for "Homemakers Organization for a More Egalitarian Society." It expresses Hayden's effort to change the privatizing logic of the typical suburban house while reimagining a more emancipatory form of life, in which domestic labor could be shared and socialized beyond the nuclear family.

At their inception, suburbs were planned with the idea that men would be the sole wage earners and homeowners, entirely responsible for the financial survival of their children and of a spouse who would take care of domestic chores. However, in the postwar period, women entered the job market while remaining the custodians of the household. Hayden's proposal started from the observation that suburban houses work against the needs of working women since they generate extra domestic work. The HOMES project was based on six principles: involving both men and women in unpaid domestic labor; involving both men and women in the paid labor force; eliminating residential segregation by class, race, and age; eliminating all federal, state, and local programs and laws which offer implicit or explicit reinforcement of the unpaid role of the female worker; minimizing unpaid domestic labor and wasteful housing consumption; and maximizing real choices for households regarding recreation and sociability.

To implement these principles, Hayden envisioned a scenario in which thirteen households would pool their resources, remove the fences that separated their yards, create new common land, and share facilities such as communal play areas for children, a collective kitchen, a daycare facility, a laundry, and a grocery depot. Additionally, all single-family houses could be gradually remodeled and subdivided into smaller units, so that up to three households could share what originally was a house for a single family. From an architectural point of view, the retrofitting process radically changed the condition of the block, which is no longer the simple accumulation of single-family houses but becomes an intermediate collective urban structure. [Fig. 11]

Transforming the single-family house from a temple of privacy and property into a more collective living environment necessarily involves tackling immaterial aspects such as land property, forms of housing tenure, and management. One alternative to current forms of private property is the Limited Equity Cooperative (LEC), an ownership model that facilitates housing accessibility for those who would otherwise be excluded, and by avoiding forms of long-term speculation can nurture collective commitment to place.[35] Another is the Community Land Trust (CLT), an ownership model based on separating ownership of the land, which perpetually rests in the hands of the trust (a local organization serving as a long-term steward for affordable housing), from ownership of the unit, which is purchased by the inhabitants, who are bound to sale clauses ensuring that housing remains affordable in the long term.

While in Europe, the operations of CLTs are confined primarily to urban areas, their impact is slowly transforming the American suburb. Although CLTs are concerned primarily with the land rather than its use, as argued by Gabriel Cuéllar and Athar Mufreh, they also "act spatially."[36] By observing the operation of CLTs in cities such as Atlanta, Minneapolis, Tampa, and New York, Cuéllar and Mufreh revealed that the ways plots are scattered in a CLT present various opportunities, from preserving the neighborhood to stabilizing real-estate values, supporting urban agriculture, and facilitating the renovation processes of dilapidated housing stock. [Fig. 12]

As highlighted by Hayden, retrofitting the single-family house into a more collective (and gender-equal) form of living could take advantage of the availability of land, the isolation of the house within the plot, and the presence of generous gardens in between properties. All this can make sharing original private properties with others more tolerable. However, real forms of communal living can only be achieved if private property can be bypassed and new models of ownership are implemented.

A Glance Forward

Although inevitably partial and discretionary, these five design trajectories make it possible to compare some of the most influential positions in the last decades of architectural and urban design discourse focused on reconfiguring the extensive single-family housing developments built in the second half of the twentieth century. Paying attention to their concrete outcomes, we can identify three critical considerations.

35. On the potential for Limited Equity Cooperatives to nurture collective commitments to place, see Hayden, *Redesigning the American Dream*, pp. 211–13.

36. Athar Mufreh and Gabriel Cuéllar, "Virtues of Proximity: The Coordinated Spatial Action of Community Land Trusts," *Footprint* 15, no. 2 (2022): pp. 23–44.

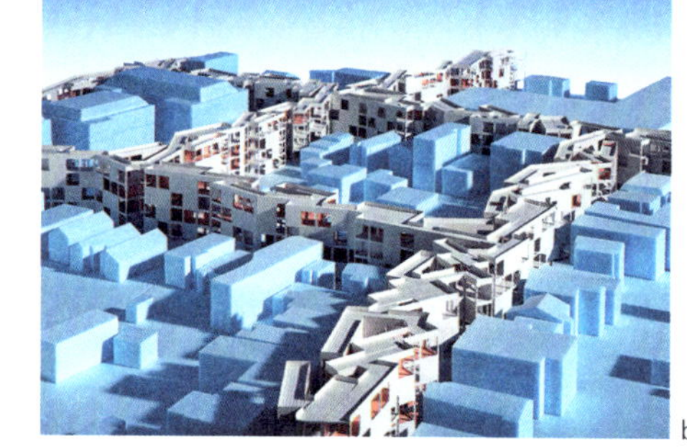

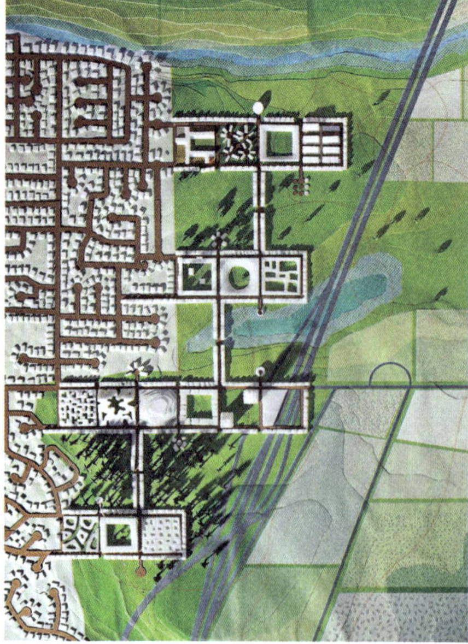

Fig. 10 — Projects to transform single-family house settlements, from the exhibition *Foreclosed: Rehousing the American Dream*, 2012: a. and b. proposal by MOS Architects for Orange, New Jersey, in which a new mixed-use development fills the street spaces between the existing buildings of a typical suburban fabric; c. and d. proposal by WORKac for Keizer, a suburb of Portland, Oregon, where a new housing development redefines the external fringe of a settlement of single-family houses.

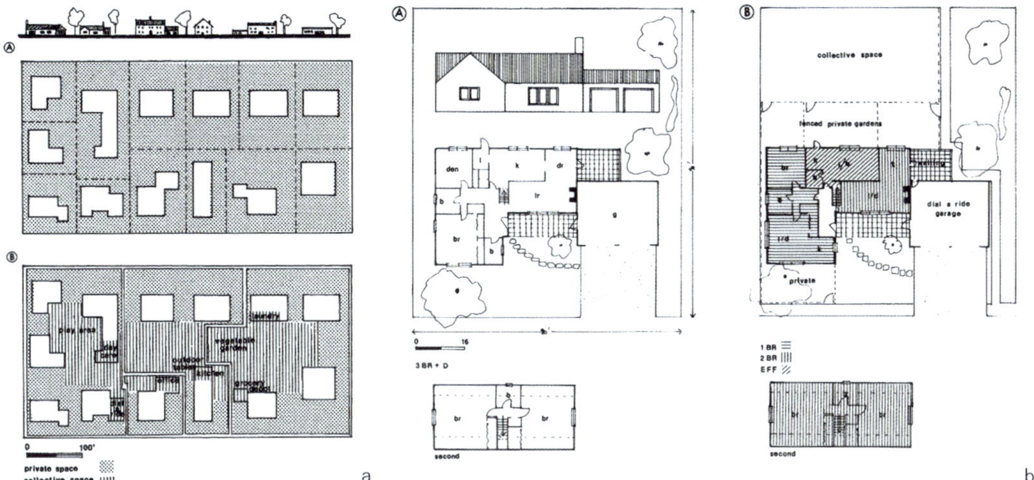

Fig. 11 — Proposal for the revitalization of a suburban neighborhood block with new common spaces and facilities. Project by HOMES (Homemakers Organization for a More Egalitarian Society), 1980s. a. the block layout before and after the interventions; b. a three-bedroom single-family house converted into three units, plus a dial-a-ride garage and a collective outdoor space.

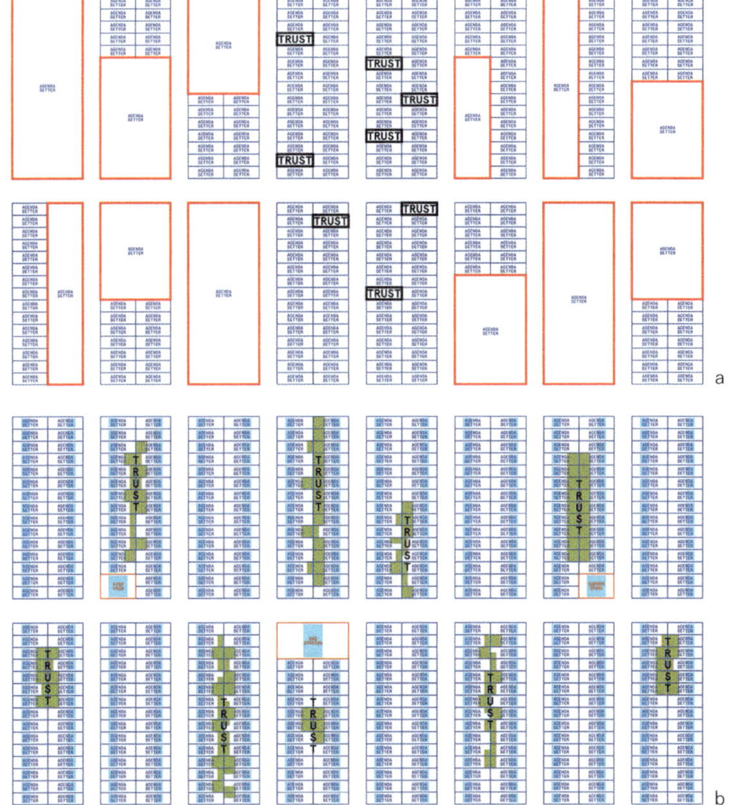

Fig. 12 — Ways to organize the property formations of Community Land Trusts. Drawing by Gabriel Cuéllar, Athar Mufreh and Clare Coburn, 2022. a. popular checkerboarding to resist commercial real estate land acquisition strategies; b. yard consolidation to assemble partial interests into larger interconnected surfaces suitable for urban farmers.

37. Laurence Troy and Ryan Van Den Nouwelant, "Accessory Dwelling Units and Incremental Urbanism: Becoming 'Urban' or just 'Intensive Suburban'?," *Built Environment* 49, no. 1 (2023): pp. 39–57.

The first relates to projects that focused on the energy performance and the technological and material aspects of single-family housing. In general, these initiatives remained anchored to the development of technical solutions for individual houses, with the wider goal to improve the environmental sustainability of the housing stock. In this sense, proposals were often made regardless of the urban contexts in which the buildings were located, and failed to consider changes in the functioning of domestic spaces. This leaves the single-family house model, the forms of life it embodies, and its monofunctional settlements essentially unchanged. Bearing in mind the shortcomings of this approach can help us to reflect on the limits of the purely technological and digital conception of the present-day ecological transition, and instead to base strategies for intervention on a richer understanding of the built environment as a field of interaction between social and technical elements.

The second consideration concerns initiatives that aimed at fostering incremental densification and typological adaption of the single-family housing type. There are good arguments for such processes under certain conditions: for instance, when there is good connection to public transport or other public amenities, as mentioned above, and when the diversification of residences can introduce multiple, more flexible, and more affordable housing typologies. Beyond this, these types of projects raise a twofold issue. In cases where densification has been allowed and incentivized through zoning and building codes, its diffuse and cumulative outcomes may sometimes undermine the intended enhancement of urban quality. This is not just an issue related to architectural incongruity, but also to the speculative potential of such densification projects, as previously mentioned. Beyond this, however, increasing the number of residents in an area may create a heightened dependence on existing public equipment and congestion. Not developing corresponding projects for new amenities and improved public accessibility results in an "intense suburban" rather than more "urban" environment.[37] Conversely, in projects where densification and typological adaptation were explored through architect-led experimental prototypes, these designs often avoided focusing on a real subject or client (with specific spending capacity, life expectations, and domestic needs). As a result, they often remained confined to the realm of theoretical speculation or to a small number of constructed buildings "signed" by distinguished architects.

The third consideration relates to projects that proposed a more radical reconfiguration of the single-family-house parceling schemes, at both the neighborhood and block scale, advocating for their replacement with different urban and architectural models that subvert their individualistic character of dwelling. These proposals often underestimated the "obduracy" of the single-family house—a term used by Wouter Bervoets and Hilde Heynen in their research on Flemish suburbanization to identify the resistance of this type to any change—and the intrinsic difficulties connected with thoroughgoing land re-parceling schemes.[38] Consequently, their outcomes were often limited, or rather than triggering an effective widespread transformation of the existing settlements, they inspired the construction of new greenfield developments, largely for the affluent.

Overall, the projects and reflections here constitute a first, useful repertoire of conceptual tools and intervention techniques that should remain on the drawing tables of architects and urban planners who are engaged in rethinking territories dominated by the presence of the single-family house. However, honest reflection on the limits of these schemes and the reasons behind their partial outcomes is equally necessary, as is an up-to-date outline of the evolutionary history of the single-family housing type and its varied combination patterns. Holding these different strands together appears key to embrace new projects and policies that are both effective in producing the substantial and urgent changes required by a socio-ecological transition and responsive to the spatial needs of the subjects that progressively re-inhabit the mature single-family housing stock.

38. Wouter Bervoets and Hilde Heynen, "The Obduracy of the Detached Single-Family House in Flanders," *International Journal of Housing Policy* 13, no. 4 (2013): pp. 358–80.

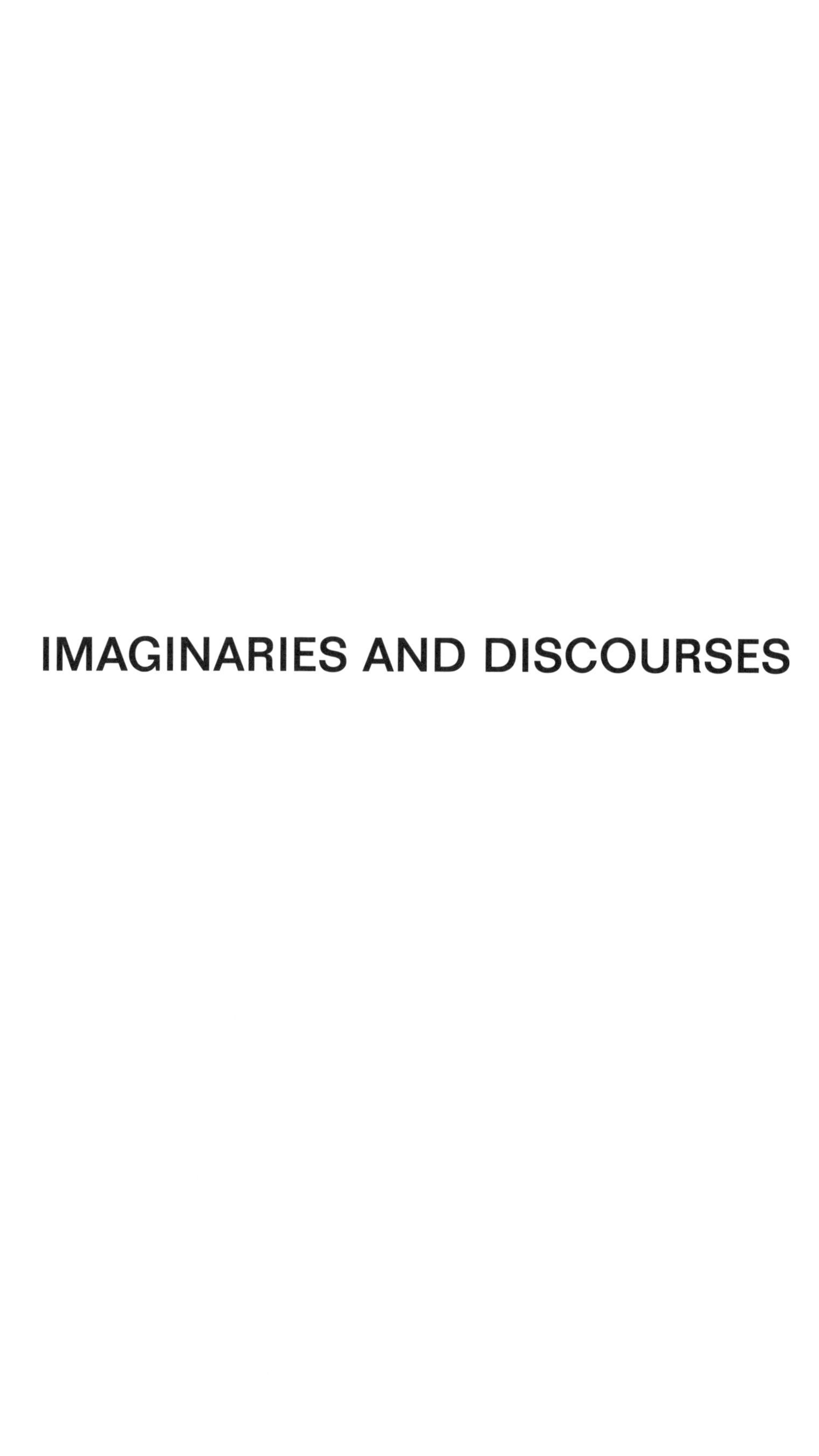

IMAGINARIES AND DISCOURSES

The Single-Family Home in Flanders: The Emergence and Decline of a Popular Housing Type

Hilde Heynen

In Flanders, the northern part of Belgium, the single-family home is the dominant housing typology and makes up a majority of the urban sprawl that the region is known for. In this essay, I will first trace the historical circumstances that gave rise to this situation. In the second section of this essay, I will discuss the criticisms that the single-family home raised from the 1960s onwards, especially among architects. In the third and last section, I will indicate the major concerns nowadays regarding this typology and its future in Flanders.

Housing Policies in Belgium

There is a well-known saying that "Belgian people are born with a brick in their stomach," which indicates that Belgians aspire towards building and owning a family home. This motivation, supposedly a part of the Belgian "character" (whatever that may be), was historically produced by a specific housing policy that was initiated already before the World War II and came to fruition in the immediate postwar period. The most important law in this regard was the De Taeye Act, authored by Alfred De Taeye, a Catholic politician and Minister of Health and Families and approved by the parliament in 1948. [Fig. 1] The act encouraged small-scale private initiative by offering subsidies to private builders, and by setting up a mortgage system that allowed builders to borrow up to 90 percent of the value of their property. The effects of this act reached about 100,000 beneficiaries during the first five years, which meant 20,000 new dwellings were annually built according to this system, or about 75 percent of all new homes. Most of these dwellings were built not as part of a bigger planning scheme, but as a one-time enterprise initiated by the owner/inhabitant who hired an architect to design the house and a contractor to build it.[1] The design of individual homes thus became a major occupation for Belgian architects. Structured neighborhoods with public housing did exist—and some rather good ones, like those by Renaat Braem in Antwerp and Brussels—but quantitatively they never formed a major component in the construction of new homes. Basically, the Belgian postwar housing plight—as far as it existed—was met thanks to the De Taeye Act.

Officially, all these homes had to be designed by an architect since building applications needed to be signed by a registered professional. However, the impact of the owners themselves on the design of their homes was considerable. There were several sociocultural organizations that helped people in the decision-making process by offering home education. These were connected to different social groups, such as Catholics, socialists, or liberals, and subdivided into social classes such as farmers, laborers, and the middle class. The organizations' advice was thus colored by their political background. Compared to the interwar period, when these organizations were also active in the field of home culture, there was a growing sense of convergence between divergent outlooks. In the 1920s and 1930s, there were serious differences of opinion among these organizations regarding themes such as: the adequacy of apartment living (desirable or not?—the socialists said yes, the Catholics no); the parlor (separate from the living kitchen or not?—no according to the socialists, yes according to the Catholics); the chimney (place for the cross, according to Catholic organizations); or the kitchen (a small working kitchen or a large living kitchen?).[2] Such differentiations became less prominent in the postwar decades, but each organization still had its own favorite themes and methods for mediating between experts and the organization's members.[3] The overall effect of these varying mediations was that the impact of lay people became much stronger. Since organizations were competing with one another to attract members, their offerings in terms of services and advice shifted quickly in response to feedback from the member base. The modernist ideals that experts tried to convey to members were easily modified when it became clear that these did not match well with their expectations of what a home should be.

A telling example of this development can be found when considering efforts for home culture education in *de*

1. Hilde Heynen, "Belgium and the Netherlands: Two Different Ways of Coping with the Housing Crisis, 1945–70," *Home Cultures* 7, no. 2 (July 1, 2010): pp. 159–77.

2. Sofie De Caigny, *Bouwen Aan Een Nieuwe Thuis: Wooncultuur in Vlaanderen Tijdens Het Interbellum* (Leuven: Universitaire Pers Leuven, 2010).

3. Els De Vos, *Hoe Zouden Wij Graag Wonen? Woonvertogen in Vlaanderen in de Jaren Zestig En Zevntig* (Leuven: Leuven University Press, 2012).

Fig. 1 — Minister Alfred De Taeye officially marks the start of construction for the 100,000th home built under the subsidy program he introduced, 1954.

Fig. 2 — The festive inauguration in 1962 of the 150th exemplary dwelling of the Catholic Association of Farming Women.

4. Els De Vos and Hilde Heynen, "Shaping Popular Taste: The Belgian Farmers' Association and the *Fermette* During the 1960s–1970s," *Home Cultures* 4, no. 3 (November 2007): pp. 237–59.

5. Dolores Hayden, *The Grand Domestic Revolution: A History of Feminist Designs for American Homes, Neighborhoods, and Cities* (Cambridge: MIT Press, 1981); Sun van Meijel, ed., *Vrouwendomicilie En Mannendominantie: Reader over Vrouwen, Wonen En Gebouwde Omgeving* (Amsterdam: SUA, 1982); Dolores Hayden, ed., "Building Suburbia: Green Fields and Urban Growth, 1820–2000" (New York: Vintage Books, 2004), p. 318.

6. Renaat Braem, *Het lelijkste land ter wereld* (Leuven: Davidsfonds, 1968).

Boerinnenbond (the Catholic Association of Farming Women). This association regularly published books with examples of model homes intended for a large audience, and it supported a well-organized *Dienst Wonen* (Home Service), which offered advice to members regarding the building or transformation of their homes. The books were remarkably successful and became widespread manuals read by a variety of prospective homebuilders (not just farmers). The association moreover promoted so-called exemplary dwellings, which were "show houses" inhabited by members and open for visitors at regular intervals. [Fig. 2] Whereas early publications and the exemplary dwellings of the 1950s and early 1960s favored modernist design ideas, later ones were far less strict in obeying modernist dos and don'ts. Thus, in the late 1960s, the association started to support a hybrid kind of dwelling that was modern in its floor plan and equipment, while traditional in its appearance. This evolution was because the organization was client-oriented rather than committed to modernism as such.[4]

The feminist critique that developed in the United States and the Netherlands vis-à-vis suburban development also applied to the Belgian version of urban sprawl.[5] Single-family homes found in suburban and peripheral neighborhoods limited opportunities for women by making it difficult to reach places of employment. The result was that only one family member—the one with a car—was fully mobile and therefore assigned as the breadwinner. Subsequently, the full burden of childcare fell solidly on the shoulders of the stay-at-home mom. Second-wave feminists thus criticized the zoning and suburban sprawl that had such a negative impact on emancipatory potentials for women.

Architectural and Planning Discontents

Modernist architects in Flanders became frustrated with what was happening on the ground, because their ideas about planning and design were scarcely taken into account. This frustration came most clearly to the fore in Renaat Braem's publication *Het lelijkste land ter wereld* (*The Ugliest Country in the World*).[6] In a chapter on the "dissolution of the urban and the rural," he states that: "everything is increasingly dependent on traffic" and the city had become "a shapeless, amorphous blotch on the earth's surface, without a recognizable order, grown along the path of the least resistance."[7] Built "according to special zoning plans ... haphazardly, following spec-builders' land-subdivision-schemes,"[8] he pinpoints the single-family house as one of the main culprits of this spatial disarray and consequently lashes out at its visual traits:

> built according to plans in which the involvement of the architect is restricted to placing his signature, [these] ersatz houses are a covered and sheltered place, but not a living space. Everything about them is deceitful. The façade has no relation with the plan [but] ... has to provide an illusion of wealth through the use of pseudo-keystones, fake bluestone, and window-frames. The windows are leadlight, to enhance coziness and block off the outsider's gaze. In the front garden, decorative metal framing. Next to the entrance, a planter with plastic plant. In front of the voile-curtain, a "*Diane à la chasse*," bronze in plaster, neither visible from inside or to be admired by the passer-by outside.... An exaggeration? Look around. Ninety-nine percent of what has been built after liberation looks like this. We were freed from barbarity to be occupied by ugliness.[9]

Braem's criticism of the Belgian built landscape was manifold: he thought that it represented chaos rather than order; he blamed the single-family homes for being artificial rather than authentic; and he saw an overall prevalence of sentiment over rationality and clarity. Many modernist architects and intellectuals shared his feelings. In 1974, for example, journalist Johan Struye published a booklet that denounced the so-called *fermette* (a single-family home in the image of a farm) as a fake status symbol: "Nowadays the Flemish intellectual, the 'young executive,' lives in a farmhouse. Those who don't own a 'fermette' do not dare to invite friends for the weekend."[10] [Fig. 3] He opposed the old, self-made Flemish farmhouses, ill-provided with tiny windows and just one stove for the whole house, "shyly hidden away" in the landscape, with what he called "pepped up fermettes." The latter, he observed, had nothing in common with the agricultural cottages of the hard-working, poor crofters. In these new fermettes, plain walls and the horizontality of surfaces are replaced by large sliding windows, artificial oak beams, and cartwheels on the wall. Its modern, large windows look out "on the right to the Spanish villa of the neighbors who work for the railway company

7. Braem, p. 38.

8. Braem, p. 50.

9. Braem, p. 51.

10. Johan Struye, *De Pastoor Wist Wat Goed Was: Bouwen in België* (Brussel: Knack, 1974).

Fig. 3 — A typical *fermette* from the 1970s or 1980s in Limburg, Belgium, 2017. This type can be found everywhere across Flanders.

and on the left to the small castle in a Moresque style of the glass dealer." "Of course you don't reach a totally rural character on plots of 36 feet [11 meters wide]," remarked Struye.

Whereas criticism regarding the look of single-family homes prevailed in the 1970s, in the 1980s and 1990s concern shifted more towards issues of land use and mobility. After the publication of the UN Brundtland report on sustainable development,[11] there was a growing awareness in Belgium that suburban sprawl contributed to the decline of natural ecosystems and, moreover, required high levels of car mobility, which had a negative impact on sustainability. This awareness resulted in a new planning policy in Flanders, which came into effect as of 1997. By that time the Belgian state was federalized, and the region of Flanders could autonomously decide about its spatial planning. The so-called Structure Plan for Flanders (*Ruimtelijk Structuurplan Vlaanderen*), which was created by an expert group led by Louis Albrechts and Charles Vermeersch, advocated for a region that would be "open and urban." This meant that further development should be steered towards city and town centers, whereas the countryside should remain open.[12] The idea was that housing should be concentrated rather than sprawling, in order to be nearer to amenities and to facilitate the organization of public transport (higher densities are needed to make public transportation cost effective). Plots should diminish in size to ensure more efficient land use, and open landscapes should be protected against further encroachments to stop the ongoing onslaught on nature.

This plan was never fully implemented. The idea to channel most new housing construction to urban areas did not work out. Whereas the goal was to have 60 percent of new dwellings in urban areas, and only 40 percent outside of them, this was hampered by the drawn-out process of determining which areas would count as "urban" and which as "countryside." Moreover, it proved expensive and difficult for municipalities to change the legal status of land that was zoned for dwelling (or as "reserved for dwelling"), which there was a lot of. Lastly, municipalities did not have any incentive to block new parcellations and new constructions. This all resulted in well more than 40 percent of new building permits being granted in nonurban areas. The implementation of the Structure Plan for Flanders was deficient, and its ambitions were never realized.[13]

11. Brundtland Commission, *Our Common Future* (Oxford: Oxford University Press, 1988).

12. Louis Albrechts, "Planners as Catalysts and Initiators of Change: The New Structure Plan for Flanders," *European Planning Studies* 7, no. 5 (1999): pp. 587–603.

13. Peter Renard, Tom Coppens, and Guy Vloebergh, *Met Voorbedachten Rade: De Sluipmoord Op de Open Ruimte* (Leuven: Kritak, 2022).

14. Renard, Coppens, and Vloebergh, p. 12.

15. Will Steffen et al., "Planetary Boundaries: Guiding Human Development on a Changing Planet," *Science* 347, no. 6223 (2015): p. 736.

Contemporary Matters of Concern

Although the Structure Plan for Flanders was supposedly put in place in 1997, the actual construction of new dwellings and other buildings largely continued according to business-as-usual. A multitude of single-family homes thus continued to be built in either new residential developments or alongside roads (so-called ribbon developments). [Fig. 4]

Flanders currently has more than 7,500 miles (12,000 kilometers) of such linear developments, which is outstanding given its rather small territory of 5,200 square miles (13,500 square kilometers). The built landscape is thus fragmented and dispersed, occupying one third of Flanders' surface area, with half of it sealed. This largesse is reflected in the homes themselves: in Flanders, dwelling units measure on average 1,420 square feet (132 square meters) versus the European average of only 1,030 square feet (96 square meters).[14]

Spatial planners and other experts view this situation as concerning due to a range of both ecological and socioeconomic factors. This section will first explore sustainability challenges, such as biodiversity loss, climate change, and water shortage. Secondly, it will highlight key socioeconomic issues, including underutilized housing, affordability, and the organization of care services.

Spatial Sustainability

In recent years the scholarly understanding of how land use and mobility patterns contribute to the ecological crisis has only deepened. It has become clear that planetary boundaries are being transgressed. According to the Stockholm Resilience Center, there are several areas where human activities threaten to disturb and destroy ecological balances that were prevalent for millennia. The Center lists climate change alongside biosphere integrity, land-system change, freshwater change, biochemical flows, ocean acidification, atmospheric aerosol loading, stratospheric ozone depletion, and "novel entities."[15] Sprawl-based land use patterns contribute to the loss of nature and thus the loss of biodiversity. In a region such as Flanders, suburban sprawl contributes to the loss of open, unbuilt landscapes. The general tendency remains to claim unbuilt areas for development, which today happens at a rate of five hectares per day (12.3 acres).[16] The remaining open space is therefore increasingly fragmented, which harms the regeneration of biodiversity. Old and established forested areas are encroached upon, whereas newly planted woodlands that supposedly compensate for the loss of old forests are home to far less biodiversity.[17]

As for climate change, it has only become clearer that it is truly happening, and that greenhouse gases drive this process. In Flanders, it is estimated that buildings are responsible for 29 percent of these emissions (mostly due to heating and cooling), whereas transportation contributes for 36 percent of the total.[18] This means that more than half of Flanders' emissions have something to do with the organization of the built environment. The further proliferation of suburban sprawl only enhances this phenomenon. Even if this development happens with only energy-neutral buildings, and even if the growth of private mobility is entirely taken up by electric cars, the net impact on greenhouse gas emissions is still considerable because of the embedded energy needed to produce building materials and because electricity production has not yet been fully decarbonized. This means that white papers calling for drastic climate policies invariably mention spatial policies (including land use) as one of the important areas for intervention.[19]

Belgium has traditionally seen itself as a country with a lot of rain—reputedly almost as much as in England, where cloudy skies and drizzly weather are hallmarks of its national identity. In recent years, however, experts have been warning the public about potential water shortages.[20] This is partially due to climate change, which has an impact on rainfall patterns: rainfall will be rarer, but possibly more extreme. A major factor, however, is the impact of spatial elements. Sprawl means that a lot of soil is sealed—in 2018, this amounted to 15 percent of the region's surface area.[21] Water coming down on these sealed surfaces does not percolate into the ground, but is instead directed towards the sewage systems and the rivers. These rivers are canalized and wetlands around them have been drained to become more suitable for agriculture, which together result in water rapidly being deposited in the sea, rather than being kept in place to charge groundwater reservoirs. Hence, average groundwater levels are dropping, which causes serious problems for the drinking water supply. Flanders and Belgium are thus confronted, much more than before the onset of climate change, with periods of drought that result in water shortages.

16. Ann Pisman et al., "Ruimterapport Vlaanderen 2021: Een Ruimtelijke Analyse van Vlaanderen" (Brussel: Departement Omgeving, 2021).

17. Arne, "Bossen op wandel—bescherm onze bossen deel 1," *BOS+* (blog), June 28, 2023, https://bosplus.be/.

18. "Ontwerp Vlaams Energie-En Klimaatplan 2021–2030" (Brussels: Departement Omgeving, 2023).

19. "Panel voor klimaat en duurzaamheid" (Brussels: Klimaatpanel, 2019).

20. Erik Mathijs, Willy Verstraete et al., *Vlaanderen Wijs Met Water: Waterbeleid in Transitie, Standpunten 42* (Brussel: KVAB, 2016).

21. Pisman et al., "Ruimterapport Vlaanderen 2021," p. 35.

22. "Huishoudensvooruitzichten: aantal en groei," Statistiek Vlaanderen, May 23, 2024, https://www.vlaanderen.be/statistiek-vlaanderen/.

23. Wouter Bervoets et al., "Towards a Sustainable Transformation of the Detached Houses in Peri-Urban Flanders, Belgium," *Journal of Urbanism: International Research on Placemaking and Urban Sustainability* 8, no. 3 (2014): pp. 302–30.

24. Filip Canfyn, *Woon(on) Betaalbaarheid: Over Problemen, Randfenomenen En Oplossingen* (Oud Turnhout: Gompel & Svacina, 2023).

Socioeconomic Issues

From a socioeconomic point of view, one of the main problems is that the large single-family houses that are located throughout Flanders do not match the evolution in household types. Households are getting smaller because families are now having less children and there is more divorce. Furthermore, higher lifetime expectancies mean more people grow older, so more couples and singles continue to occupy the large family homes they once built. Such underused houses do not necessarily pose a problem for their inhabitants—most people like having surplus space in their homes and use it for guest rooms, hobby rooms, or storage. On a macro level of the population, however, it is unwise to have so many underused houses, especially when there are so many new households in need of accommodation. Indeed, the number of households in Flanders is expected to continue growing at a rate of 7 percent between 2020 and 2030, meaning that some 160,000 additional dwelling units will be needed.[22] A straightforward solution to this would be to promote the subdivision of larger single-family homes into two or more smaller units, rather than building new homes from scratch. There are, however, many practical, logistical, and even regulatory reasons why this is not as straightforward as it seems. Individual homeowners do not feel the need to subdivide; they like the surplus space they have. Moreover, given that all these homes are "one-of-a-kind," each individual home needs to be redesigned by an architect to make it into two or three units, rendering the process lengthy and expensive. And lastly, many zoning regulations prohibit the establishment of multifamily dwellings in residential areas.[23]

There is also a substantial problem of affordability. Single-family houses make up the largest part of the Flemish housing stock, but most of them were built before the 2000s and do not meet current energy standards. However, the real estate market is as strong as ever, with relatively high prices for such houses, even if they need a costly overhaul.[24] Conversely, only six percent of the Flemish housing stock consists of social housing, which is far from enough: there are twice as many families eligible for this type of housing than the actual number of available units. Since there is not enough affordable rental housing on the private market, a lot of underprivileged groups pay rents that are too high, often for substandard living conditions. Women, the

Fig. 4 — Aerial photograph of the northern part of the village of Stekene, Belgium, 2018. Photo by Lionel Callewaert.

Fig. 5 — A typical ribbon development in Limburg, Belgium, 2017. Aging in place presents unique challenges in this typical car-dependent environment, characterized by ribbon development along a main road.

25. Sien Winters et al., *Vlaamse Woonmonitor 2021* (Leuven: Steunpunt Wonen, 2021).

26. Wesley Grijthuijsen and Dominique Vanneste, "De Geografie van Het Ouder Worden in Vlaanderen," in *Ongehoord En Ongezien: Hoe Vlaanderen Vergrijst*, ed. Jan Vranken et al. (Sint-Niklaas: Gompel&Svacina, 2023), pp. 167–86.

27. Emma Volckaert, *Oud vasthouden: over vergrijzing, wonen en beleid* (Antwerpen-Hertogenbosch: Gompel&Svacina, 2022).

elderly, large families, and single parents are disproportionally affected by this issue.[25]

Another type of socioeconomic problem related to sprawl has to do with the organization of care for the aging population. Aging-in-place is promoted by the Flemish government, even though it means that many aging people stay put in a home that is often too large for them, not adapted to their needs, and not well located with respect to amenities such as shops, medical facilities, and cafés or restaurants.[26] [Fig. 5] It also means that nurses and care providers from homecare organizations have to drive long distances on their way from one client to the next. This is only exacerbated by the fact that there are many competing private organizations who do not pool resources to rationalize their logistics.[27] Again, there seems to be a mismatch between the needs of an aging population, which predictably will become less mobile and more care-dependent, and their spatial distribution across the thinly spread suburban landscape, where distances can only be negotiated by car and where amenities are few and far between.

Conclusion

Since the early postwar period, the single-family house has been the dream for many people in Flanders and Belgium. For a long time, it seemed to offer an affordable, highly attractive, and manageable housing option that allowed many middle-class families (and especially dads) to make their home into their castle. This source of individual pride, however, generates many collective problems. It gives rise to unsustainable patterns of land use and mobility, and contributes to climate change, water shortages, and biodiversity loss. Moreover, it struggles to adapt to new types of residents while aggravating societal problems related to the organization of care for the elderly. Therefore, from the perspective of urban planners and architects, a further proliferation of this type of housing seems untenable. For the foreseeable future, however, there will be a large amount of homes that will need to be subdivided, renovated, reorganized, and densified—in short, considerably altered—to somehow meet sustainable development goals.

This societal challenge is enormous, because what is needed on the level of the collective (reducing greenhouse gas emissions, preserving open space, transforming the water system) does not match with the needs of individual households. The distance between the current living conditions in Flanders and what would be necessary to live within our planet's boundaries is vast. A recent master's thesis at KU Leuven determined that, to begin meeting the targets set during the 2015 Paris Climate Conference, the average living space per person in Flanders would need to be reduced from the current 538-646 square feet (50-60 square meters) to just 194 square feet (18 square meters).[28]

There are some trends that go in the right direction. There is a shift towards more multifamily homes, towards smaller plots and smaller units, and towards densification. There are initiatives promoting cohousing, and there are community land trusts. Some people build tiny houses, while others stimulate the provision of care units. All these initiatives are worthwhile, but they need to be scaled up and gain momentum before they start having real impact. Planning departments, city administrations, social housing associations, and private partners all need to play a role in that. And architects could do their bit by developing and visualizing attractive alternatives, which might make these new ways of living desirable rather than threatening.

28. Robine Verhaeghe, "Ontwikkeling van milieubenchmarks voor de woonfunctie in België op basis van de planetaire grenzen" (Master's Thesis, KU Leuven, Faculty of Engineering Science, 2023).

Domestic Spaces, Family Models, and Gender Roles: Investigating the Imaginary of the Villetta Housing Type in Italy

Michela Bassanelli

Urbanization Processes in Postwar Italy and the Multiple Models of a Single-Family House

The twenty years between 1955 and 1975 represent both an exceptional and an ambiguous time in Italian history. Also known as the "economic miracle," this period hosted a phase of great economic growth with direct consequences on the country's urban and territorial development. Italy also witnessed remarkable transformations in its social structure and consumption habits, particularly with regards to consolidating the link between the nuclear family and the homeownership regime, which is understood as an element of social stability.[1] The housing stock built in Italy during this time is highly diversified and roughly associated with two main phases of urbanization. The first, which took place immediately following the end of World War II, included the rapid growth of both mid-sized towns, most of which were located in the northern part of the country, as well as emerging industrial metropolitan areas such as Milan, Turin, and Rome. These industrial areas were exposed to large internal migration fluxes and hosted new, dense neighborhoods, where an apartment in a multistory condominium became the predominant housing solution.[2] The second included low-density urbanization in more peripheral territories, such as smaller villages in rural areas and the central and southern parts of the country.[3] In this second phase, which started in the mid-1960s and continued into the 1980s, the dominant building type was the single-family house, or the so-called *villetta* (literally a small villa).

The villetta incorporates varying roles and meanings within different territorial conditions. In the Milan area, for

1. Valerio Castronovo, *L'Italia del miracolo economico* (Roma-Bari: Laterza, 2010); Stefano Cavazza and Emanuela Scarpellini, eds., *Storia d'Italia. Annali 27. I consumi* (Torino: Einaudi, 2018).

2. Filippo De Pieri, Bruno Bonomo, Gaia Caramellino, and Federico Zanfi, eds., *Storie di case. Abitare l'Italia del boom* (Roma: Donzelli, 2013).

3. Alberto Clementi, Giuseppe Dematteis, and Piercarlo Palermo, eds., *Le forme del territorio italiano* (Roma: Laterza, 1996).

4. Stefano Boeri, Arturo Lanzani, and Edoardo Marini, *Il territorio che cambia: ambienti, paesaggi e immagini della regione milanese* (Milano: Abitare Segesta, 1993).

5. Stefano Munarin and Maria Chiara Tosi, *Tracce di città. Esplorazioni di un territorio abitato: l'area veneta* (Milano: Franco Angeli, 2001); Chiara Merlini, *Cose/Viste. Letture di Territori* (Santarcangelo di Romagna: Maggioli, 2009).

6. *Ville in pianura: ville residenziali, ville da fine settimana, case di campagna* (Milan: Görlich, 1961); Cristina Moro, "The 1960s Italian Summer Houses from Domus Archive," *Domusweb*, August 15, 2023, https://www.domusweb.it/.

7. Dolores Hayden, *Redesigning the American Dream. The Future of Housing, Work, and Family Life* (New York: W.W. Norton & Company, 1984).

instance, the detached house embodies an exclusive residential dimension, and generated repetitive suburbanization patterns within the emerging multiform landscape.[4] In other places, the house incorporates productive activities and integrates itself with other buildings—such as a shop, an artisan workshop, or a warehouse—replicating the hybrid schemes that were typical of rural areas and often coupled with a multi-family model in the northeastern and central parts of the country.[5] Still in other cases, the house responds to the need for leisure in the form of a secondary residence located along the country's coastline and mountain landscapes.[6] As Dolores Hayden argues, the proliferation of the single-family house embodies a capitalist agenda that establishes itself as a political project in this architectural form and aims to control not only productive and reproductive working time, but also leisure time.[7] In this framework, this essay investigates the villetta as an exclusive place of privacy and domesticity, and where the nuclear family model becomes consolidated. The aim is to investigate the origin, evolution, and architectural typologies that have marked, and still characterize, a large portion of the Italian housing stock to understand its current impact and possible future uses.

Introducing the Villetta Housing Type

The *villetta* has been a prominent model for city villas and holiday homes, appearing in renowned architecture magazines like *Domus* and *Casabella* since the late 1920s. Since the 1950s, however, it has acquired a more defined typology and has deeply influenced the multifaceted diffusion of the single-family house in Italy. The villetta, and particularly its internal spaces, is investigated here as a housing model in which specific issues relating to social stratification, consumption patterns, domesticity, and family roles are condensed, allowing us to reflect on the evolution of these aspects over time.

First, the term villetta needs to be clarified to define its main features. According to the Treccani Encyclopedia, villetta refers to a small villa or a house with a garden, mainly located in the suburbs. The term villetta refers both to detached and semidetached houses, while *villetta a schiera* refers to terraced houses. Regarding typological and construction characteristics, most of the *villette* are built in masonry with gabled roofs and plastered façades. They are usually developed on a two-story layout, dividing the living area on the ground floor and the sleeping area on the upper floor. They often expand by adding an inhabitable attic to the upper floor, or a multipurpose space (a so-called *taverna*) along with a private garage in the basement.

Since the 1950s, several books focusing on this type have been published by Italian publishers, such as Hoepli and Görlich.[8] These catalogs—which usually feature a selection of country houses, weekend houses, villas, and bourgeois and stately homes, all designed by distinguished architects—offer a range of stylistic and technical solutions to be followed and replicated by design practitioners throughout the country. In this way, they disseminated a specific design culture encompassing not only housing types but also design solutions for specific rooms (living room, bedroom, kitchen) and furnishing elements. [Fig. 1]

One main example is the book edited in 1957 by the Milan-based architect Mario Ravegnani Morosini, dedicated to the *casa individuale* (detached house). Through a selection of twenty-four single-family houses built in central-northern Italy, the book promotes the suburban house as a healthy and low-cost housing solution—in line with British and American trends—according to which the family can achieve a higher degree of wellbeing outside the city. The book explores additional aspects related to a proper integration of the buildings into the landscape and the adoption of local building techniques and materials, highlighting the predominantly rural character of these traditional structures. In contrast, the interior spaces possess traces of the latest influences of modern styles and flexible organization. The author takes into careful consideration the organization of such interior spaces that must be "inhabitable": "The house must be a series of spaces, related to the measure of the ordinary man, tailored to his needs, it should offer in every hour … an area in which one can take refuge, gather, be able to live joyfully."[9]

The villetta model embodies the residential imaginary of many families belonging to the emerging postwar middle class, who in this architectural typology identify the ideal place for the affirmation of their social status. It represents the house where family time is realized and cultivated under the watchful eye of the woman-mother who is its main inhabitant, creator

8. See: Alessandro Lissoni, *Ville Casette* (Milano: Görlich, 1952); Mario Ravegnani Morosini, *La casa individuale in Italia* (Milan: Görlich, 1957); *Villette moderne. Esempi di architettura di ville con studi, progetti, realizzazioni* (Milan: Görlich, 1967).

9. Morosini, *La casa individuale in Italia*, p. 48.

VILLETTE MODERNE

esempi di architettura di ville con studi, progetti, realizzazioni

a

b

c

Fig. 1 — Book covers. a. of *Villette moderne. Esempi di architettura di ville con studi, progetti, realizzazioni* (Milan: Görlich, 1967); b. Mario Ravegnani Morosini, *La casa individuale in Italia* (Milan: Görlich, 1957); c. *Ville—Casette al mare, al lago, in collina, in montagna* (Milan: Görlich, 1971).

Fig. 2 — National Homes Corporation.
a. exterior view of the prototype for a $12,500 house, 1955; b. interior view of the kitchen of the prototype for a $14,000 house, 1955.

Fig. 3 — "Casetta di Grazia," Prefabricated Sector, Milano trade fair, 1960.
Photo by Ancillotti & Marinotti.

and consumer of domestic space and its equipment.[10] The influential role of the housewife-consumer initially came from the United States and spread into European culture through advertisements in women's magazines aimed at the general public offering household appliances, hygiene and care products, and furniture ideas.[11] The spaces of the house themselves reflect male and female domains. Within the villetta, the woman's principal space was the kitchen—a place originally designed according to the modernist functional project. The lower floor or basement—initially intended for car storage, food storage (cellar), and boiler room—was repurposed starting in the mid-1950s to host a more secluded living area with a small kitchen, often furnished in masculine tones for the family man's leisure activities.[12] It was also used as a play space for the children during the day.[13] Another element that relates the villetta housing typology to the emerging consumption models in the postwar years is the growth of the car market, which, starting from the 1950s onwards, enabled the extensive use of the territory and the possession of single-family houses in ever-more distant suburban or rural locations.[14]

Defining the Imaginary of the Villetta: The Role of Exhibitions and Fairs

In defining the imaginary of the Italian villetta, a prominent role was played by some exhibitions and fairs that took place in key Italian cities over a decade starting from the mid-1950s. These exhibitions welcomed the rise of the single-family housing model, as well as the diffusion of light prefabrication systems in the building sector. They also conveyed a lifestyle characterized by precise family roles. A breakthrough, Paolo Scrivano argues, first came with the traveling exhibition "Main Street U.S.A.," which passed through Milan, Paris, Barcelona, and Bari, and was conceived to "show Europe how Americans live."[15] The event—promoted by the United States Department of Commerce and sponsored by several companies in the American building sector—played a decisive role in the development of construction language and internal stylistic features that looked primarily at women's domestic role.[16]

The exhibition hosted two villetta prototypes. The first, costing 14,000 dollars and distributed by Scholz Homes, was

10. Roberta Sassatelli, *Consumer Culture. History, Theory and Politics* (London: Sage 2007).

11. Michela Bassanelli, "Corpi e domesticità in mostra. Le riviste specialistiche, i settimanali femminili, 1958-1972," in *Spazi delle donne. Casa, lavoro, società*, eds. Michela Bassanelli and Imma Forino (Bologna: DeriveApprodi, 2024), pp. 157–170.

12. Imma Forino, *La cucina. Storia culturale di un luogo domestico* (Torino: Einaudi 2019).

13. James A. Jacobs, "Social and Spatial Change in the Postwar Family Room," *Perspectives in Vernacular Architecture* 13 (2006): pp. 70–85.

14. From 1958 to 1963, the presence of cars in Italy had nearly tripled, surging from approximately 1.4 million to almost 4 million. It escalates further to 5 million in the subsequent year. See: Castronovo, *L'Italia del miracolo economico*, p. 95.

15. Joseph A. Barry, "Proudly House Beautiful shows Europe how Americans live," *House Beautiful* 7 (1955): pp. 86–95.

16. See Paolo Scrivano, "Signs of Americanization in Italian Domestic Life: Italy's Postwar Conversion to Consumerism," *Journal of Contemporary History* 40 (2005): pp, 317–340, and Paolo Scrivano, *Building Transatlantic Italy: Architectural Dialogues with Postwar America* (Farnham: Ashgate, 2013).

initially built in Ohio, photographed, and then rebuilt at the Milan trade fair in 1955.[17] The second, costing 12,500 dollars, was built by the National Homes Corporation in Lafayette, Indiana, and then rebuilt in Bari the same year. Both villette are single-story houses with pitched roofs and a covered garage. [Fig. 2] Inside there is a fully equipped independent kitchen with adjoining living and dining rooms, three bedrooms, and a bathroom. The main stylistic innovations are found in the kitchen: the walls are canary yellow, the table and chairs are made of steel, and it contained electrical appliances. The other rooms combine the modern lines of sofas and lamps with classical elements such as sideboards, armchairs, and upholstered chairs. In the images featured in the exhibition catalog, there are no women. However, at a closer glance, there are endless signs that let us imagine a woman's presence with very precise roles connected to domestic work and leisure activities, such as embroidery.

A few years after this event, in 1960, the Milan Trade Fair—one of the main postwar players promoting domestic appliances and prefabricated elements in the building sector—launched the *Casetta di Grazia* (Grazia's small house), a prefabricated single-family house designed by architects Antonio Corradi and Luigi C. Olivieri and produced by an Italian building company.[18] [Fig. 3] The house was named after a women's magazine with the same name that first featured the prototype in 1959. The two-story house was designed for a young middle-class family with two children: the ground floor was for parking the car; the first floor—accessible through an external staircase—included four rooms and a small fully-equipped kitchen.[19] The exterior volumes of the Casetta followed the simple, stereotyped shape of the pitched roof house. At the same time, the interior spaces were characterized by more marked stylistic choices, such as colored plasters and modern furniture. [Fig. 4, 5] The prefabricated model of the Casetta was cheap—it cost 2,400,000 lire—and could be adapted to different contexts, such as residential or holidays settings. A second prototype of the same Casetta was published in 1960 by the magazine *Grazia*, with a focus on the affordability, practicality, and solidity of home furnishing.[20] This second prototype was also exhibited at the Milan Trade Fair, in both 1962 and 1965, with some innovations: a large space was dedicated to the

17. The Trade Fair of Milan had been selected by a high-ranking official of the U.S. Department of Commerce as "the most gigantic and perfectly organized market of a universal character that exists today." Fiera di Milano, "USA per la prima volta ufficialmente presenti in fiera," *Bollettino quotidiano d'informazione dell'ente fiera* 7 (April 20, 1955): p. 4.

18. The first Trade Fair of Milan in 1946 presented electric cookers, removable hobs, and the Candy Modello 50 (model) washing machine.

19. Maria Pia Rosignoli, "La casetta per tutti," *Grazia* 947 (April 12, 1959): pp. 60–74.

20. "Arredati quattro locali con meno di seicentomila lire," *Grazia* 1000 (April 17, 1960): pp. 118–123.

Fig. 4 — "La casetta per tutti," cover of *Grazia* no. 947 (1959).

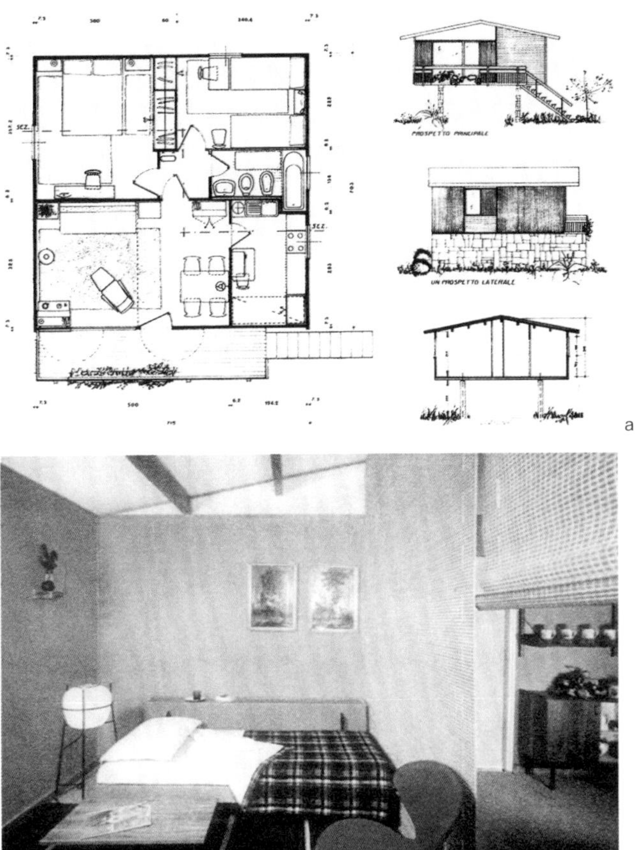

Fig. 5 — "La casetta per tutti,". a. drawings; b. view of the living room
with converted sofa for the night. From *Grazia* no. 947 (1959).

Fig. 6 — "Casetta di Grazia," Prefabricated Sector, Milano trade fair, 1962.

21. Paolo Scrivano, Signs of Americanization in Italian Domestic Life (2005): p. 326.

22. Savorra Massimiliano, "La X Triennale di Milano e la casa prefabbricata," in *Casa per tutti. Abitare la città globale*, ed. Fulvio Irace (Milano: Electa, 2008), pp. 49–61.

23. Graziella Leyla Ciagà, "La casa unifamiliare prefabbricata alla Triennale di Milano," *Rassegna di architettura e urbanistica* 162 (September-October 2020): pp. 23-32.

24. *12. Triennale di Milano* (Milano: Arti Grafiche Crespi, 1960), pp. 68–70.

swimming pool, which enriched the imaginary of the suburban house with pleasant comforts. [Fig. 6]

Another venue that also played a crucial role in the diffusion of single-family house prototypes and the related consumerist model was the Triennale di Milano, which had been active since the 1920s. Starting from the IX Triennale exhibition, held in 1951, architectural and design elements typical of the American way of life were progressively showcased. The US Pavilion, designed by Studio BBPR, featured a selection of household objects including kitchen furniture, toilet equipment, and appliances that highlight the woman's role as the consumer of the domestic space.[21] The X Triennale exhibition in 1954 addressed the emerging subject of the leisure and holiday home by setting up six prototypes, including a prefabricated wooden and aluminum house designed for weekend rest.[22] Among the most interesting examples is the industrialized country house by architects Luciano Baldessari and Marcello Grisotti: a single-story house featuring a pitched roof that encloses two volumes; a smaller one with the kitchen and the bathroom, and a larger one for living and sleeping areas within the same space.

While Baldessari and Grisotti's proposal remained tied to some more traditional architectural elements, the project by architects Gio Ponti, Antonio Fornaroli, and Alberto Rosselli was entirely focused on the language of prefabrication.[23] [Fig. 7] While the exterior façades express a rigid and strong style, the composition of the floor plan creates internal movements through the disposition of three distinct blocks. Finally, in the "Home and School" exhibition hosted in 1960 as part of the XII Triennale exhibition, several life-size housing solutions were displayed, including a proposal for a suburban home developed by architect Fredi Drugman. This proposal aimed at meeting the needs of a typical middle-class family, consisting of a father, mother, and two children, "oriented towards modern lifestyles." The prototype featured a large living area, designed to provide spatial continuity, consisting of a dining area with a fully equipped open-plan kitchen, with several models that underlined women's domestic roles.[24] The photographs that accompany the home prototypes presented at exhibitions and fairs often portray women at work in them or interacting with the new appliances. From these representations, the development of

Fig. 7 — a. Architects Luciano Baldessari and Marcello Grisotti, *Casa industrializzata di campagna* (Industrialised country house), X Triennale exhibition, Milan, 1954; b. Architects Gio Ponti, Alberto Rosselli, and Antonio Fornaroli, single-family house, X Triennale exhibition, Milan, 1954; c. Architect Fredi Drugman, life-size model of a suburban house, XII Triennale exhibition, Milan, 1960.

a

b

Fig. 8 — "La casetta che costa un milione," from *Grazia* magazine no. 896 (1958). a. view of the garden and ground floor plan; b. view of the living room.

Fig. 9 — *"Il Casamodello,"* from *Annabella* no. 15 (1961).

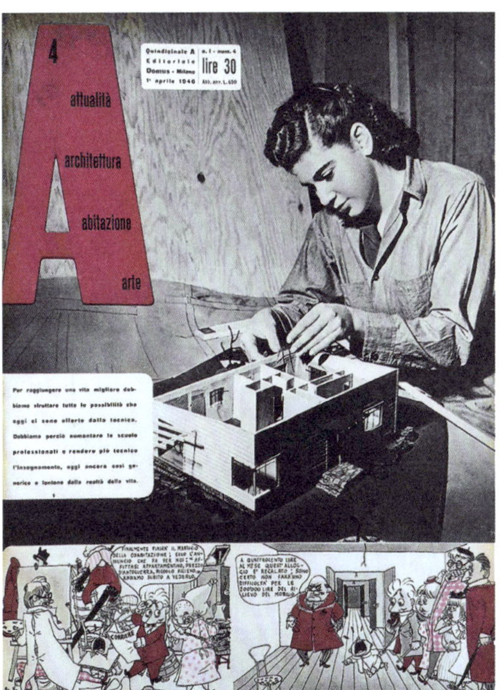

Fig. 10 — Covers of the magazine *A. Attualità Architettura Abitazione Arte*, edited by Lina Bo, Carlo Pagani and Bruno Zevi (1946).

25. Joann Vanek, "Keeping Busy: Time Spent in Housework, United States 1920–1970" (PhD diss., University of Michigan, 1973). See also: Tersilia Faravelli Giacobone, Paola Guidi, and Anty Pansera, *Dalla casa elettrica alla casa elettronica* (Milano: Arcadia, 1989).

26. Among the magazines: *Rivista dell'arredamento* then *Interni* (1955–), *Ville e Giardini* (1956–), *Abitare* (1961–). See also Maria Teresa Feraboli, *Case da sogno. Storie del paesaggio domestico 1840–2019* (Bergamo: Bolis Edizioni, 2019).

27. Among the main magazines: *Annabella. Rivista di moda e attualità femminile* (1938–1984); *Gioia! Settimanale femminile di politica, attualità e cultura per le donne* (1937–2006); *Grazia. Un'amica al vostro fianco* (1938–). For a more detailed discussion, see Alex Banali, "Interni immaginati. La casa italiana degli anni Cinquanta e Sessanta nelle riviste femminili dell'epoca" (Master's thesis, Università degli Studi di Padova, Scuola di Scienze Umane, Sociali e del Patrimonio Culturale, 2015).

28. The full name of the magazine is *Grazia. Un'amica al vostro fianco*. It was established in 1938 in Milan and released on a weekly basis. Inside, there are sections dedicated to the home and interior design, such as: *L'architetto risponde* ("The Architect Answers") and *Arredamento* ("Furnishing").

29. *Annabella. Rivista di moda e attualità femminile*, was a weekly magazine active from 1938 to 1984 and published by Rizzoli, Milan. The columns dealing with interior design include *La vostra casa, Annabella in casa*, and *l'architetto*. "La villetta prefabbricata," *Annabella* 15 (1961): pp. 34–45. Laura Arrighi, "Case, riviste e sogni. Spazi di carta del secondo dopoguerra in Italia e Stati Uniti," in *Interni. Nuove geografie della ricerca*, eds. Jacopo Leveratto, Viviana Saitto, and Valeria Sansoni (Santarcangelo di Romagna: Maggioli, 2020), pp. 35–39.

the household appliance industry emerges as one of the major signs of women's superficial liberation from reproductive labor. The introduction of these appliances proved instead, as was known already in the 1970s, to be yet another instrument of oppression in women's lives.[25]

Defining the Imaginary of the Villetta: The Role of Italian Women's Periodicals and Interior Magazines

During the postwar period, alongside exhibitions and fairs, specialized magazines dedicated to interiors and the home played a key role in disseminating the imagery of the Italian villetta.[26] Certain trends, particularly in terms of décor and furniture, were also covered by general women's magazines, which contributed to the spread of the single-family house model and the dream of a fresh start for new families, realized far away from the city's hustle and bustle.[27]

In 1958, *Grazia* presented the design project titled *La casetta che costa un milione* ("The small house that costs a million lire").[28] In the idyllic opening image, a couple—still wearing their wedding clothes—was portrayed entering into a small house among dense vegetation for the first time. [Fig. 8] The single-story house was built with traditional masonry systems, and the interior was presented as a single living space divided by wooden partitions, furniture elements, and curtains. The house was a mere 430 square feet (40 square meters) total in size, and consisted of a small kitchen of 54 square feet (5 square meters) open to the living room with a sofa bed for guests, a bathroom, and a bedroom with a double bed and a small bed for a child. In the center of the house, a fireplace—built from brick and open on two sides—provides heating. Photographs of interior spaces exclusively depict a woman engaged in household tasks. Again, a simple exterior volume contrasts with interior rooms rich in color as well as innovative space design solutions.

A few years later, the magazine *Annabella* first proposed four solutions for prefabricated homes to be built in the countryside, and then a solution for the "Ideal House," designed by architects Mario Brunati and Sandro Mendini and intended to host a family of four to five people.[29] This second house model, titled *Casamodello* ("The model house"), featured a typical suburban house surrounded by a garden and was equipped with a car. [Fig. 9] Compared to the casetta proposed by *Grazia*, the house has one level but with much larger spaces. The volume is more articulated, not only in plan but also in the slopes of the roof. The interior spaces consist of an entrance hall, a living/dining room, a wardrobe kitchen, a bedroom each for the parents and the children, toilets, and covered outdoor spaces. Total freedom is left in the choice of building materials, as the house "can be located anywhere (countryside, seaside, city, mountain)."[30] The innovative element of this project consists in the repeatability of this "ideal home": the magazine attaches the executive plan of the accommodation that can be presented directly to the building company.

In 1967, the magazine *Abitare* also offered a solution for a quiet life away from the city in just 388 square feet (36 square meters).[31] Architect Carlo Santi's project envisaged a small masonry building with a gable roof for a young couple with three children. The house was situated in the upper part of Brianza (near Como) and cost 3,000,000 lire. On the ground floor was the living/dining room, the kitchen, and the children's room; on the mezzanine was the master bedroom and a small guest room. As in the Casamodello, a role is given to covered outdoor spaces, and the protective character of the building is accentuated by the extension of the roof to form two large lateral porticoes.[32] The interior spaces are meticulously designed to make the best use of space; the interior partitions and the mezzanine are made of spruce wood. The focus of the photographs depicting the space is on the children, who are portrayed at different times of the day as the true owners of this space. In the definition of a new culture of living, children's rooms and their furnishings were of central importance in educational development, as they enable children to develop their character and identity.[33]

Among the magazines that emerged immediately after the war, a less-known role was played by *A. Attualità Architettura Abitazione Arte*, edited by architects Lina Bo, Carlo Pagani, and Bruno Zevi. Inaugurated in 1946 and publishing only nine issues, it was the mouthpiece of certain trends coming directly from the United States: prefabricated houses, American-style kitchens, and modular furniture, such as George Nelson's storage wall.[34] The eye-catching covers show women scrutinizing models of single-family houses or attending to household tasks

30. Mario Brunati and Sandro Mendini, "La casa ideale," *Annabella* 14 (1961).

31. *Abitare* is a monthly magazine that has been running since 1961 with the aim of promoting a new vision of living.

32. Carlo Santi, "Bastano tre milioni per vivere in pace fuori dalla città," *Abitare* 53 (1967): pp. 28–39.

33. "Per bambini mobili e giocattoli," *Domus* 394 (1962): pp. 48–49.

34. Baldo Bandini, "Pareti ed armadi per gli alloggi sinistrati," *A attualità, architettura, abitazione, arte* 3 (March 15, 1946): pp. 8–10.

with care, embracing the prevailing gender culture. [Fig. 10] The magazine also held a referendum (as was customary in women's magazines) open to all Italian women to design the "ideal home," which was introduced by the following:

> Men make houses: they alone calculate pillars, beams, walls... [B]ut in the house formed by walls there is the "house," made up of rooms, appliances, furniture... [O]f things that make the house habitable. In all this, women must be able to speak their mind: whereas for men the house is a place of rest and relaxation, for women ... it is a place of work, it is a school for children's education, it is a hospital when someone falls ill, it is a temple of the family, it is ambition, it is hard work.[35]

The most frequently represented and described interior spaces in all of these examples are the living room and the kitchen. From 1955 to 1975, these two rooms underwent significant transformations, as they embodied the most important social, cultural, and political places of the domestic model. Many of the articles published in women's magazines are devoted to the presentation of all types of kitchens and of living room furniture: armchairs, sofas, bar, and TV equipment—everything that had to be ready for family relaxation and conversations with guests.[36] All these elements contributed to portrayal of the Italian middle-class family in a precise way, through correlation to specific domestic spaces.

Imaginaries and Models Tested by Time

Most of the house prototypes examined above showed construction and typological solutions aimed at both the emerging needs of a postwar, consumerist middle-class society and aligning with developments in the building sector. Building innovation at the time was mostly concerned with two issues. The first involved light prefabrication techniques, which, despite numerous prototypes and the promotion of new construction materials at trade fairs, continue to be an area of experimentation today. In Italy, although there are attempts to steer the construction sector towards prefabrication, and even though many distinguished designers had advocated for dry construction models that could support and advance large-scale industrial building production

35. "Concorso," *A attualità, architettura, abitazione, arte* 1 (February 1946).

36. "Piccoli e grandi fanno bella la casa," *Annabella* 22 (May 1968): 108–109; "Per la casa nuova: nuove idee, colori," *Annabella* 5 (February 1970): pp. 47–53; "Briosi, sobri e comodissimi, i divani e le poltrone," *Gioia* 19 (May 1958); "Un bel divano con poca spesa," *Grazia* 899 (May 1958).

even before the war, these solutions were never able to replace traditional building systems.[37] Most construction of single-family houses has remained anchored to self-promotional dynamics, within which small construction companies dealt directly with families owning a plot of land, and followed low-tech building schemes and local construction traditions. The second issue relates to interior spaces and the innovations related to its flexibility that distinguishes most of the investigated prototypes from the American standard single-family housing model. While maintaining the functional divisions between spaces, these prototypes introduced the theme of transformation through design devices, such as replacing masonry partitions with curtains and modular furniture, the presence of folding furniture, and the introduction of a modern language open to the new research that architects were carrying out in the field of housing. However, these innovations remained mostly on paper and did not take hold in the widespread production of Italian single-family houses, which has remained mostly tied to classical functional and spatial divisions.

Beyond these missed innovations, the distance we have today to those housing prototypes is not just temporal, but also in the models of family, work, and consumption they presupposed. Within favorable territorial conditions, a villetta from the 1960s may endure today and still attract young couples with children. This is particularly true in post-pandemic times, when there has been an increase in demand for old single-family homes in suburbs close to cities due to lower prices and the presence of green areas.[38] Conversely, in more peripheral areas, this housing typology is becoming increasingly inadequate for meeting the demand and responding to current living practices, particularly to the needs of people living and aging alone.[39] For these reasons, it is necessary to reflect on this heritage and understand how it can be adapted and re-inhabited. On the one hand, most of the single-family housing stock would require substantial interventions to meet current energy standards. On the other, it would require a reconsideration starting from the use of interior spaces.[40] This represents one of the most challenging design issues for architects today, as they would need to subvert the idea of privacy embedded in the single-family house to meet current demands for collectivity and mutual support.

37. Maria Teresa Feraboli, "Prefabbrichiamo la futura civiltà," *Rassegna di Architettura e Urbanistica* 162 (2020): pp. 14–22.

38. Viviana Giavarini, Fabio Manfredini, Chiara Merlini, and Federico Zanfi, "A portrait of Italian 'Family houses': diversified heritage in a redefined territorial and demographic context," *City, Territory and Architecture* 7 (2020).

39. The percentage of people living alone exceeded that of couples with children for the first time in Italy in 2021. The National Statistical Institute/ISTAT predicts a further increase: by 2040, there will be about 10,000,000 lonely and aging people.

40. Giovanna Borasi, ed., *A Section of Now: Social Norms and Rituals as Sites for Architectural Intervention* (Leipzig: Spector Books, 2021).

The IKEA Suburb: A Cataloged Imagery of Single-Family Housing

Rebecca Carrai

Now the suburban house has an identity of scale as solidly real as the brick… Iconographically, the suburban house is as American as television.[1] [Fig. 1]

Building for Best Products was an exhibition held in 1979 at the Museum of Modern Art (MoMA) in New York. It presented specially commissioned showrooms of the American Best Products Company. In the exhibition catalog, architect and theorist Stanley Tigerman pointed out the ubiquity of the suburban house and its intrinsic links with consumer culture. While assuming different connotations, the single-family house is a vivid, widespread, transcontinental reality, first emerging in the rising consumer culture of postwar America. More than the architectural typology per se, this essay delves into what could be described as a certain "single-mindedness of living": a yearning for private property and a life goal that is detached from the broader community. This is typically seen through the spatial organization of suburban single-family houses. However, as historian James S. Ackerman suggests, it also extends further back in time and includes, for example, early Medici villas.[2]

As media scholar David Coon argues, suburbia is a utopian space filled with desirable single-family homes, happy dwellers, and carefree lives.[3] It is a concrete spatial arrangement that shapes everyday life and reflects the hopes and fears ingrained in society. This physical and imaginary space has been reinforced over time by narratives in film, television, and, more broadly, commercials, including catalogs. By acknowledging the influential role of mass media in forging certain myths about dwelling at the intersection of space and representation, this essay examines the single-family house—its inhabitants, objects, and images—as mutually constitutive elements. The world's largest furniture company, IKEA, has been a key driver of this. Suburbia is a reality that has unfolded not only in the United

1. Stanley Tigerman, "The Best Home of All," in *Buildings for Best Products* (The Museum of Modern Art, exhibition catalog, 1979), 22. Accessed September 12, 2023. https:/www.moma.org/documents/moma_catalogue_1781_300297029.pdf.

2. James S. Ackerman, *The Villa: Form and Ideology of Country Houses* (Princeton: Princeton University Press, 2017), pp. 9–34.

3. David R. Coon, *Look Closer: Suburban Narratives and American Values in Film and Television* (New Brunswick: Rutgers University Press, 2013).

Fig. 1 — The single-family house as a ubiquitous reality. Page from the catalog *Buildings for Best Products*, The Museum of Modern Art, New York, 1979.

States but also in Sweden, IKEA's country of origin, and many other countries across the globe. This global presence is partially due to the influence of prominent transnational businesses, such as IKEA itself, and their catalogs. While the Swedish furniture company is often associated with modern space-saving solutions, few have noticed IKEA's contribution to the so-called myth of suburbia: its depictions of single-family interiors and spacious living rooms, with glimpses of idyllic gardens set against a suburban backdrop.

Throughout its seventy-year history of building domestic narratives, IKEA's consumerist attitude has tapped into millions, if not billions of people's everyday lives. The IKEA catalog has played a pivotal role in perpetuating the paradigm of the heteronormative, nuclear family.[4] Its representations of domestic interiors suggest what the exterior might be like, acting as carriers of selected traditions, ideal lifestyles, and issues related to gender and race. In examining the representational agency of IKEA's catalog, a counternarrative might emerge from within its pages. This essay will investigate the development from straightforward representations of single-family interiors in IKEA catalogs to the seeming dilution of the IKEA suburb model, to argue that the company acts as a promotor of escapism and individualism. Considering the pressing need for architecture to enhance the coexistence between human and nonhuman beings and tackle urgent questions such as housing for all, it seems more crucial than ever to problematize the legacy of mass media, including shopping catalogs that, through repetitive images and inscription techniques, have infused individualistic values into the collective imagination.

The Origins of IKEA's "Myth of Suburbia"

The IKEA catalog has been idealizing the myth of suburban life since it first went to print over seventy years ago. It has since been published in thirty-two languages and adapted for and distributed to over fifty markets, with peak global distribution occurring in 2016 at two hundred million copies.[5] Preceded by a smaller brochure titled *Ikéa-nytt*, the first official IKEA catalog was published in 1951 and circulated in the same rural area where the company had been founded about ten years earlier: Älmhult. [Fig. 2] This Swedish town, located in the province

4. This analysis focuses on IKEA's Swedish catalog editions from 1951 to 2000, which served as a blueprint for catalogs in other countries. It also involves the examination of selected catalogs from other countries when necessary.

5. "After seventy great years, IKEA is turning the page," Newsroom, IKEA, December 7, 2020, https://www.ikea.com/global/en/newsroom/.

of Småland, was the result of suburbanization.[6] Despite the American suburb most being one of the earliest examples, the suburbs are not unique to the United States. One can also appreciate the influence of American consumer culture in Sweden, including, as architectural historian Joan Ockman elaborates, its unique reinterpretation of postwar modernism, infused with values of affluent consumerist societies.[7] In addition, prosperous Swedish residential neighborhoods in or near city centers can be traced back to nineteenth and twentieth century urbanization projects, which also resulted in widespread suburban expansion.[8]

Both urbanization and suburbanization processes are at the core of the Swedish welfare state, whose program *Folkhem* (People's Home) ran from the 1930s to approximately the 1970s. As the name suggests, the program revolved around the question of housing and aimed to upgrade Sweden, drawing on architectural historian Helena Mattsson's words, from a country belonging to "Europe B" to "Europe A."[9] Various figures—from politicians to municipality architects—and publications—from official manuals to shopping catalogs—contributed to the construction of the "good housing" paradigm.[10] Among them, sociologists and politicians Alva and Gunnar Myrdal played a significant role in the transformation of Sweden from an undeveloped, agricultural country into a modern, developed one.[11] Alva Myrdal's writings—partially written in the United States and influenced by American researcher Allan Carlson—seem to favor the single-family house when arguing for a suburban model based on rural rather than urban living.[12]

In *Urban Children* (1935) and *Crisis in the Population Question* (1934), Alva Myrdal argues that urban environments are not fit for children.[13] With the rise of industrialization and technological advancement, homes in the city became barren and unstimulating. Echoing the Swedish philosopher Ellen Key, Myrdal views the old peasant society as a positive model, where farms are self-sufficient and mothers can be personally fulfilled by domestic labor. Conversely, women in the city require more aid from government programs, as well as support from a male-driven society. Myrdal wrote her theories during an époque when women suffered from a particularly subordinated position in Swedish social hierarchy.

In 1951, IKEA launched its catalog, tapping into and reinterpreting Myrdal's discourse in its pages. Alva Myrdal and

6. Bertil Torekull and Ingvar Kamprad, *Leading by Design: The IKEA Story* (New York: Harper Business, 1998).

7. Joan Ockman, "Architecture and the Consumer Paradigm in the Mid-Twentieth Century," in *Swedish Modernism: Architecture, Consumption and the Welfare State*, eds. Helena Mattsson and Sven-Olov Wallenstein (London: Black Dog Publishing, 2010), pp. 170–87.

8. It is important to note that in the mid-nineteenth century only 10 percent of the Swedish population lived in towns and cities. It was not until the mid-twentieth century that half of the population lived in cities and this period corresponded to greater urbanization. See Sören Edvinsson and Hans Nilsson. "Swedish Towns during Industrialization," in *Annales de Démographie Historique 1999 2* (1999): pp. 63–96.

9. Helena Mattsson, "Designing the Reasonable Consumer: Standardisation and Personalisation in Swedish Functionalism," in *Swedish Modernism*, pp. 84–85.

10. Rebecca Carrai, "Normalizing the Home: A Synchronic Comparison Between the Ikéa Catalogue and God Bostad," *siTA* 9 (2021): pp. 29–50; Maria Perers, "Inside the Ideal Home" (PhD diss., Bard Graduate Center, 2020).

11. Myrdal Alva, *Nation and Family: The Swedish Experiment in Democratic Family and Population Policy* (Cambridge: MIT Press, 1968).

12. Hedvig Ekerwald, "Alva Myrdal: Making the Private Public," *Acta Sociologica* 43, no. 4 (2000): pp. 343–352.

13. Ekerwald: pp. 349-50.

Fig. 2 — The suburban lawn where the first IKEA store was built in 1958, next to the company's head offices in Älmhult, Sweden.

14. Confirming the modernity of their views, today there appears to be a re-evaluation of certain ideals of living; see, for example: Kristen Ghodsee, *Everyday Utopia. In Praise of Radical Alternatives to the Traditional Family Home* (London: The Bodley Head, 2023).

15. This approach can be observed throughout the catalog but see, for example, Catalog, IKEA (1951): pp. 30, 55, 61.

16. Jon Stobart and Cristina Prytz, "Comfort in English and Swedish Country Houses, c.1760–1820," *Social History* 43, no. 2 (April 2018): pp. 234–58.

Ellen Key urged for a proximity to nature, down-to-earth labor, and a connection with traditional culture as opposed to modern city life.[14] [Fig. 3] Monochrome images featuring period-style furniture and traditional plan layouts flooded the catalog's pages.[15] The dining room represented the center point of IKEA's imagined society—one which, rather than envisioning a better model of living or voicing feminist positions, imitated dated bourgeois cultures and mimicked historical styles that mark the middle-class. Despite vaguely mirroring Key's wish to return to an idyllic past, these spaces featured static layouts with uncomfortable, French-bourgeoisie inspired furniture. Such warped notions of comfort, homeliness, and warmth—the tradition of "domestic informality" shared in eighteenth and nineteenth century England and Sweden—returned uncritically to a pre-modern scenario.[16] In doing so, these catalogs also situated their products in an industrial, capitalist agenda.

Fig. 3 — A dining room in one of the early IKEA catalog, 1951. Complete with period furniture, the dining room was the core of the 1950s single-family house.

IKEA's early mass media was generally populated with richly decorated wooden wardrobes, dining tables, chairs, and knickknacks that prospective buyers could envision raising their social status. The catalog images often included pastoral paintings, evading the modern industrial society, as well as fireplaces, which represented the meeting point of the heterosexual, patriarchal family. Although images in the early catalogs were less animated than they are today, and different visual elements were not always portrayed together in the same image, their sequential position and repetition constructed a certain narrative for the reader.

Fig. 4 — View of a garden in the IKEA 1958 catalog. Outdoor spaces become new domestic commodities.

Fig. 5 — View of the living room in the IKEA 1963 catalog. The suburban, stylistically eclectic narrative highlighted in the 1960s catalogue is complemented by modernist designs and rational layout solutions.

Material Expansion: Absorbing Greater American Influences to Consolidate IKEA's suburbia

By the end of the 1950s, IKEA's catalog reinforced the suburban idyll by depicting the dining room alongside various other domestic spaces, including the outdoors.[17] [Fig. 4] As a clear asset of any single-family house, the garden in the 1958 IKEA catalog reflects a process of expansion and externalization from the domestic interior for leisure. IKEA's myth of suburbia was fully consolidated between the 1960s and 1980s. The catalog images became less static, more colorful, and began to incorporate tele-visual forms of expression, thus offering explicit suggestions for the customer. Better designed than the early, blurry, black-and-white editions, the 1960s catalog interiors helped the reader to imagine a home's exterior. [Fig. 5] For example, prominent large windows offered a vivid idea of the suburban surroundings. Usually framed by draped, kitschy curtains, these "portals" gave a clear view of idyllic gardens, pitched roofs, and fences that were protecting private property: all to show a household model that was alluded to more directly in the 1960s IKEA catalog.[18]

Together with an increase in modern storage and space-saving solutions that responded to housing shortages regulated by the Swedish Housing Board, IKEA's catalog promoted a suburban narrative, and eventually combined contrasting registers of the urban and the rural.[19] Due to its growing range of products, the 1960s was a period of increased eclecticism and aesthetic transition for IKEA's catalog. It also included images of rational lines and diagrams that illustrated how to economize both space and money. These images included a compact living room and a separate bedroom, hall, and kitchen, ideal for small urban flats, and offered a narrative aligned with a rhetoric of modernity and functionality.[20] [Fig. 6] This was presented in parallel with echoes of the 1950s catalogs, which featured spacious, pompous, fully accessorized rural interiors offering a very different narrative—one aligned with the postmodern allure of pastiche and collage.[21] Yet, despite the various trends on display, the single-family house as a whole became more refined, with an increasing number of new objects, functions, and rooms. This is clearly represented by the old-fashioned Antiquva chair that appears in the 1964 catalog and is portrayed with the woman of the house reclining in the chair and knitting.[22]

17. Catalog, IKEA (1958): p. 39.

18. For example, Catalog, IKEA (1964): p. 205.

19. Carrai, "Normalizing the Home," pp. 29-50.

20. Although this is not the only time that an illustration suggests a whole interior decoration and ideal floor planning, see, for instance, Catalog, IKEA (1962): p. 19.

21. Fredric Jameson, "Postmodernism and Consumer Society," in *The Anti-Aesthetic: Essays on Postmodern Culture*, ed. Hal Foster (Washington: Bay Press, 1983), pp. 111–26.

22. Catalog, IKEA (1964): p. 54.

While in 1950 it was typical for a family home to have one or two bedrooms and a kitchen, during the 1960s, most homes included three or more rooms.[23] It is during this shift from a housing shortage to a surplus, and during this period of economic growth, that the IKEA catalog increased both the number of products included in its pages and number of copies printed—up to two million per year by the mid-1960s.[24] As a result, there were even more visitors to IKEA's newly opened stores, firstly in Älmhult, and subsequently in Stockholm. Simultaneously, in 1965, the Swedish government launched the Million Program, which is continued till 1974 and identified by some as the pinnacle of the Swedish welfare state.[25] During these ten years, one quarter of Sweden's housing stock was built, with approximately one third consisting of single-family dwellings. The program also entailed the development of urban and suburban infrastructures, including shopping centers and malls. The purchasing power of Swedish consumers doubled between 1950 and 1975, and the country embraced unbridled consumerism. This included driving, with Sweden having the highest number of cars per capita in Europe.[26] Residential settlements, usually built in the untouched countryside outside or near cities, were conceived as commuter areas that would have bolstered infrastructures, small stores, day care centers, schools, and various other service facilities close by.[27]

IKEA's Americanism

Although links between American and Swedish cultures can be identified in the preceding centuries, they were reinforced starting in the mid-1950s, and particularly from the 1960s, by a clear growing interest in American domestic culture. This phenomenon can be observed in the popular Swedish magazine *Allt I Hemmet,* which advocated for large family kitchens inspired by the postwar American "family room," a space devoted to the family's activities and hobbies.[28] In Sweden, single-family houses [Fig. 7] were usually located in smaller communities separate from the main urban centers. They were built by private developers and usually comprised of prefabricated elements, in line with the American Levitt & Sons' catalog houses.[29] The affordable wooden constructions built in Sweden featured traditional saddle roofs and convertible lofts.[30] Echoing the American

23. Thomas Hall and Sonja Vidén, "The Million Homes Programme: A Review of the Great Swedish Planning Project," *Planning Perspectives* 20, no. 3 (January 2005): pp. 301–28.

24. Eva Alte Bjarnestam, *IKEA: Design & Identity* (Verona: TITEL Books AB for IKEA of Sweden, 2013).

25. Erik Stenberg et al., *Structural Systems of the Million Program Era* (Stockholm: KTH School of Architecture, 2013).

26. Helena Mattsson, "Where the Motorways Meet: Architecture and Corporatism in Sweden 1968," in *Architecture and the Welfare State*, eds. Mark Swenarton, Tom Avermaete, and Dirk Van den Heuvel (Abingdon: Routledge, 2015), p. 159.

27. Jennifer Mack, "Impossible Nostalgia: Green Affect in the Landscapes of the Swedish Million Programme," *Landscape Research* 46, no. 4 (May 2021): pp. 558–73.

28. Perers, "Inside the Ideal Home," pp. 76–78.

29. Paul D. Naish, "Homegrown History: Popular Historiography on Exhibition at the Levittown Mini-Museum," *The Columbia Journal of American Studies* 3, no. 1 (1998).

30. Stenberg et al., *Structural Systems of the Million Program Era*, pp. 8–9; 106–7.

Fig. 6 — View of the living room in the IKEA 1964 catalog. Large windows offer expansive views of the suburban landscape, subtly emphasizing the single-family home as the preferred model of homeownership.

Fig. 7 — View of Bankekind, Linköping ,1966, showcasing a residential area from the Million Homes Program, characterized by single-family houses set in a rural landscape. Photo by AB Flygtrafik, Bengtstors.

model, the Swedish home was envisioned as a set of modular parts meant to be assembled in various ways that, as understood by Ockman, allowed for a relaxed, integrative relationship with one's surrounding landscape.[31] Among many other locations, single-family houses in Sweden were built in the cities of Växjö, Alvesta, and Lund—all less than one hour away by car from the flagship IKEA store in Älmhult. There is no direct evidence of any official involvement of IKEA in furnishing homes during the Million Program era, but considering their product range, catalog imagery, and, more generally, promoted lifestyles at the time, it seems highly likely that residents furnished their homes by shopping at IKEA.

IKEA also promoted American car culture, introducing highway maps into their catalogs in the 1960s which high-lighted routes to their stores out in the periphery. More broadly, IKEA transformed the experience of retail from pure commerce into a social activity that can build a sense of community, particularly in rural areas otherwise lacking in gathering places. This resonated with concomitant American retail and urban planning theories, such as those of Victor Gruen and Larry Smith.[32] IKEA founder's, Ingvar Kamprad, went on a field trip to the United States in 1961.[33] Interested in the drive-in and motel model of shopping, he returned to Älmhult with the idea to design the first IKEA motel, which he commissioned to company architect Claes Knutson, who had also travelled to the USA.[34] [Fig. 8] Recalling the elongated single-story plan of postwar American motels, along with their visibility and easy access from the road, the 1964 IKEA motel became a public attraction in the suburban landscape.[35] As well as offering a com-fortable overnight stay and a large car park, the motel featured highly desirable amenities such as a swimming pool and sauna. Kamprad wanted to create a suburban facility that praised both modernity and countryside living. In creating such a facility, Kamprad also aimed at the growing number of customers throughout Sweden who travelled to the Älmhult store by car.

IKEA's adherence to what architectural historian Jean-Louis Cohen defined as "Americanism" is apparent as it began to construct its imagery in line with what was disseminated in American media.[36] This often reflected a sense of forward-look-ing optimism and highlighted an innovation-obsessed, hedonis-tic culture. IKEA's catalogs from the 1960s and 1970s present

31. Ockman, "Architecture and the Consumer Paradigm in the Mid-Twentieth Century," pp. 170–87.

32. Victor Gruen and Larry Smith, *Shopping Towns USA: The Planning of Shopping Centres* (New York: Van Nostrand Reinhold Company, 1960).

33. "IKEA till Tony och Hugo," Archive & Collection, IKEA Museum AB, Älmhult.

34. Samuel Palmblad, *Arkitekt Claes Knutson – Du Får Aldrig Stunden Tillbaka* (Växjö: Kulturspridaren Förlag, 2020).

35. Geoffrey Baker and Bruno Funaro, *Motels* (New York: Reinhold Publishing Corporation, 1955); John A. Jackle, Keith A. Sculle, and Jefferson S. Rogers, *The Motel in America,* (Baltimore: John Hopkins University Press, 1996).

36. Jean-Louis Cohen, *Building a new New World: Amerikanizm in Russian Architecture* (New Haven: Yale University Press, 2020).

the suburban dream by promoting the importance of the family, leisure, nature, and community within a perfectly charming, quiet, idealized American postwar suburban environment. Despite modernized solutions for home management and childcare, heteronormativity and patriarchal values were still at play, with women still being portrayed as chief protagonists of the home in IKEA's catalog images. There was no hint at the possibility of being both a mother and a wage earner. Instead, nuclear families consisting of a mother, father, and child were portrayed in ideal domestic scenes. Once the housing question was solved, IKEA catalogues started featuring larger living rooms with more commodities, thus portraying wealthy domesticity: dressing tables for the housewife's make-up; various cozy accessories, such as bed throws; and an increasing amount of outdoor equipment and furniture.

Bigger furniture pieces offered organization systems for larger interiors, such as bookshelves designed to contain all the diverse accessories now entering the home like televisions, radios, and other entertainment devices. Large wall-to-wall storage units, particularly suited for spacious suburban houses, were not only designed in different sizes, but could also be assembled according to a customer's personal preferences and needs. During the 1960s and 1970s, the "do-it-yourself" concept which IKEA is now famous for, from browsing the catalog to the in-store experience, became fully developed. This enabled the company to cut costs, while the catalog advertised self-sufficiency as a form of household entertainment. At the same time, the size of rooms depicted in the catalog grew larger, with extra domestic spaces and activities becoming included, which were all in need of additional furniture and equipment: from broad corner sofas and bigger bathrooms with hot tubs, to new wardrobes and storage spaces, laundry and bicycle rooms, garages, outdoor recreation areas, and so on. They even included office corners, a clear demonstration of IKEA's historical role in shaping new lifestyles and what has become today's commingling between living and working.

Another way that IKEA promoted the suburban dream was by depicting a second home. This paradigmatic single-family typology fostered an intrinsic motivation for private property, as well as the image of a green idyll. By the mid-1970s, IKEA was capitalizing on these ideals even further: while gardens

Fig. 8 — Visitors experiencing the newly built IKEA motel, circa 1964, Älmhult, Sweden.

37. Catalog, IKEA (1980), cover.

38. Perers, "Inside the Ideal Home," p. 431.

39. More on the final phase of the Swedish welfare system in: Helena Mattsson, *Architecture & Retrenchment: Neoliberalisation of the Swedish Model across Aesthetics and Space, 1968–1994* (London: Bloomsbury, 2023).

40. Catalog, IKEA (1989), cover.

had always been present in catalogs, as backgrounds of interior images, images of lush Swedish nature and serene outdoor vistas became increasingly common, and even linked to IKEA's brand identity. Nature was not the only object of commodification: childhood, too, through the increasing prevalence of children's furniture.[37] Indeed, the perfect suburban single-family house required a child's room, and why not, a dog. [Fig. 9]

The Dilution of IKEA's Suburban Myth

From the mid 1970s onwards, IKEA's myth of suburbia seemingly started to falter, concomitantly with the business's global expansion, the end of the Million Program, and the beginning of the Swedish housing market's deregulation. As argued by design historian Maria Perers, the following two decades marked the turning point when "ideals [became] more wholly driven by the market."[38] Indeed, IKEA had always represented market forces, yet during this time, a certain predisposition to align with Swedish state-led housing norms and visions became clearly discernible. From 1973, when IKEA opened its first store outside of Scandinavia, to the end of the 1980s, the company had become a conglomerate with around eighty stores around the globe. Throughout that time, and into the early 1990s, when the welfare state system was considered over and radically new attitudes about housing—including furnishing standards— came to the fore, IKEA adapted its agenda in accordance with the wider Swedish national narrative.[39] In other countries, the catalog served as a model for the store. Its task, following meticulous market research, was to adapt their advertisements to local cultures.

Nevertheless, the 1980s Swedish catalogs largely consolidated IKEA's suburban narrative through the repetitive presentation of single-family houses. The catalogs continued to portray spacious and luxurious domestic interiors with bay windows, elegantly laid dining tables, and floral patterns. The occasional appearance of a modern technological device or a piece of edgy furniture dispelled the myth and reminded the audience that times were changing. On the cover of the 1989 catalog, a living room was portrayed from an elevated standpoint, suggesting a mezzanine more in line with a loft typology.[40] The same catalog featured a new furniture line, Sätta Bo, which was designed to address different generational needs, such as young couples moving from the countryside to the city who needed cheaper, compact furniture.[41] Sätta Bo alludes to a fleeting style of living, rather than a peaceful and grand idyllic past.

Over time, views through windows became hazier, eventually no longer suggesting the home's exterior at all, instead implying the potentially ubiquitous character of IKEA's products.[42] And, as much as the furniture, styles, and domestic typologies diversified, so did the family models. Women began to be portrayed engaging in nondomestic activities, and men were pictured more involved in childcaring, though local

41. The furniture line had been introduced some years earlier already, but it starts gaining more visibility with the 1989 catalog.

42. Catalog, IKEA (1996), p. 80; Catalog, IKEA (1996): p. 51.

Fig.9 — View of the living room with a chimney in the IKEA 1981 catalogue. In the luxurious setting of a spacious, elegantly decorated living room, even dogs become part of the IKEA range of commodities.

catalogs and digital media adjusted to varying political contexts surrounding gender in different countries. For instance, IKEA's first advertisement featuring a nonheteronormative couple aired in 1994 on American television, while images in the 2013 catalog for Saudia Arabia excluded women. It was not by chance that IKEA's broader vision of diverse domestic cultures came about as the company was expanding to new markets. Its target had shifted from the local to the global, and as with the introduction of children's furniture in the 1980s, the more variegated the target, the greater the income.

IKEA's "Single-minded" Living

Before the publication was discontinued in 2021, the IKEA catalog had formed an immense archive of objects, values, and traits designed and curated by the company. This archive was opened up and communicated through continuously evolving techniques of inscription. Conceiving of the IKEA catalog as

43. Ursula Lindqvist, "The Cultural Archive of the IKEA Store," *Space and Culture* 12, no. 1 (February 2009): pp. 43–62.

44. Gendered narratives are particularly frequent in the 1950s, 1960s, and 1970s editions, but they continue to also exist later. See, for example, Catalog, IKEA (1985): pp. 212; Catalog, IKEA (1999): pp. 213, 221. Records from women employees at IKEA, particularly since the 1960s, come from the Archive & Collection, IKEA Museum AB, Älmhult.

an archive allows us to underpin the power and authority of the company's long-lasting authorial medium. IKEA's myth of suburbia, whether focused directly on single-family housing, or diverging from this typology in the phase of its apparent dilution, has been historically constructed through romanticized images of IKEA's hometown, Älmhult, and rural life more widely, complete with farmhouse-style furniture and single-family home interiors. At the center of this narrative has always been the desire to detach from reality and live in a dreamy, private—obviously IKEA-decorated—space. But this seemingly idyllic, easy-to-assimilate archive of visual, material, and textual narratives has, as suggested by Scandinavian studies scholar Ursula Lindqvist, simultaneously archived other stories.[43] The preponderant incorporation of typical characteristics from Sweden and pandering to the welfare state system made the IKEA catalog, for much of its existence, a vividly nationalistic project. Eugenics and patriarchal discourse are often interwoven in the catalog pages and represented through a seductive serial juxtaposition of text and images, while neglecting any divergence from "the norm." Flipping through the IKEA catalog today, one cannot help but notice the predominance of white bodies and heteronormative domestic scenes. There is no LGBTQ+ representation and no diverse family models. The images situate women—regardless of their presence in the professional work force—not as empowered agents, but as figures upon which masculine narratives are imposed.[44]

Although these images disseminate a subjective view of powerful hierarchies both in the family and society, the agency of the catalog has been particularly effective in introducing nuances and replacing certain values with trends that are tangential to the mainstream. This has contributed to its great commercial success: from the incorporation of American influences to the dilution of a nationalist agenda and its appeal to foreign cultures. An exemplary product of capitalist mass media, the real power of the catalog lies in its skills of abstraction and a representation of relatable lifestyles that are attached to domestic scenes. These scenes altogether shape the *topoi* of IKEA's myth of suburbia. The catalogs depicted a new economy, consisting of a series of discrete buildings and interiors, usually displaying an air of good taste, dreamy landscapes, and social order. The IKEA suburb unfolds both in a (literally) represented and metaphorical form throughout the catalog's lifespan.

More straightforward representations of IKEA's suburban myth are evident, for example, in the STOCKHOLM collection, a sort of sub-brand launched in 1985 to sponsor nationalistic designs and attract more up-market consumers. The 2020 catalog, which was published in tandem with pandemic de-urbanization, also carries traces of a supposedly escapist rural life.[45] Further evidence of IKEA's myth of suburbia is subtly intertwined with other mismatched elements, such as a more contemporary aesthetic or more contemporary materials. One could argue, then, that a major feature of the IKEA catalog is what designer Clino Castelli describes as "transitive design," a phenomenon that—though now widespread in contemporary material culture—the company had long been experimenting with. By playing with the viewer's imagination, the IKEA catalog attempted to connect the past and future without any nostalgic intent or futuristic ambition.[46] In Castelli's words, transitive products are "temporal ferries": products, images, or signs filled with eclectic references and specifically designed to depart from an accurate depiction of reality.[47] These familiar objects evoke homely sensations and memories that are easily interiorized by the reader.

Assimilations and reinterpretations of the IKEA myth of suburbia can be observed around the world. Not only is the suburban house an enduring icon of contemporary living, disparate replicas and interiorizations of its alluded way of living are easily observed. This can be seen in "trad wife" and "cottagecore," recent trends romanticizing patriarchal family models and Western agricultural lifestyles, mirroring the ideal perpetuated in IKEA's catalogs and in the current demand for more spacious single-family houses, resulting from and exacerbated during the COVID-19 pandemic.[48] Whereas sociologist Henri Lefebvre expressed his doubts in the 1970s concerning a possible return to nature by conceptualizing what he calls "complete urbanization," the IKEA catalog has concealed the intrinsic business nature of its mythicized domesticity. Therefore, it gives the impression of operating outside of industrialized society. While reality is complex, hyper-productive, dynamic, and conflicting, the company presents an enduring and reliable sense of inactivity, stillness, and happiness at home.[49]

IKEA's suburbia, whether figurative or literal, promotes passive viewing and individualism. It presents its interior designs

45. Catalog, IKEA (2020): pp. 8–9.

46. Clino Trini Castelli, *Transitive Design: A Design Language for the Zeroes* (Milan: Mondadori Electa, 1999).

47. Castelli, *Transitive Design*.

48. Sophie Elmhirst, "The Rise and Fall of The Trad Wife," *The New Yorker*, March 29, 2024; Alexandra Petri, "Goblincore? Cottagecore? Here Are Some More-Cores, since We're Doing This," *Washington Post*, September 18, 2021.

49. This argument is also suggested in Andrés Jaque, *Ikea Disobedients* (2011).

as a way to escape the hectic lifestyle that most of us lead, drawing connections between beauty and nature. By treating domestic reality and images of interior design equally, the IKEA catalog flattens the nuance and complexity of home life, while suggesting that owning cozy domestic products can allow individuals to liberate themselves from day-to-day reality. The images present a static utopia that leaves one's relation to society unquestioned and eschew the significant role that capitalist corporations and their allies, such as advertising, have in shaping dominant lifestyles. By analyzing the images in IKEA's catalogs, we are able to not only disclose its logic of archiving, representing, and perpetuating domestic narratives over its seventy-year lifespan, but also underpin IKEA's cultural, authorial influence on the single-family housing market, or better, a "single-mindedness" of living that surpasses its typological setting.

CHANGE

"Invisible" User-Generated Change: Coping with Housing Insecurity in Portland, Oregon

Kateryna Malaia

There is no doubt: the United States, like many other places around the world, is in a socially universal housing crisis. What is so universal about it? Housing unaffordability no longer exclusively affects those devoid of resources. Now it also affects middle class urbanites who, according to American economic stereotypes, should be able to secure housing without an issue. They have to be proactive and resourceful if they want their housing security to last.

"We got so lucky with this house in 2015. I realized that we were getting priced out of Portland, and if we didn't buy a house then, we never would have," says Pandora S., a small-business owner in her early thirties.[1] Her business is in the vibrant and gentrified neighborhood of Southeast Portland, Oregon. Her home, however, is in Vancouver, Washington—Portland's bedroom community. "Our house is very small, only 800 square feet (74 square meters). It was built as temporary housing for the docks' military personnel in 1942." The story is as old as time: there is nothing more permanent than the temporary. Since 2015, Pandora and her partner have been modifying the house to gain more space. They did not get a permit to turn the garage into a studio/office "because it would have been a bureaucratic nightmare." Their contractor from Portland was not licensed to work in Washington. "If we were to sell [the house], we would not add the square footage of the garage to the overall house footage; we would just call it a special feature," she explained.

Peter Marcuse and David Madden identify that the language of the "current" housing crisis refers to the American middle class experiencing housing unaffordability, while for the oppressed, housing has never really been affordable or readily available.[2] The 2022 Harvard University Joint Center for

1. Names of all homeowners are changed. Pandora S., interview by author, Portland, Oregon, May 2020.

2. David Madden and Peter Marcuse, *In Defense of Housing: The Politics of Crisis* (New York: Verso, 2016), pp. 9–11.

3. *The State of the Nation's Housing 2022* (Cambridge: Joint Center for Housing Studies of Harvard University, 2022), p. 4.

4. Teresa A. Sullivan, Elizabeth Warren, and Jay Lawrence Westbrook, *The Fragile Middle Class: Americans in Debt* (New Haven: Yale University Press, 2020), p. 242.

5. Sullivan, Warren, and Westbrook, p. 202.

6. Matthew Desmond, *Evicted: Poverty and Profit in the American City* (New York: Crown, 2016).

Housing Studies report identifies that access to homeownership for middle-income and first-time homebuyers has become progressively more difficult everywhere in the United States, not just in expensive metropolitan areas:

> At today's prices, the down payment that a first-time buyer would have to make on a median-priced home—typically 7.0 percent of the sales price—amounted to $27,400 in April 2022. Without help from family or other sources, this requirement alone would rule out 92 percent of renters, whose median savings are just $1,500.[3]

Moreover, for those who are able to purchase a home, homeownership may hold an "important place in financial distress" because "homes join credit card debt" as one of the "voluntary sources of money troubles."[4] Teresa A. Sullivan, Elizabeth Warren, and Jay Lawrence Westbrook remark that although homeownership should signify the "solid financial stability of the middle class," bankruptcy data suggests that homeowners are not immune to financial struggles, and home-ownership itself may be a part of the problem, especially in the context of increasingly pricey housing that is rampant nearly anywhere in the country.[5]

The laws and financial opportunities, as well as the homes and residents examined in this essay, perfectly fit the definition of this seemingly secure middle or lower-middle class: practically none of the materials below concern the urban poor and homeless. The questions of homelessness and evictions that are more relevant than ever in the United States are effectively addressed in other research, such as Matthew Desmond's re-markable and infamous book *Evicted: Poverty and Profit in the American City*.[6] This essay, on the contrary, chooses to concentrate on those who have housing and who most likely own their homes. This is not out of disregard for the problem of homeless-ness, but because of an interest in a different dimension of what it means to dwell and adjust to economic precarity—namely, the home's physical qualities, and the practice of modifying one's home to fit one's needs, especially when those needs are determined by changing economic or social conditions.

Housing Stories

A first-time home buyer wants to purchase a house. To receive a mortgage in the United States, this home buyer needs to demonstrate a stable income, make a significant down payment, beat other buyers with an offer, and finally, be able to sustain their dream home for the years to come. Although affordable housing programs and underwriting criteria help avoid foreclosures, the sheer number of foreclosures shows that these safety measures are often ineffective.[7] On a large scale of housing policies, real estate economies, and planning, precarity in the lives of housed individuals may not seem apparent. Yet, it only takes a few stories about buying and remodeling a house to clearly recognize the materiality and space-use patterns of precarity in contemporary single-family homes.

In gentrified and gentrifying cities, the sense of insecurity that comes with housing is omnipresent. At the same time, this growing homeowners' insecurity is difficult to discern in large numbers, statistics, social policies, and other wide lenses of knowledge. This is perhaps even more true for familiar domestic architecture that we often inhabit instinctively without questioning our ways or the challenges we face on an everyday basis. Only when architectural comforts are compromised do we realize that those comforts even existed. As residents, we rarely verbalize the changes we can feel in the bones and muscles of our lived environments—until we happen to tell a story about the architecture we occupy. Homelessness is often apparent to a passer-by; an eviction, although a relatively short moment in time, can be a terribly traumatic experience precisely due to the visibility and shame attached to it. But housing insecurity is often invisible until it manifests in an eviction or foreclosure, especially if it is covered up by the seemingly solid façade of the employed urban middle class. Behind these façades, urbanites are hastily adapting the architecture of their homes to new precarious economic conditions. To understand these conditions, I choose to focus on two different realities of resident-generated housing modifications: the formal reality of legal and financial regulations and trends, and the informal reality of unpermitted housing modifications often performed by residents without bank financing and oversight from governing bodies. I will do this through two different types of lenses: an inquiry into the

7. See Barrett Lee and Megan Evans, "Forced to Move: Patterns and Predictors of Residential Displacement During an Era of Housing Insecurity," *Social Science Research* 87 (March 2020).

8. *Accessory Dwelling Unit Cost and Financing Guide*, Santa Cruz County, September 2018, p. 8.

9. "Accessory Dwelling Units," San Francisco Planning, accessed May 27, 2024, https://sfplanning.org/.

10. "Portland, OR," Help Center, Airbnb, accessed May 27, 2024, https://www.airbnb.com/help/article/875/portland-or.

taxonomy of home modifications, built on formal definitions and statistics, and an inquiry into the everyday lived qualities of these spaces.

Taxonomy

There are several categories of modifications that should be considered. Currently, many municipalities around the country have adopted the language of an Accessory Dwelling Unit (ADU) that has effectively replaced many historic terms, such as granny flats and in-law suites. In this essay, I will adopt a widely used definition of these modifications, employed in cities such as San Francisco and Santa Cruz. The City of Santa Cruz identifies the following types of modifications that fit into the definition of an ADU:

> (a) A converted space within an existing house or accessory structure; (b) New space built above a garage; (c) Addition to existing house; (d) New detached building.[8]

San Francisco further provides a reference to historic definitions in relation to current day terms:

> Accessory Dwelling Units (ADUs), also called secondary units, in-law units, or cottages, are units added to existing residential buildings.[9]

The next taxonomy lines are drawn between the homeowners that have and those that have not received permits for their ADUs and modifications. The presence or the lack of a permit affects the location and quality of an ADU; an unpermitted ADU is highly unlikely to be obvious from the street. Hence, it would likely appear in the back of the lot or hidden within the existing structure. Furthermore, the lack of a permit limits the types of uses that are possible for an ADU. In Portland, an unpermitted ADU will be difficult to use for short-term rentals, since rental platforms such as Airbnb require every host to obtain an accessory rental short-term permit, register with a transient-lodging tax program, and report short-term renting as a business.[10] Long-term rentals, however, present no problem, as the city does not heavily regulate them.

Alternatively, long-term rentals can also be occupied without any legal contracts or oversight whatsoever. Furthermore, some Accessory Dwelling Units may appear as simply invisible from the outside: as housing prices rise, many owners choose to subtly convert single-family residences into multiple-unit homes in ways that are unknown to the city.

Every modification, no matter how subtle, requires funds. Therefore, the availability of financing tools for ADU construction is among the most important changes that have taken place in recent years. Together with city tax initiatives, newly available financing mechanisms are arguably the biggest driving force for some types of residential modifications, besides gentrification and general population growth. One such example is the Pacific Northwestern nonprofit Craft3—a community development organization that lends money for ADU construction to homeowners who may not have enough home equity to qualify for traditional home equity loans or do not want to deal with ill-famed second mortgages.[11] A couple of decades ago, financial instruments for ADU construction virtually did not exist. This used to be a chicken-and-egg problem: banks did not have the tools to estimate the risks of ADU investments based on property value increase, hence they did not issue loans. But the more ADUs were getting built, the more data emerged on how they were affecting property values. For large banks, and even more so for local credit unions, this data was an encouraging reason to work with homeowners and find ways to provide them with financing tools.

Cities where ADU construction is on the rise also actively work with banks to establish new rules and financing opportunities. For example, in 2022, the city of Seattle was negotiating with financial institutions to establish a practice of estimating future rent from a permitted ADU into loan calculations:

> If you are planning to either buy or build a home with an ADU, keep in mind that, at this time, most lenders "generally" do not include the potential rental income from the ADU in computing your income, for purposes of determining the value of loan you can qualify for. ARCH [A Regional Coalition for Housing] and the City of Seattle are actively working with the lending community to modify this practice. At this time, we are not aware of any bank that includes a portion of rental income in determining the amount of a loan.[12]

11. "Loans for Accessory Dwelling Units (ADUS)," Craft3, accessed August 15, 2022, https://www.craft3.org/.

12. "Lending Assistance," A Regional Coalition for Housing, accessed August 15, 2022, https://www.archhousing.org/.

Fig. 1, Fig. 2 — Fourplexes in Portland, Oregon, 2022. Photos by author.

Starting in 2010, the city of Portland—like many other cities facing housing shortage conditions—established a temporary System Development Charges (SDC) Waiver Program for ADU construction.[13] In 2018, this temporary program became permanent. The only condition of the waiver program, which can save homeowners thousands of dollars, is that the ADU should not be used for short-term rentals for 10 years after its construction.[14] With this initiative, Portland tried to curb the short-term rentals for tourists that are among the factors blamed for skyrocketing rental prices, housing shortages, and the growing homeless population. Finally, in 2020, Portland became the first city in the country to allow two ADUs on the same property.[15]

Almost simultaneously, in July 2019, Oregon's governor signed a bill that essentially cancels single-family residential zoning throughout the state, and hence, at least on paper, allows for multiple-unit construction on a piece of residential property.[16] This bill cancels long-standing legislation that had initially prohibited multifamily construction in many Portland neighborhoods in 1924. This restriction then expanded in the 1950s, resulting in most housing construction being single-family for decades. Curiously, this happened with input and support from Robert Moses, the infamous public official responsible for many urban planning problems of New York City.[17]

Since single-family zones ceased to exist, many new multi-unit buildings emerged throughout Portland. Their forms vary: they can be duplexes, triplexes, and fourplexes, but they are usually found in the neighborhoods of the city that do not have a protected historic district status. [Fig. 1, 2]

What is perhaps most curious about Portland is that in the recent years—despite the new legislation making the construction of ADUs even easier than it was—the number of newly permitted ADUs in the city has declined.[18] ADU advocates in Portland suggest that this might be because everybody who wanted and could afford building an ADU already did so in previous years.[19]

While city initiatives like the SDC Waiver program can offset the costs of getting a proper permit, some homeowners still find it more financially savvy to simply not register the changes they are making and the new structures they are building. There is more to the costs than just the permit: a proper

13. "Deadline to Finalize ADU Permits Submitted for Review Prior to July 31, 2018 is June 30, 2020," City of Portland, Oregon, April 1, 2019.

14. "Welcome to the ADU SDC Waiver Program," City of Portland, Oregon, accessed August 14, 2024, https://www.portlandoregon.gov/.

15. "Zoning Requirements for an Accessory Dwelling Unit," City of Portland, accessed July 11, 2022, https://www.portland.gov/.

16. Laurel Wemsley, "Oregon Legislature Votes To Essentially Ban Single-Family Zoning," *NPR*, July 1, 2019

17. Jenna Huges, "Historical Context of Racist Planning: A History of How Planning Segregated Portland," City of Portland, (September 2019), p. 5.

18. Kol Peterson, "Portland, Oregon's ADU Permit Data for 2020: Observations About ADU Permit Data Trends," *Accessory Dwellings,* July 22, 2021.

19. Kol Peterson, "Portland, Oregon's ADU Permit Data for 2020."

ADU or modification must follow the city's structural and fire safety requirements, and involve licensed construction professionals, which may significantly raise the costs. It also increases the tax value of the property. Therefore, many homeowners find it cheaper to design and construct an ADU according to their own knowledge and judgement, avoiding the tax increase by simply never reporting their changes. Such modifications are "invisible," and since they are not as standardized through the city's regulations, they are even more tempting to study. Below I analyze three examples of such transformations.

Behind the Scenes

The three cases chosen here represent two different taxonomic units: interior modifications and ADUs. These cases include one of internal modifications that convert a single-family residence into a multifamily structure; a case of internal and external conversions that do not allow for a separate household; and, finally, a stereotypical ADU—a free-standing structure meant for a single individual or family, built next to the main house.

The first case—a basement conversion—is invisible from the outside of the house. The owner, Eric M., purchased the house knowing the potential for conversation. However, he also recognized that he would not want to pursue a formal permit since he was qualified to know that the structural change would be minor and safe. The home in question is a typical split-level ranch built on a sloped plot of land originally zoned for a single-family residence. Split-level ranches were particularly popular in the United States between the 1950s and 1970s. In Portland, this type of home fits well with the hilly landscapes of the city and its suburbs. The house's main level is on the upper floor, which is where the main entry is located as well. The original bottom level of the house consisted of one large room, two small rooms, and a bathroom with a door leading outside. Eric M. had construction-related expertise, so he decided to do the remodeling work on his own. First, he removed the original finishes from the 1950s. After that he and his partner moved in and continued doing other construction that was still possible while also living in the house. Most of the work that was performed after the owner moved in was on the bottom floor—a daylight basement. Although the house was meant to be a single-family residence, the owner saw the daylight basement as a resource that had potential to help offset mortgage expenses [Fig 3].

> Downstairs we want to convert into an apartment…. As far as the solution for the unit downstairs, we opened up the wall, and put a new beam here; where it used to be a single door, it will be a studio…. This downstairs will essentially pay for a lot of the improvements, as you just pour money into the house.[20]

In other words, the typical single-family split-level ranch will be effectively converted into a multifamily residence. The project is ongoing but—considering that Portland market remained stable even during the pandemic—Eric M. is likely to realize his intent and rent the space out to offset expenses. At the same time, he indicated that due to a long experience of living in unaffordable cities, he and his partner are used to having roommates. They perceive the unit downstairs not only as an economic asset, but also as a social benefit. They can share the house and backyard with another individual, potentially a friend, without completely sacrificing the privacy of both their home and the renter's spaces.

Eric M.'s case is not unique. It is typical for split-level ranches to have more than one level and easy external access to both. But it is also a very likely scenario for another wide-spread typology: Portland foursquare craftsmen homes that often have a kitchen door in the back in direct proximity to a daylight basement. While a daylight basement or an attic may not be the most upscale accommodation, such units are nevertheless very popular in the extreme Portland rental market. [Fig. 4] However, even in Portland, with its progressive legislation for ADUs, there is a significant investment one must make if they are willing to officially transform their home's basement or attic into a separate unit. To list a few: it must have a separate HVAC system, a separate electrical panel, and potentially a separate water meter. Yet all of this investment may not result in higher rent or returns.[21]

In Portland, if an ADU is constructed without a permit, it can be legalized retrospectively. However, that would require checking if the insulation, the plumbing, and the HVAC comply with the city's requirements. This could entail opening walls or floors. It also puts an ADU owner at the mercy of the

20. Erik M., interview by the author, Portland, May 2020.

21. "Accessory Dwelling Unit (ADU) Connections for Water, Sanitary and Storm Sewer," City of Portland, accessed July 11, 2022, https://www.portland.gov/.

Fig. 3 — Existing situation (left) and modified condition (right) of lower-level plan of single-family housing in Portland, Oregon. The wall between two existing rooms is removed, and the remaining alcove is converted into an open living room/kitchen (1). The laundry room (2) and bathroom (3) are divided into separate spaces. Elaboration of original drawings by author.

Fig. 4 — An occupiable daylight basement with a separate entrance under construction in Portland, Oregon, 2022. Photos by the author.

authorities: "verification of the compliance of concealed building components that were covered without inspection will be at the discretion of the building inspector," states the City of Portland website.[22] At the same time, little prevents homeowners from keeping the house as one unit on paper, because, when sold, a separate unit in the basement or attic can be listed as a "special feature."

Perhaps the most significant issue with not having a house legally split into two units is insurance. For example, personal injury insurance is a standard policy for homeowners in the United States where the insurance company will step in to pay if the property owner has legal liability for a guest's injury. This, however, does not apply if it is revealed that the injury is related to a tenant. This potential problem is just as real as the insured cases themselves: although injuries may not happen often, when they do happen, legal and financial consequences for the property owner may be severe.

The second case in the taxonomic unit of interior modifications is also an example of undocumented construction—this time both inside and outside of the house. This home is in central Portland in one of the particularly desirable and expensive residential areas. It is a simple bungalow with a basement constructed in the first decade of the twentieth century. During its over one-hundred-year history, the house has seen many changes. Older changes include a closet constructed between two original bedrooms in place of a former hallway and an extended dinner nook added to the kitchen in the back of the house. These changes were made when the house still served as a single-family residence. The new changes inside the existing structure, although almost as subtle as the previous ones, completely shift the house's performance.

The house's owner, Gabriel Z., purchased it in the 1990s and lived there with his partner and children. After the children grew up and his partner moved out, Gabriel rented out one of the rooms on the main level and the small room in the basement under the front of the house. Originally, the house had two bedrooms and one bathroom. Over the years, the owner built another bedroom in the basement facing the backyard. At this point, there were four residents in the house: the owner and three renters. All residents were using the same bathroom situated between the two original bedrooms on the main floor.

22. "Accessory Dwelling Unit (ADU) Permits," City of Portland, accessed July 12, 2022, https://www.portland.gov/.

23. Gabriel Z, interview by author, Portland, Oregon, May 2020.

24. Gabriel Z, interview by author, Portland, Oregon, May 2020.

As this presented an issue, the owner decided to build another bathroom in the basement. After that, he constructed an ADU with a kitchenette, a bedroom, and a bathroom in the backyard, next to the previously existing shed. [Fig. 5, 6] Gabriel says that he "wants to rent it through Airbnb."[23] However, that appears unlikely as becoming an Airbnb host requires going through a permit process that involves a city inspection, and the owner never received any documentation for the construction that he did. At the time of this interview, the unit in the back was rented to the owner's acquaintance for a stay that was expected to last several months. Although the house remains a single-family two-bedroom, one-bathroom home on paper, in reality, it has been effectively converted into a communal household, analogous to the historic example of a boarding house.

Although this example may seem like a wise property investment, that is hardly the case. The owner, who is now retired and lives in one of the property's bedrooms, uses rent money to pay for minor repairs and property taxes: "I have always lived with roommates and the house pays for itself," he stated.[24] His investments into the modifications may pay themselves off (not in the case of the ADU), but they do not produce significant passive income. However, despite the outdated interior and limited amenities, the rooms in the house are rarely unoccupied for a long time. Portland rent is expensive in comparison to the nationwide average, and there are always takers for an inexpensive room in a city that has many students and service workers earning minimal wages.

The final example is a free-standing ADU, one of the earlier ADUs built in Portland prior to the current legal simplification. Unlike the previous two cases, this ADU was built with a permit. As it is a free-standing separate building, it is a great illustration of another dimension of Portland regulations and architectural and planning taxonomies: there is a five-foot (one-and-a-half-meter) setback requirement for all structures on any residential city lot. Portland's setback requirement was put in place even before the cancelation of the single-family residential zone. This resulted in a relatively dense city fabric for single-family neighborhoods.

In other American cities, setback and lot-size regulations in single-family zones can be significantly bigger, making legal detached ADUs practically impossible. For instance, according to 2019 research, Miami-Dade County has a major housing shortage problem and happens to have plenty of unpermitted ADUs.[25] Yet, in the City of North Miami, 2021 regulations stated that the minimum lot size to build an ADU in a single-family (R1) zone had to be 12,500 square feet (about 1,150 square meters), while a typical single-family lot size in North Miami is under 10,000 square feet (about 930 square meters).[26] Moreover, the 2021 regulations established that an ADU cannot be larger than 25 percent of the main residence. A typical single-family home in North Miami can be anywhere between 1,000 and 2,000 square feet, or approximately 90 to 190 square meters. Therefore, in theory, prior to the 2022 regulatory change in Miami-Dade County, a potential ADU in the city of North Miami would have been limited to a maximum of 500 square feet, or 47 square meters—a very small dwelling by American standards—if it was permitted at all. In practice, this means that in order to build an additional structure near a house, a homeowner must own a very large lot and a very large primary structure. Ironically, those homeowners who own extremely large lots in Miami-Dade County are hardly the ones who need to build ADUs to house extended family or supplement their income through rent. And Miami-Dade County made sure that everyone who did not comply with the regulations was prosecuted and fined.[27]

At the same time, Miami-Dade County allowed for the construction of sheds as long as they were set five feet (1.5 meters) away from the property line at the back.[28] The county's definition of what constituted a shed was rather broad—anything under 400 square feet (37 square meters) was allowed. A shed could be electrified, and the code did not specify if they were allowed to have conveniences such as plumbing or not. Five feet is a reasonable regulation for many single-family lots in Miami and elsewhere in the United States.[29] Finally, in November 2022, the City of Miami acknowledged the problem and its informal solution. In this most recent development, and in recognition of a serious housing problem, Miami-Dade country passed a new set of ADU regulations that lowered the minimum single-family lot size to 7,500 square feet (696 square meters) and increased a permissible ADU size to 800 square feet (74 square meters), an equivalent of a typical two-bedroom apartment.[30]

25. Richard Florida, and Steven Pedigo. *Miami's Housing Affordability Crisis* (Miami: Florida International University, 2019).

26. Ordinance No. 1466, City of North Miami, August 24, 2021.

27. "RU-1 – Single-Family Residential District," Miami-Dade County, accessed July 13, 2022, https://www.miamidade.gov/zoning/district-ru-1-sf-residential.asp.

28. "Utility Shed Permit Requirements," Miami-Dade County, accessed September 30, 2023, https://www.miamidade.gov/.

29. "Utility Shed Permit Requirements," Miami-Dade County.

30. Sophia Hernandez, "Miami Dade County Commissioners Approve Second Units for Some Homeowners," *ABC Action News*, November 8, 2022.

Fig. 5 — Street and backyard views of an ADU built behind a house in Portland, Oregon, 2022. Photos by author.

Fig. 6 — Main floor and basement plans of Gabriel Z.'s house modifications, Portland, Oregon. Main floor: 1. breakfast nook, 2. kitchen, 3. dining, 4. bedroom, 5. den, 6. bedroom and kitchenette, 7. garage. Basement: 1. unused bedroom, 2. remaining unfinished basement, 3. bedroom, 4. laundry. Elaboration of original drawings by author.

Between the lines of these dimensions, one may discern the resulting architectures and living scenarios: in North Miami, a "shed" could be built and used as an additional residence, as long as it was not claimed as such, and as long as it remained within the family. Extended family could live on the same property, and unregistered ADUs could be rented cheaply to family and friends. Not only did this way of construction and living help mitigate the strict Miami zoning regulations that disadvantaged low-income populations, but it also spared residents the permit and certified-contractor costs that the city would unavoidably enforce.

Unlike Miami, in Portland, an ADU or a house extension can be relatively easily approved for a permit, yet a legally qualified contractor still needs to be hired, which makes an ADU a long-term, high-stakes investment. Despite the potential high costs associated with hiring a licensed contractor, people build ADUs and have been building them for a long time. My interviewee, James P., built his ADU many years ago when Portland laws were less easy to navigate. During his construction, James relied on several architectural rules determined by the inherently small size of ADUs. James's free-standing ADU is connected to the outside through large windows and French doors; it has an open plan kitchen and living room, high ceilings, and double-height spaces. James emphasized the importance of not having major windows face close neighbors, as a free-standing ADU is essentially urban infill.[31] He lived in this ADU at first, renting out the main house to various unrelated tenants until he relocated to a different property in a different part of the city, where he also built an ADU. He was recently forced to move back into his original free-standing ADU due to an unruly tenant in the main house. Portland is a so-called "renter's state," where laws mostly side with renters, not landlords. Subsequently, the landlord cannot evict a tenant, even with advanced notice and even if the tenant causes complaints from other renters—unless the landlord resides at the same property as the tenant. Since he relocated onto the property, James was able to issue an eviction notice for his troubled tenant without having to move into the main house.

31. James P., interview by author, Portland, Oregon, May 2022.

32. Pandora S., interview by author, Portland OR, May 2020.

33. See, for example, Le Corbusier, *The Athens Charter* (New York: Grossman, 1973).

Epilogue

During the pandemic summer of 2020, Pandora and her partner tried to buy a bigger home. They were preapproved for a mortgage despite her "nebulous" income as a small-business owner, but then were outbid by another buyer. She was not bitter about the fact:

> With the equity we had in our house, we could buy a bigger home, but that would mean we would lose the return on investment. My parents do not have equity in their mortgages. I do not come from money, and I want my son to have the equity.[32]

This story is becoming the new narrative of American housing: middle-class urbanites en masse no longer seek housing that they see as fit for the persistent conspicuous American ideals, but rather, housing that they can afford and that gives them some sense of financial security and a chance for wise investments. However, the needs residents have for their homes do not disappear; instead, they transition from the domain of real estate to that of architecture. This story revolves around architectural and urban planning terms: building and site taxonomy, residential zone types, square footage, permits (or not), insulating previously cold spaces, appropriate daylight, openings, and fire hazards, to mention a few.

It is not unlikely that history is repeating itself today: rapid industrialization and urbanization in the nineteenth and twentieth centuries generated a revolution in architectural vocabulary and form. Back in this formative period of Western architectural modernity, the overpopulation of industrial centers led to the reconsideration of what constituted healthy housing. Conversations about architecture and planning in this period revolved around proper daylight access and ventilation of residential units, as well as access to green spaces and other recreational environments.[33] Although some planning principles developed at that time are now considered obsolete, many rules pertaining to an individual dwelling are still actively in use.

Currently, we are witnessing a similarly powerful moment. Not just the innovation in luxury residences, but also the lack of affordable housing is beginning to drive architectural discourse on housing form. Moreover, it is not just affordable housing per se, but the involvement of residents in housing production processes that has become a sign of the times. This is most apparent in the iconic status recently achieved by social housing projects that, by design, involve residents in changing them over time, such as Elemental/Alejandro Aravena's Half a House, OMMX's Naked House, and Tatiana Bilbao's housing in Ciudad Acuña. With all of their imperfections, these projects signify a trend and set a tone for the development of architectural discourse, where architects may for once step back and learn from residents already at the frontlines of remodeling and fighting against housing insecurity.

As for the residents, they are actively modifying their homes inside and out, densifying the many suburban neighborhoods of American cities from within. Single-family living in a large house with a vast lawn of inefficient turf grass is no longer universally affordable to the American middle class. It is symptomatic that there is now a general name—an ADU—for all forms of dense living in formerly single-family-home neighborhoods. Perhaps we are about to witness a powerful qualitative leap that will reveal and address the "invisible" pressure on single-family homes. Perhaps we are already witnessing it without even knowing.

Mixing Metabolisms: New People in Aging North American Sprawl

Lawrence Davis

Introduction

For at least three decades, a consequential demographic and cultural change has taken place in the suburbs of North America. There has been abundant discussion about how the original culture and form of suburbia can be adapted to reconstruct future suburbs, most notably through the work of the Congress of New Urbanism. There is less conversation from architects and urbanists about the innovation new immigrant cultures and their spatial practices have on the shape, space, and character of the metropolitan periphery. After seventy years, what is commonly known as postwar sprawl is at the end of its first material phase. Seldom easy, such an infusion of new cultural energy and related spatial practices can, like all successful settlements over time, force sprawl to transform into a more responsive and interesting place to live. [Fig. 1]

Fig. 1 — Detail of the racial dot map of Northern Orange County, California, based on the 2010 US Census. Map by William Cooper Center for Public Service, University of Virginia, Charlottesville, 2013.

The suburbs' newest residents are part of a global transformation that started in the 1960s and accelerated after the end of the Cold War.[1] Beginning with the Industrial Revolution, immigrants traditionally landed in or near city centers. The

1. Susan F. Martin, "Heavy Traffic: International Migration in an Era of Globalization," *Brookings Institute,* (September 2001); "International Migrants by Country," *The Pew Research Center,* (January 30, 2019).

2. Jill H. Wilson and Nicole Prchal Svajlenka, "Immigrants Continue to Disperse, with Fastest Growth in the Suburbs," *Bookings Institute* (October 29, 2014).

3. Wei Li, "Anatomy of a New Ethnic Settlement: The Chinese Ethnoburb in Los Angeles." *Urban Studies* 35, no. 3 (March 1, 1998): pp. 479–501.

most recent cohort, the largest being from East Asia and Latin America, now arrive from all parts of the globe and move directly to the metropolitan perimeters of the United States and Canada.[2] In most cases, the first generation of immigrants typically attempts to assimilate and buy into the traditional American suburban dream portrayed in popular media.[3] However, more recently, as more communities have started to incorporate different cultures, immigrants have gradually exerted increasing influence on local governments. Expats are more likely to push for zoning regulations that match their values and everyday needs. This has begun to transform spatial purposes and patterns, as well as social practices in communities that were originally dominated by the twentieth century European American nuclear family.

In the last two centuries, the North American suburb was an inhabited perimeter designed to be the pastoral opposite of the industrialized city. The separation of domestic life and work, the fabrication of class and racial exclusion, the promotion of better health and the creation of an investment tool for producing family wealth were key drivers to suburbia's common form. Exceedingly popular, postwar suburbia developed access to this type of built environment for the working class. In part because of its popularity and related populist character, the suburbs became the subject of immense criticism. It was critiqued for its homogenous culture, its role as an asylum for white Americans attempting to control their relationships to those of other social and ethnic backgrounds, and more recently, its contribution to global warming. Preserving this pattern of inhabitation increased the amount of power over property value and even more importantly, the social characteristics of daily life. The recent change in the background of new residents, their cultural values, and spatial practices represents a serious challenge to the suburban way of life and form of self-definition. More broadly, it also represents an evolution of the larger social identities of both the United States and Canada and how they correspondingly transform their inhabited environments.

In North America, California, and Arizona have the highest concentration of postwar suburbs that are transforming due to demographic change. More than any other state or province, California is currently at the forefront for both formal and informal applications of new zoning regulations, functional repurposing, and spatial adaptation in existing communities. For architects and urban designers, this recent culturally diverse resettlement of postwar sprawl is an opportunity to rediscover the now aging suburbs as a site of spatial experimentation and a place to reimagine community. Ultimately, this new metropolitan redevelopment is most optimistically viewed as not against or replacing the city or suburbs that preceded it. Instead, it is seen as an emerging environment that renews a region through its social and spatial complexity and brings a new cultural energy that, in the process of its making, becomes more inclusive and desirable for many more people.

Demographic Change

The end of the Cold War around 1990 represents the start of the economically and culturally globalized world that we inhabit today.[4] Increased mobilization between, and awareness of, other parts of the world fueled immigration to more developed nations. In the United States and Canada, new arrivals from Asia, the Middle East, and Latin America bypassed central cities and landed directly in the suburbs.[5] This complicated the ethnic and social composition of these traditionally white metropolitan territories. Although at a diminished rate in virtually all categories, the 2020 US census reflects a continuation of this trend, mapping a consistent migration from the metropolitan center to the outskirts, but also an increase of nonwhite residents in the existing suburbs.[6]

Since 1990, while the overall suburban and exurban population has continued to grow, there has been—as was projected as far back as 2001—an approximately 20 percent drop in the amount of white residents in North American suburbs.[7] Nonetheless, there has still been a modest increase in the overall number of European Americans in the suburbs during the last three decades. However, the percentage difference is principally driven by a significant increase in African American, Hispanic, and Asian populations in the metropolitan periphery.[8] [Fig. 2] During this same period, the African American population in the suburbs increased an average of 12 percent,[9] with the suburban communities of some metropolitan areas increasing over 50 percent.[10] Two reasons that are cited for this change are: first, a displacement of low-income African Americans from central

4. Wilson and Svajlenka, "Immigrants Continue to Disperse."

5. Wilson and Svajlenka, "Immigrants Continue to Disperse."

6. "Movers and Shakers; Internal Migration," *The Economist* (December 16, 2021); Richard Florida, "The Changing Demographics of America's Suburbs," *Bloomberg City Lab* (November 7, 2019).

7. F. Mitchell, N. Smelser, and W. Wilson, "An Overview of Racial and Ethnic Demographic Trends," *America Becoming: Racial Trends and Their Consequences: Volume I* (Washington, DC: The National Academies Press, 2001): pp. 43–45; William Frey, "Melting Pot Cities and Suburbs: Racial and Ethnic Change in Metro America in the 2000s," *Brookings Institute* (May 2011): pp. 3, 4, and 10; A. Micklow and M. Warner, "Not Your Mother's Suburb: Remaking Communities for a More Diverse Population," *Urban Lawyer* 46, no. 4 (Fall 2014).

8. Florida "The Changing Demographics of America's Suburbs."

9. Frey, "Melting Pot Cities and Suburbs."

10. Florida "The Changing Demographics of America's Suburbs."

11. Florida "The Changing
Demographics of America's
Suburbs."

12. Li, "Anatomy of a New Ethnic
Settlement," p. 479.

Fig. 2 — Percent of
residents residing in exurbs
in 100 of the largest
metropolitan areas in the
USA (1990, 2000, 2010,
2020). Diagram by author
based on data by William
H. Frey.

cities to lower-income inner suburbs due to urban gentrification; second, an increase in the number of middle-class and upper-middle-class African Americans settling in more affluent suburbs.[11]

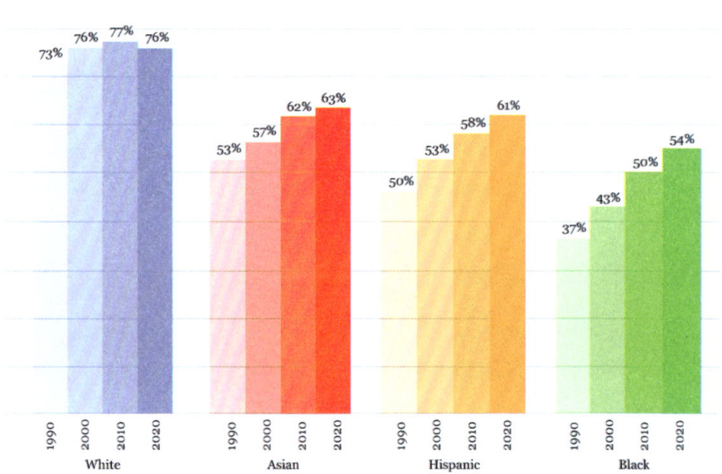

In both cases, spatial practices are not noticeably different from European Americans who are living in the same type of place. Unlike other newer arrivals moving to the suburbs, this group has been in North America for as long as European colonists: over four hundred years. In addition, the horrendous and forced displacement of Africans across the Atlantic Ocean has created an erasure of shared cultural memories and practices. This may be part of the explanation as to why racial diversity in the suburbs tends not to drive spatial change. New spatial patterns in existing suburbs are more often the result of an ethnically specific concentration of relatively newer immigrant groups. When these groups amass enough local political power, they can change zoning ordinances and the spatial patterns that historically have reflected the white, middle-class values.

The Rise of the Ethnoburb

In 1997, Wei Li—then an assistant professor of geography at the University of Connecticut—coined the term "ethnoburb" in a paper that examined the growing suburban Chinese population in Los Angeles's San Gabriel Valley.[12] This launched an academic arena of social research that focused on new immigrants of East

Asian and Latino descent in the aging suburbs of Los Angeles and other cities such as San Francisco, Vancouver, Toronto, New York, Philadelphia, and Washington, DC. These older inner-ring suburbs offered low-cost housing and commercial properties that were conveniently located near the centers of large metropolitan regions. Despite being slightly dated, the typical suburban community became an important symbol of success and assimilation with one's new country. As is often the case throughout history, this recent generation of immigrants departed their home nations for a variety of reasons, most commonly to create a better life for themselves and their families. Like previous generations that arrived in central city neighborhoods, the transition from one life to another—now directly to the suburbs—became easier by landing in a community with similar backgrounds and whose social needs, practices, and languages were familiar. The support within ethnic communities also includes vital, yet informal, financial systems that allow new residents to maneuver around legal and social impediments to funding major necessities, like housing or maintaining a business.

The forms and investments in ethnoburbs are as diverse as the types of cultures that compose such communities. In low-income areas, organizations like Rotating Savings and Credit Associations (ROSCAs) are locally formed to pool and loan money. There are also various types of "hawalas," a South Asian term used to describe an informal system to internationally transfer funds. These two unofficial practices are used to finance renovations and new construction.[13] In more affluent Asian ethnoburbs, large financial institutions—especially from China or Taiwan—have established branches in American ethnoburbs to directly offer residents more conventional banking instruments like mortgages and construction loans. More recently, established American and Canadian banks recognize the potential of ethnoburbs and are offering their financial products to the growing market. The processes of renovation and construction are also diverse, ranging from collective do-it-yourself projects that would use various informal financing mechanisms to more conventional contractor-client agreements that are required to have bank loans and building permits.

Wei Li's initial 1990s study on increased Asian immigration focused on Monterey Park, a suburb of east Los Angeles. The aging inner suburb was thick with comparatively affordable

13. Jamie Johnson, "What is a Rotating Savings and Credit Association?," *The Balance* (April 26, 2022); Mohammed El-Qorchi, "Hawala," *Finance and Development: Quarterly Magazine of the IMF* 39, no. 4, (December 2002).

14. Li, "Anatomy of a New Ethnic Settlement," p. 484.

15. Wei Li, *Ethnoburb: The Ethnic Community in Urban America* (Honolulu: University of Hawi'i Press, 2009): p. 75.

16. Li, *Ethnoburb*, p. 83.

17. Li, *Ethnoburb*, p. 90.

18. Elisabeth Rosenthal, "North of Beijing, California Dreams Come True," *New York Times*, (February 3, 2003); Teresa Pires do Rio Caldeira, "City of Walls: Crime, Segregation, and Citizenship in São Paulo," (PhD diss., University of California at Berkeley, 1992).

19. Willow S. Lung-Amam, "*That Monster House is My Home*," *Trespassers?: Asian Americans and the Battle for Suburbia*, (Oakland: University of California Press. 2017), pp. 138–174; Margaret Crawford, "Asian Garden Mall" (paper presentation, Civic Space in Scattered Cities/Lo Spazio Pubblico nella Città Diffusa symposium, Florence, Italy, 2009).

20. Lung-Amam, "*That Monster House is My Home*," pp. 162–167.

and conveniently located single-family houses.[14] Monterey Park is emblematic of this first wave of ethnoburbs that were, on one hand, characterized by East-Asian-specific businesses and public celebrations of new immigrants, but on the other, exhibited little change to the spatial pattern and practices of the original Euro-American residents and other similar suburbs.[15] [Fig. 3] Li's research suggests that the main factor in the rise of the LA ethnoburb was a desire by Asian residents, similar to white Americans, to leave the challenges of the city center and to "make it" in the suburbs.[16]

After the initial wave of local Asian migration from neighborhoods near downtown LA to the suburbs in the early 1970s, a second, more intense surge of newer residents, starting in the 1980s, immigrated directly from their home countries to Asian-dominated suburbs like Monterey Park. This more direct path was driven by the image of the Euro-American suburb across the world through television and film. American and Canadian suburban lifestyles are both familiar and highly valued internationally and are critical for the direct advertising of North American properties in foreign countries. In the case of Monterey Park, its available real estate holdings are not only promoted in the Los Angeles Basin, but in various media outlets across Taiwan as well.[17] Additional evidence of the American suburb's popularity is found in new peripheral development abroad, from Ju Jun, known locally as "Orange County," north of Beijing to the dozens of gated Alphaville projects across Brazil. In such post-Cold War peripheral communities, American suburbia is a commodity packaged and sold to those who can afford it.[18]

Mission San Jose, of Fremont in the Bay Area, and Westminster in Orange County are two California postwar suburbs, demographically dominated by Chinese and Vietnamese immigrants respectively, that changed either the residential zoning or the existing shared space of their communities. In Mission San Jose, affluent Asian residents were attracted to its good schools, access to Silicon Valley jobs, and related technology-sector investments.[19] Over time, the Asian community was able to exert enough political power on the local government to change zoning laws to allow greater Floor Area Ratios (FAR) on residential lots.[20] New residents purchased low-slung 2,500 to 3,000 square foot (230 to 280 square meter) single-floor ranches featuring a relaxed indoor-outdoor connection between the home's shared interior living spaces and rear gardens. These were then torn down and replaced by larger, loftier homes of up to 5,000 square feet (465 square meters). [Fig. 4] Disparagingly referred to as "monster homes" by locals who did not like them, these slightly extravagant structures contain more formal inward-focused interiors and are less connected to the now smaller exterior spaces ringing the house. These larger structures mark a changed sensibility from a home that is "in and of the garden" to one that emphasizes the material success of its inhabitants, thus contributing to a significant transformation in the community's spatial pattern and identity.[21]

Westminster, south of Los Angeles in Orange County, also experienced a transition in the residential fabric of its formerly dominant postwar ranches. Less affluent than Mission San Jose's new residents, Vietnamese immigrants arrived shortly after the end of the Vietnam War. [Fig. 5] Unlike Mission San Jose, these ranches, built in the 1950s and 1960s, were not torn down, but renovated through smaller additions and the introduction of culturally specific symbolic forms. As with the well documented modification of Levittown homes, the original texture was maintained and adapted to new cultures through more subtle changes and through overtly emblematic Southeast Asian roof designs and garden practices.

At the same time, Westminster is an example of cultural adaptation going both ways. It is now common for the original grass front yards of its residential streets to be completely paved. The hard surfaces can accommodate several cars of a multigenerational family, or it can provide space for a single automobile that is needed when the garage itself is converted into additional residential space. Both practical and a conspicuous symbol of material success, these wide front driveways, ideally filled with flashy cars, are a form of assimilation because automobiles are one of the most highly prized elements of American society.

More subtle changes to the overall design of the house are just as instrumental to the transformed structural texture of this exurban city. [Fig. 6] The original homes are single floor and "L" shaped, with the short wing being the garage on the street side. The modified version often introduces a new section facing the garage that creates a "U"- or (tighter) "C"-shaped footprint. A gateway might frame an open passage to an inner-entry courtyard that acts as a transition from the driveway to the

21. Lung-Amam, *"That Monster House is My Home,"* pp. 155–160.

Fig. 3 — Taipei Shopping Center, Monterey Park, California, 2023. Photo by Chenhao Luo and Zhi Zheng.

Fig. 4 — Exterior and interior of a typical new 5,000-square-foot (464.5 square meters) single-family house on lots that formerly contained 2,500-square-foot (232.2 square meters) mid-century ranch houses in Mission San Jose, California, 2015.

Fig. 5 — Typical transformed mid-1960s ranch houses in Westminster, California, 2019. Photo by author.

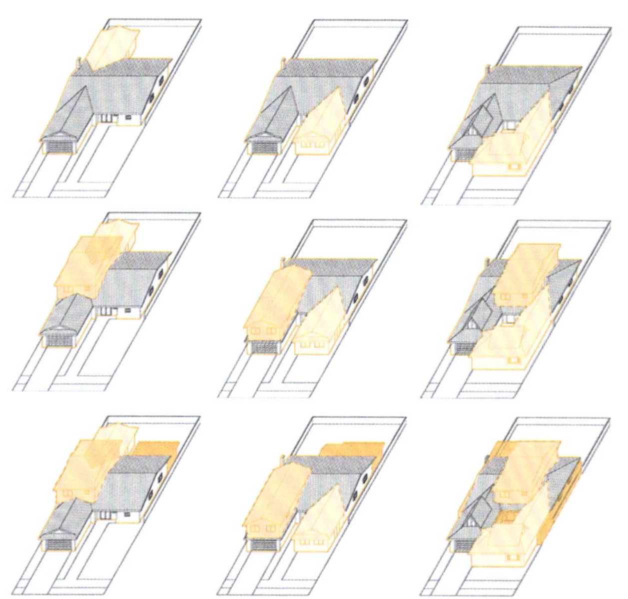

Fig. 6 — Typological transformations in the Vietnamese Ethnoburb of Westminster, California. Drawing by Chenhao Luo and Zhi Zheng.

Fig. 7 — Composite transformations in the Vietnamese Ethnoburb of Westminster, California. Drawing by Chenhao Luo and Zhi Zheng.

22. Crawford, "Asian Garden Mall."

23. Crawford, "Asian Garden Mall."

24. Crawford, "Asian Garden Mall."

front door, now more secluded from the street. This small, new garden space offers a serene and private transition as one enters, analogous to the traditional Southeast Asian courtyard house. Taken together, these elements constitute a basic renewed design alphabet that combines with original mid-century forms and themes to produce a set of hybrid symbols, figures, and spaces for the original Euro-American suburban homes. [Fig. 7] This emerging grammar re-energizes what was once an aging postwar residential texture. It also reveals a promising model of exurban change that advances incrementally over time and, like any socially healthy city, is part of a continual process of cultural renewal and related spatial morphologic invention.

In Westminster, cultural and spatial changes are not confined to domestic space. The Asian Garden Mall—known locally as Phước Lộc Thọ and named after three deities for fortune (Phước), prosperity (Lộc), and longevity (Thọ)—re-invents the tired typology of the suburban shopping mall as a dynamic multifunctional cultural center.[22] The mall runs along an endless commercial strip that is characterized by Vietnamese owned businesses and signage but, like Monterey Park, is no different spatially from other suburban strips that saturate metropolitan North America. Nevertheless, the Asian Garden Mall is a creative example of the potential future of public exurban space. It contains small-scale, culturally specific retail, dining options, religious spaces, and community event spaces, as well as a functional reconsideration of the most ubiquitous surface of postwar suburbia: the parking lot.[23] [Fig. 8, 9] Typically located in the front of the building, the mall's parking area is the site of shared symbols, monuments, and frequent night markets and important festivals, such as the Lunar New Year festival.[24] What is usually a dead no-mans-land becomes a flexible and valued public space. [Fig. 10]

While culturally engaged and functionally rich and dynamic, the Asian Garden Mall is still physically isolated from what could potentially be a larger, more socially intimate network of space and movement. Like most commercial properties in Westminster, pedestrians are not connected any better to the larger community than in other typical postwar suburbs. For that, bicycle paths, sidewalks, and shared landscapes must be introduced to make connections within, and between, neighborhoods.

As much as Westminster is a pithy example of the ethnic transformation of a postwar suburb, it is still typical of the effects that such a space and culture have on its new arrivals. Orange County's sprawling layout and faster pace make public life and social interaction more challenging. In particular, the dispersed car-driven world of Southern California offers less socially intimate and more consumptive lifestyles compared to those of urban or rural Southeast Asia. On the other hand, notably for the young who were eager to conform and build an accepted life in their new home, many adapted quickly and embraced this new way of living. Automobiles are a key element in this assimilation of Asian youth. As creative symbols of power, ethnic identity, and self-assurance, cars and their customization, and sometimes illegal racing, are a modern and ethnic version of age-old hot-rod cultures found across the United States, especially in the Los Angeles Basin.

A more patchy but socially effective method for enriching connections and developing cultural texture in the suburbs can be found in Riverside, California. In January 2020, the city changed its zoning laws to permit micro-enterprise, home-kitchen operations that allow for limited dining, most often in backyard patios.[25] [Fig. 11, 12] Clandestine at-home restaurants have existed for decades in California and other parts of the United States and legalizing them solves many problems. Most importantly, it embraces the cultural diversity of a community. In Riverside, there are now African American, Caribbean, Asian, and Mexican home kitchens. These small-scale dining spaces are a new frontier for restaurant culture. They can also be a piece of the solution for addressing the challenge of food deserts.[26] Finally, in an era of pandemics, it is easy to imagine at-home restaurants as a key element in making small-scale social bubbles for residential blocks or neighborhoods.

The transformation of space around residential suburban units is important when considering their future quality. Historically, this area is covered in grass and gardens to promote the residents' privacy. By changing the purpose and material of these suburban green surfaces and making them more public, the social nature and cultural character of the overall built environment changes. For communities who now have a new cultural identity, the transformation of these outside spaces can better match the aspirations of new residents. It can also offer a

25. Farley Elliot, "Riverside's Newly Legal Home Restaurants Look to Revolutionize California's Food Scene," *Eater Los Angeles,* (September 2, 2020).

26. Elliot, "Riverside's Newly Legal Home Restaurants."

Fig. 8 — Buddhist Shrine to Di Lặc in Phước Lộc Thọ (Asian Garden Mall), Westminster, California, 2019. Photo by author.

Fig. 9 — Night Market, Phước Lộc Thọ (Asia Garden Mall), Westminster, California, c. 2016.

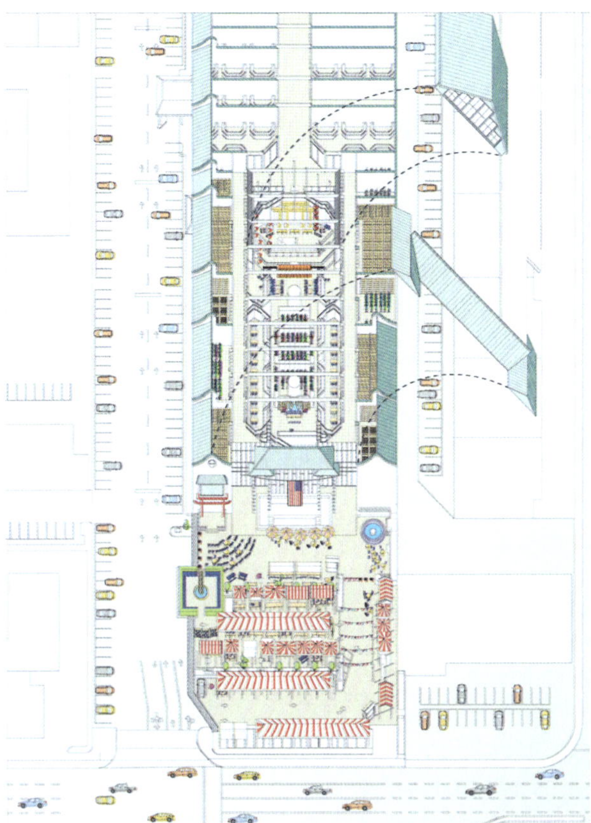

Fig. 10 — Axonometric view of Phước Lộc Thọ (Asia Garden Mall), Westminster, California. Drawing by Chenhao Luo and Xinyu Tang.

Fig. 11 — Barra de Pan, Backyard Kitchen Restaurant, Corona, California, 2020. Photo by Clay Larsen.

Fig. 12 — Axonometric view of Barra de Pan, Backyard Kitchen Restaurant, Corona, California. Drawing by Chenhao Luo and Zhi Zheng.

27. Joel Budd, "Places Apart;
Essay: A planet of suburbs," *The
Economist* (December 6, 2014),
pp. 48–54.

28. Budd, "Places Apart," p. 53.

novel experience for people of all backgrounds who visit or want
to live in a unique environment. On a regional level, this could
make a metropolitan area more spatially varied and could create
a more competitive choice relative to other cities that remain
trapped in less imaginative patterns. Additionally, these outdoor
spaces could counter dense, mixed-use city centers with conventional privatized suburban peripheries.

Many of Riverside's informal and clandestine home
kitchens are run by Mexican American families. It is customary
to find other functionally and spatially inventive examples
throughout Latino suburban neighborhoods. [Fig. 13] This is especially true in the Southwest. In such places, social interaction
occurs both on a family and neighborhood scale and is highly
valued, encouraging alternative ways of using space around
suburban structures. [Fig. 14, 15] In Latino culture, it is more
common to see the front yard as a site of social engagement
and cultural representation. Maryvale, Arizona was originally
a desert Levittown for white retirees moving to the Phoenix
area.[27] Today, Maryvale is a largely Latino neighborhood with
familiar challenges associated with low-income communities.
Nonetheless, the front yards of these postwar suburban homes
are less often a spatially transitional, picturesque private garden
that is framed by the window of an interior living room. Instead,
they are more commonly used for communal activities that can
connect the front yard to adjacent sidewalks and streets. The
backyard, originally a private yet social space, is more frequently
used for utilitarian purposes, such as outside sheds, gardens,
or storage.[28]

This pattern also exists in San Ysidro—a diverse suburb
south of San Diego at the border with Tijuana, Mexico, that features many variations to the reconsidered front yard. In addition
to being a functional alternative to the private garden, the front
yard is also transformed into a symbolic landscape of cultural
identity. Often religious, small monuments and other decorative
artifacts in the yard represent values that residents are proud
to illustrate to others. The front yard's fence is also sometimes
rethought as a highly symbolic surface, as well as an improvisational commercial space along the sidewalk, where clothing and
other items are presented for sale to pedestrians.

San Ysidro is also the site of one of the most inventive and
conscious reconsiderations by architects of an aging suburb

transformed by nonwhite spatial practices. Casa Familiar is a project designed by Estudio Teddy Cruz+Fonna Forman for a community-service organization. The project attempts, through a relaxed and informal sensibility, to increase density in suburban sprawl.[29] [Fig. 16] By increasing physical density and functional complexity through the addition of both building mass and mixed uses, the ground floor can be better activated for multiple uses and cultural readings. Such hybrid occupations of a standard suburban lot increase social interaction. As a result, the definition of "urbanity" is no longer reliant on traditional compactness, but on the amount and character of functional and social interface of a given location. This more liberal and intricate understanding of the term opens the way for suburbs to become urban.

Consciously Moving Forward

The ethnic suburbs noted in this essay are emblematic of new settlement patterns and related spatial practices that are occurring more frequently in the periphery of North American cities. The deep and complex history of urban change is littered with examples triggered by the arrival of new residents and circumstances. This makes it easy to argue that such mutations are common and that the most successful and livable cities adapt their built texture in a way that's linked to constantly shifting social and economic facts. Well known examples include Florence that began as a Roman city, Madrid, which began as a Moorish fortress, and Shanghai, which began as a colonial trade city. All three continue to speak to an interaction of cultures over a large span of time. Their capacity to thrive is the result of periodic—though, at times, contentious—adjustments to the rules of building that adapt to their transforming populations.

Like in Rome, Madrid, and Shanghai, cultural growing pains also exist in the suburbs. Those who embrace postwar suburbia's original white, Euro-American culture are often threatened by change. Nevertheless, the processes of transformation currently underway presents an opportunity to rejuvenate a type of aging built environment that is ripe for reconsideration. Architects, planners, and politicians can read this popular, chiefly subconscious phenomenon and develop strategies for reorganizing the spatial DNA of these existing

29. Teddy Cruz, "The informal as inspiration for rethinking urban spaces: architect Teddy Cruz shares 5 projects," *TED Blog* (February 5, 2014); Teddy Cruz, "Casa Familiar" (paper presentation, Civic Space in Scattered Cities/Lo Spazio Pubblico nella Città Diffusa symposium, Florence, Italy, 2009).

Fig. 13 — Latino Front Yards, Los Angeles Basin, California, 2019. Photo by James Rojas.

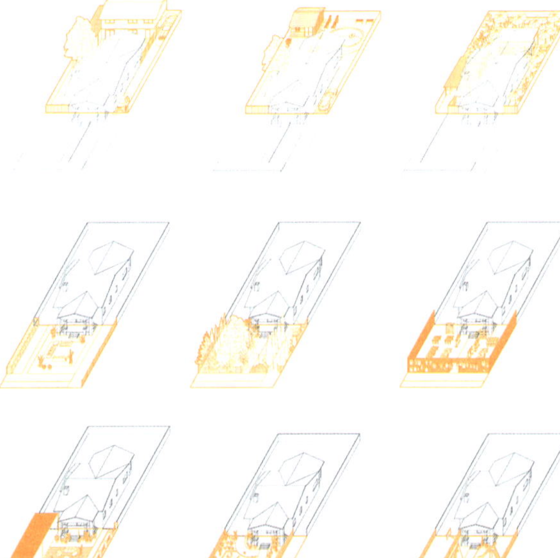

Fig. 14 — Typological transformations in Latino Neighborhoods, Los Angeles Basin, California. Drawing by Chenhao Luo and Xinyu Tang.

Fig. 15 — Composite Transformations in Latino neighborhoods, Los Angeles Basin, California. Drawing by Chenhao Luo and Xinyu Tang.

Fig. 16 — Estudio Teddy Cruz and Fonna Forman, Casa Patio, Living Rooms at the Border, San Ysidro, California, 2020. Photo by Estudio Teddy Cruz and Fonna Forman.

30. "Accessory Dwelling Units," *American Planning Association,* accessed February 2021, https://www.planning.org/; Vinit Mukhija, *Remaking the American Dream: The informal and Formal Transformation of Single-Family Housing Cities,* (Cambridge: MIT Press, 2022), pp. 236–240.

31. Manuela Tobias, "Duplex housing law met with fierce resistance by California cities," *Cal Matters,* blog, (April 11, 2022).

32. Muhammad Alameldin and David Garcia, "State Law, Local Interpretation: How Cities Are Implementing Senate Bill 9," Terner Center for Housing Innovation, University of California Berkeley, (June 8, 2022).

33. Stephen Dow, "'That's not Sheridan': Residents express concerns about accessory dwelling units," *The Sheridan Press* (August 9, 2021).

communities. Doing so can strengthen the social and economic metabolism of these environments and position them for a richer second life.

A growing body of conceptual and administrative tools are emerging that encourage this phenomenon. Riverside's functional rezoning for microenterprise is just one way to reimagine how diverse cultures reoccupy suburbs. Continued experimentation with accessory dwelling units (ADUs) is a strategy that is generally driven by housing affordability, but can also accommodate various kinds of culturally diverse family arrangements.[30] Variants of ADUs could also allow for nonresidential life and work activities that encourage functional complexity and an increased density of social interaction.

Enacted in January 2022, the California Senate Bill 9 (SB9), also known as the California Housing Opportunity and More Efficiency (HOME) Act, is a state-wide ADU law. The act makes it possible for owners to split their property and build up to four homes on a single-family parcel, despite local zoning laws that may prevent such a change in occupational and spatial density.[31] Reinforced in January 2023 with the More HOMES Act (SB50) that legalized increased housing near key job centers and public transportation points, the new laws are perceived as a threat by those who embrace the original, suburban single-family home arrangement. This has ignited a series of local counter-regulations by Californian suburban communities that, in effect, prohibit SB9 and SB50's implementation. In most cases, the local authorities attempting to prevent the new laws' enactment represent very high-income suburbs. Initially, many local governments attempted to ignore this issue, but when that failed, they quickly produced legal loopholes to resist the mandate. These counter-regulations can be quite inventive: they create architectural historical districts, declare neighborhoods a wildlife habitat, remove parking and simultaneously require vehicle ownership, or require arbitrary amounts of mature vegetation and minimum backyard sizes. The last two standards are nearly impossible to meet with the increased density that comes with ADUs.[32] Resistance to change this iconic built environment is occurring in other parts of the United States as well, especially in the Northeast, where some governments are attempting to implement state-wide zoning laws that encourage greater density.[33]

The primary source of opposition to these kinds of changes comes from the perceived negative effects of density and mixed functions on the character of what was previously a leafy, low-density, mono-functional community. This includes a change in the "appeal" of a neighborhood that—because of an increase in population, noise, traffic, and lack of driveway parking—leads to a fear of the reduction in property value for homeowners, as well as in the community's overall tax base. Insufficient infrastructure for water, sewage, and public transport that would serve these greater levels of habitation are also cited as rationales to resist the new state-wide laws.[34] In addition, ADUs are comparatively expensive per square foot to build and are not within reach for many homeowners, suggesting that funding such projects is not as easy as it might initially seem. Furthermore, additional financial stress on existing property owners comes from the possibility that the increased value and property tax of a typical lot—even without an ADU—could become based not on its actual occupational density, but its potential. If the political obstruction to these types of zoning changes is successful, maintaining a higher average cost of residing in a single-family neighborhood will, at the very least, exclude low-income groups. And if one agrees that such systemic practices disproportionally affect people of color and other minorities, preserving existing zoning can also be viewed as an exclusionary housing practice.[35]

The collision of visions for the exurban city between state and local governments is relatively new and uncharted legal territory for zoning cases. Eventually this conflict may need review by the Supreme Court. Since the 1920s, many of the zoning arguments have been between individuals and local authorities.[36] What is uncommon with the disputes over state ADU laws is that it is a struggle about zoning between various levels of government. In most cases, the authority of the state supersedes that of local control. However, given the recent politicization of the courts on other contentious cultural matters, it is unclear what the outcome of such a case might be.

A third instrument allowing for shifts and experimentation in the changing suburbs is "hyperlocal zoning."[37] This practice allows small groups of residents to change the zoning of a particular area as small as four lots. This is to "up-zone" (densify) a given suburban set of tracts occupying a group of

34. Tobias, "Duplex housing law met with fierce resistance by California cities"; Dow, "'That's not Sheridan.'"

35. David Brand, "Hochul, Lawmakers Look to Override NY's Exclusionary Zoning Amid Housing Crunch," *City Limits,* (February 4, 2022).

36. "Foundational Land Use Law Cases," *APA Planning and Law Division,* American Planning Association, 2019.

37. John Myers, "Hyperlocal zoning: Enabling Growth by Block and by Street," *Manhattan Institute* (February 3, 2021).

lots, a street, or an entire neighborhood. Hyper-local zoning begins to address the political challenge of zoning adjustments experienced on the scale of the city by focusing the negotiation on a smaller group of residents. In this way, smaller groups can create policies that suit them best.

Hyper-local zoning can open both front yards and back-yards to ADUs, businesses, restaurants, and other functions that a neighborhood may need. In addition, when land parcels are connected, the center of a block can open to create a shared and protected space that can be used as an entry courtyard to auxiliary apartments. Center blocks can also offer the surface and space for community playgrounds, gardens, libraries, cafes, day cares, and other social spaces for residents to gather.

Importantly, hyper-local zoning can protect minority constituents from a large-scale change in the urban texture that may not illustrate or accommodate their values or way of life. This type of zoning allows a community to truly preserve its social and cultural diversity by responding to both the cultural aspirations of a newer majority and those in the minority. Some believe that the image and space of such a policy can lead to an inconsistent neighborhood space and form. However, such messiness in terms of community image can speak not only to social diversity, but also to the functional and social invention that allows for a neighborhood to adapt to all types of change in ways that make it more attractive on a regional, national, or global scale.

Conclusions

Demographic change in aging suburbs is a fact that architects, urban planners, and civic leaders need to view as an opportunity for renewal in the spatial patterns of suburbia. New values and identities are the fuel that drive this change. The number of in-formal and improvisational transformations of suburban spatial practices continues to grow. These transformations are also productive inspiration for thinking about various possibilities for modifying the suburbs.

For civic leaders and designers of the built environment, there is more than meets the eye in this change. The collision of the historical Euro-American suburb based on the lawn and the house with new cultures, forms, functions, and spatial practices create a new type of urbanism defined not by physical density, but by functional variety and the concentration of social inter-action. A future suburbia that is less formula driven can be a place that addresses more needs for a greater variety of people. This can eventually become a better place where new, engaging, and yet-to-be imagined personal and shared stories can develop and play out for those who live and work there.

While such change remains threatening to some, existing suburbs that adapt will not only creatively address the identity and meet the needs of their new residents, but more likely make places that attract people from other backgrounds. This allows the community and the larger metropolitan area to not only be more competitive—by adapting to changes in human behavior and harnessing the potential energy and innovation of new residents—but also better speak to the ethical responsibility of providing places that accommodate and illustrate the values of all residents.

Balancing Energy Challenge Adaptation and Heritage Preservation: The Evolution of Single-Family Houses in 1950s Residential France

Céline Drozd and Daniel Siret

Improved Energy Efficiency in Postwar Urban Single-Family Houses

In comparison with 1990 levels, France has set targets to cut its greenhouse gas (GHG) emissions by 40 percent by 2030 and by 75 percent by 2050. Although all sectors may be considered actors in this collective undertaking, the construction industry, which accounts for 20 percent of greenhouse gas emissions and 40 percent of end-use energy in France, has a pivotal role to play. The housing sector in particular is responsible for 28 percent of energy consumption and 13 percent of greenhouse gas emissions in France.[1] With ever-ambitious regulatory measures becoming a reality, new construction does what it can in the overall struggle to reduce greenhouse gases, but alone, its efforts fall short of the objectives in place.

Of all existing dwellings, single-family houses are the most common in France, making up nearly 60 percent of all housing or the equivalent of 19.2 million units. Thus, it goes without saying that the transformation of single-family houses is a key issue in the battle to reduce energy consumption. In line with this reasoning, public authorities have implemented new measures over the past several years to encourage owners to renovate their houses. These include laws, planning tools, and a number of initiatives to provide funding, in addition to assistance, awareness-building, and training opportunities.[2] Despite these movements oriented towards the energetic renovation of single-family houses, a recent survey shows that efficiency improvements have thus far been unsatisfactory.[3] In more concrete terms, only 5 percent of all single-family-house renovations in France met a minimum of two energy rankings on the Energy Performance

1. Data issued from the following reports: *Energy Performance in France for 2019*, ed. Statistical Data and Studies Department (Tours: Efil Agency, 2021), p. 156, and *2021 Key Climate Figures, France, Europe, World*, ed. Statistical Data and Studies Department (Tours: Efil Agency, 2021), p. 92.

2. Refer to the report overview on the role of public administration in single-family-home energy rehabilitation in France: Joël Idt, Margot Pellegrino, Jérôme Rollin, and Lucas Spadaro, *Energy Rehabilitation of Single-Family Homes in France: A Cross-Analysis of Public Administration Initiatives and Household Action* (PIA City of Tomorrow—EcoCité du Grand Roissy, 2021).

3. *TREMI Survey—Energy Rehabilitation of Single-Family Homes* (Ademe, 2018).

4. In 2015, France adopted the Energy Transition for Green Growth Act (ETGGA) aimed at reducing the country's impact on climate change. In construction, the leading measures favor the renovation of existing construction, developing new and more energy-efficient buildings, and fighting energy poverty.

5. Constructions classified in the National Register of Historical Monuments or those bearing the "Remarkable Contemporary Architecture" label require the assessment of the architect overseeing the French Listed Buildings prior to the start of any work.

6. In France, Local Urban Planning Schemes (LUPSs) refer to the documents that set out for a municipality or an ensemble of municipalities, such as metropolises, the overall orientations of territorial planning and the urban architecture regulation that applies to them.

7. This article is based on research whose purpose was to examine the different adaptation and transformation triggers to which the single-family house community was subjected in light of present-day energy transition efforts. Several research methods were used, including the consultation of city archives, the listing of home renovations visible from the public space, interviews with various Claire Cité specialists, and residents via visits and target questionnaires.

Certificate (EPC), a condition that must be fulfilled as per the Energy Transition for Green Growth Act.[4]

One explanation for this may be that renovations that have been done with the assistance of these programs are generally not part of a more comprehensive undertaking, but are rather designed to improve one or two elements, at most, of the building envelope or specific elements. Another reason could be that the heritage value granted to a number of these houses inhibits certain types of renovation from being carried out. Some more modest twentieth century dwellings have been spared the same restrictions as heritage-listed properties, but are still classified and regulated as what is referred to as *small heritage*.[5] Given their social history and their spatial and construction qualities, not to mention their place within the urban fabric, they attract inhabitants and local authorities alike. As a result, they tend to meet resistance when faced with modern-day environmental concerns.

Local Urban Planning Schemes often tilt the scale in the direction of excessive heritage preservation, sometimes immobilizing construction.[6] At other times, however, the scale tilts the other way, towards increasingly demanding energy efficiency, even if that ultimately means sacrificing the heritage value of a building or area. In addition to addressing the energy transition question, these houses are also expected to reflect the ongoing changes in living and working patterns, such as blended families, remote working, increased spatial demands, and fewer partitions. It has therefore become crucial to explore a dwelling's capacity to respond to current environmental concerns, while also ensuring that heritage characteristics are preserved. Mediation is necessary between inhabitants and public authorities to balance comfort, urban planning, and heritage value.

A Neighborhood Designed According to the Garden City Model in the Context of a Housing Shortage

Immediately following the end of World War II, the municipality of Rezé's population grew exponentially thanks to the construction of a new tram, which enabled residents to easily commute to and from the center of Nantes for work.[7] Multiple construction projects of varying sizes quickly emerged, from large-scale apartment complexes to more modest individual

Fig. 1 — Views of Claire Cité in 2020. Photos by authors.

Fig. 2 — Aerial view of Claire Cité.

8. Julie Boustingorry, *From Self-Build Pioneers to Cooperators: The Castor History in the Aquitaine Region* (Pau: University of Pau and the Pays de l'Adour, 2008), p. 245.

9. Daniel Pinson, "Rezé—1954, Between the Vertical and Horizontal Subdivision, or the Castors of Claire Cité and the Radiant City of Le Corbusier," *Parallel Cities* 14 (1989): pp, 88–105.

10. Charles Richard, *A Village Within the City (Claire Cité)* (ELOR Publishing, 1996), p. 153.

accommodations in residential neighborhoods, both of which offered solutions to the postwar housing shortage. One example is Claire Cité, [Fig. 1, 2] which was built between 1949 and 1954 and consists of 101 single-family houses ranging from approximately 645 to 1,000 square feet (60 to 93 square meters) in size, with a density of around five homes per acre (thirteen per hectare). On an urban scale, it was designed according to a branch-and-cluster model, with primarily square-shaped parcels of land, whose variability is driven by dwelling placement and overall site layout. The dwellings are oriented at a 45-degree angle in relation to the cardinal points—northwest/southeast or northeast/southwest. The houses sit approximately 6 to 16 feet (2 to 5 meters) back from the street, leaving room for a drive-way or other sidewalk-like space. Historian Julie Boustingorry describes the factors that determine a neighborhood's quality in densely populated urban areas as peacefulness, tranquility, and beauty.[8] She viewed the understated charm of Claire Cité as a successful combination of the built-up area and what surrounds it: the fruit of years of extensive and relentless dedication. This "harmony" today mirrors the seemingly effortless union formed by the architecture, urban planning, and vegetation.

Using the model of garden cities from Ebenezer Howard, the plans drawn up by Claire Cité's urban planner, Roger Vissuzaine, differ radically from the principles of modernity that were being applied elsewhere in the postwar years. If the reputation of large-scale apartment buildings today leaves little to be desired—although they are diamonds in the rough for the urban renovation sector—access to this type of housing in the early 1950s was a boon, given the modern advances in technology and the comfort it offered.[9] Boasting a very different architectural imprint, Claire Cité sits at the cutting edge of what owning a home in France still means in contemporary terms: the dream of acquiring a single-family house, whose importance would overshadow that of multi-unit dwellings starting in the 1970s.

Claire Cité further stands out due to its construction method: it was built by its inhabitants, who formed a cooperative to do so, inspired by the "Castor" (or "Beaver") method.[10] This was part of a movement that originated in the principles of Gëorgia Knap (1866–1946), who in 1921 began to promote building techniques that required little or no qualified manual labor. Referred to as "public cottages," and at one point backed financially by the Loucheur Act, Knap's undertaking brought self-builds into the spotlight. Resident-builders worked when time permitted and did so in groups. As its name suggests, a "Castor" (or "Beaver") may therefore be qualified as an individual to take part in a greater whole for the purposes of building a housing ensemble. Individuals' physical contribution compensates for the financial investment that would otherwise be allotted to the manual labor necessary to build that individual's house.

At the same time as Claire Cité, and with the same intentions, several other groups throughout France arose striving for the same result: building houses to counteract the postwar shortage of housing. To transform this reverie into reality, future Claire Cité residents established the following six principles to successfully complete the project: a) the pooling of resources; b) substituting financial contributions for labor-driven investments; c) forming an approximately one-hundred-member body to allow for cost-saving and public recognition; d) the creation of a building cooperative to facilitate credit approval and intermediary-free site management; e) the construction of a well-rounded garden city in alignment with modern urban planning designs; and f) the deployment of a self-managing cooperative.[11]

The Houses of Claire Cité, Traditional and Sustainable

With discussions between architect Léon Péneau and Castor residents guiding the design, the houses were built according to eight symmetrical, semidetached models. All ground floor plans were organized around a night/day unit and featured the same rooms: an entryway parlor, a living room, and a kitchen with a water heater for the day unit. Also included were bedrooms, a lavatory, and a bathroom for the night unit, as well as a pantry and convertible attic. [Fig. 3] Therefore, Claire Cité houses contain two clearly distinct categories of space: one refers to spaces meant for immediate occupation, such as kitchen, living room, lavatories, and bedrooms; the other refers to spaces like the pantry and attic, which are more seldomly used, and form a kind of reserve that awaits a function depending on the family's future needs. The pantry is in a league of its own, boasting an average surface area of around 215 square feet (20 square

11. Ninety-seven members were registered in December 1949.

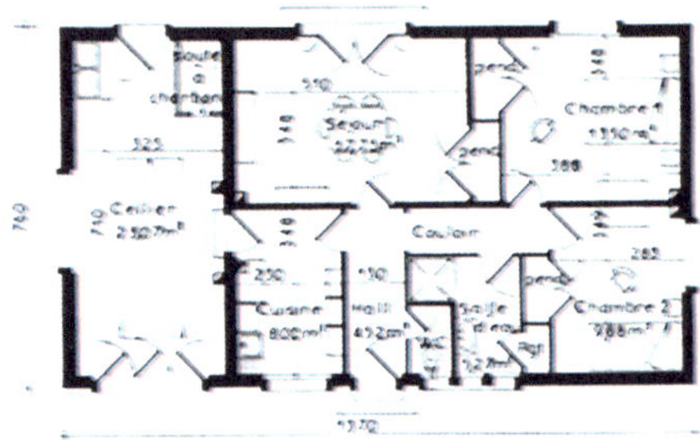

Fig. 3 — Façade and original plan of one of the eight home models by Léon Péneau Architect.

Fig. 4 — Examples of transformations in Claire Cité include the removal of a bedroom to expand the family room, the modification of the partition wall between the living room and kitchen, and the creation of a horizontal opening. Photos by the authors.

meters), which is greater than or equal to that of the living room. The attic is accessible by way of a staircase in the pantry.

For ease of implementation by an unqualified workforce, the houses were built using simple techniques and materials: concrete masonry units (CMUs, made on site due to the shortage in supplies); single-pane, wood windows and doors; a visible heating system (water heater and cast-iron radiators); and a traditional wood framework. In contrast to the building envelope, which was fabricated by the collective, each house's finishing touches are the responsibility of the inhabitants (such as wood flooring in the bedrooms or a kitchen). However, these simplified means did not imply a compromised aesthetic or quality: they all included crown molding, brick trim and elaborate woodwork on front door, large windows to maximize natural light, and high ceilings.

Transforming the Envelopes of All 101 Houses

Having all undergone visible modifications to their façades, the houses reflect both the changing nature of a family's needs and the ease with which the houses can adapt to them. This is particularly true for those founding Castors still living in the neighborhood: their houses have undergone modifications with the intention of creating additional living space (pantry-turned-family room for example), or responding to energy concerns (such as changing windows and/or doors, gable end insulation) to boost comfort or save money. That said, the modifications reveal varying levels of intervention.

Attic renovation have largely taken precedence over ground-floor extensions. At least half of Claire Cité's homeowners live upstairs. Therefore, the decision to fully utilize the interior rather than building from scratch often made the most sense. This is only furthered by the increased affordability of construction, the relative ease of intervention, the narrow nature of certain lots, and regulatory measures in place. That said, transformation strategies vary from one house to another: residents may choose to create openings in the façade to create stronger connections to the outdoors, opt for a raised roof in addition to roof windows, enlarge the family room by removing a bedroom or the pantry, or completely rethink the pantry's function through a storage build-on. [Fig. 4] What generally has the greatest impact on the types of transformation that are done to each house are the geometry of theirs plans, the location of the lavatories, the simplicity of the structural framework, the surface area of the initial dwelling, and the number of bedrooms.

Interior Transformations: Adapting to Changes in Function and Purpose

Over time, ground floor partitions have gradually been removed, giving priority to a more spacious family room. A ground-floor bedroom or portion of the pantry also often became an extension of the original living room by tearing a wall down. The open-plan kitchen overlooking the family room featured relatively defined borders, such as dividing walls with a glass partition, bar-height seating, and kitchen furniture. As a whole, however, the tendency within Claire Cité has been to create spaces that are roomy, multipurpose, and "like no other." This is in line with contemporaneous trends in the new construction of single-family houses across France. In terms of the purpose and function of a space (such as a living room, dining room, kitchen, stairwell, office, or even utility room), a revolution is underway with the removal of partitions and a desire to enhance sight lines throughout the interior. This newly open area can take up between one-fourth and one-third of the total living space. [Fig. 5, 6]

The original pantry area is considerably attractive given its potential to expand as a living space within the building's existing envelope. Initially imagined to be renovated into a garage, the 1950s pantry has proven to be a "bonus room" in the twenty-first century. By the same token, the attic is another natural candidate for renovations that aim to scale up the building's living space through the creation of additional bedrooms, with or without a bathroom. Such renovations also strive to create options for other functions that correspond to the inhabitants' lifestyle choices (such as a music room, game room, office, or TV room). Some of the houses had "pending" or "on-hold" areas meant to become future bedrooms, bathrooms, or mechanical rooms. Upstairs, the roof's slope had a strong influence on the layout. As a result, ceiling height and the location of the staircase were the primary constraints determining how the rooms upstairs are configured. [Fig. 7]

Transformations for Improved Energy Efficiency

The majority of single, wooden pane windows and doors were replaced and, for the most part, new homeowners insulated at least a portion of the walls. The original heating systems largely remain in place because they were deemed sustainable and in good enough condition by the current inhabitants, for whom levels of thermal inertia, as well as the continuous and even heat diffusion of the cast-iron radiators located throughout the house, are an advantage. The original water heater, conversely, was regularly changed out for a gas boiler, given its superior performance and the ease with which replacement could be done. However, this only deals with heating the house. Upstairs, temperatures during a heat wave can exceed 80°F or even 86°F (27–30°C), a situation described as "unbearable."

One house that has undergone a few different transformations (external gable-end insulation on one side only, double-pane windows and doors) consumes energy four times greater than that of new construction. By contrast, other houses whose inhabitants demonstrate energy efficient behavior present lower consumption levels that barely surpass those required in new construction. We can thus confidently point out that Claire Cité houses boast tremendous potential for energy improvement, with possible consumption levels nearing those established by the BBC Rénovation label.[12] Despite this, the prioritization of energy efficiency was absent among nearly all inhabitants, as renovation costs were unreasonable. Some were unaware of their house's wall composition or the work done by the previous owners. This has somewhat changed, however, given the recent hike in energy prices.

Four energy-efficient houses in Claire Cité underwent a complete makeover with wall renovation (interior and exterior) and roof insulation, changes in windows and doors, and the addition of a single- and dual-flow Controlled Mechanical Ventilation (CMV) unit, some of which are now equipped with real-time energy tracking systems. A programming system enables the set daytime and nighttime temperatures to be lower for three of the households whose primary heating source is a gas boiler, while the fourth features a wood-pellet fireplace. The occupants of these homes include families with children, with individuals who work outside the home.

12. The BBC Rénovation or "Energy-Saving Building Renovation" label establishes the energy efficiency requirements more than the thresholds set out by the thermal regulation in place for existing built-up areas. By doing so, it shines a spotlight on renovations that outdo expectations. In the residential sector, it is granted to renovations whose primary energy consumption is less than 80 kWh/m2/year (or 80 kWh/±11 ft2/year). In 2024, requirements were revised to also include a maximum threshold for greenhouse gas emission production of 11 kg CO2eq/m2/year (or ±24 lb. CO2eq/±11 ft2/year).

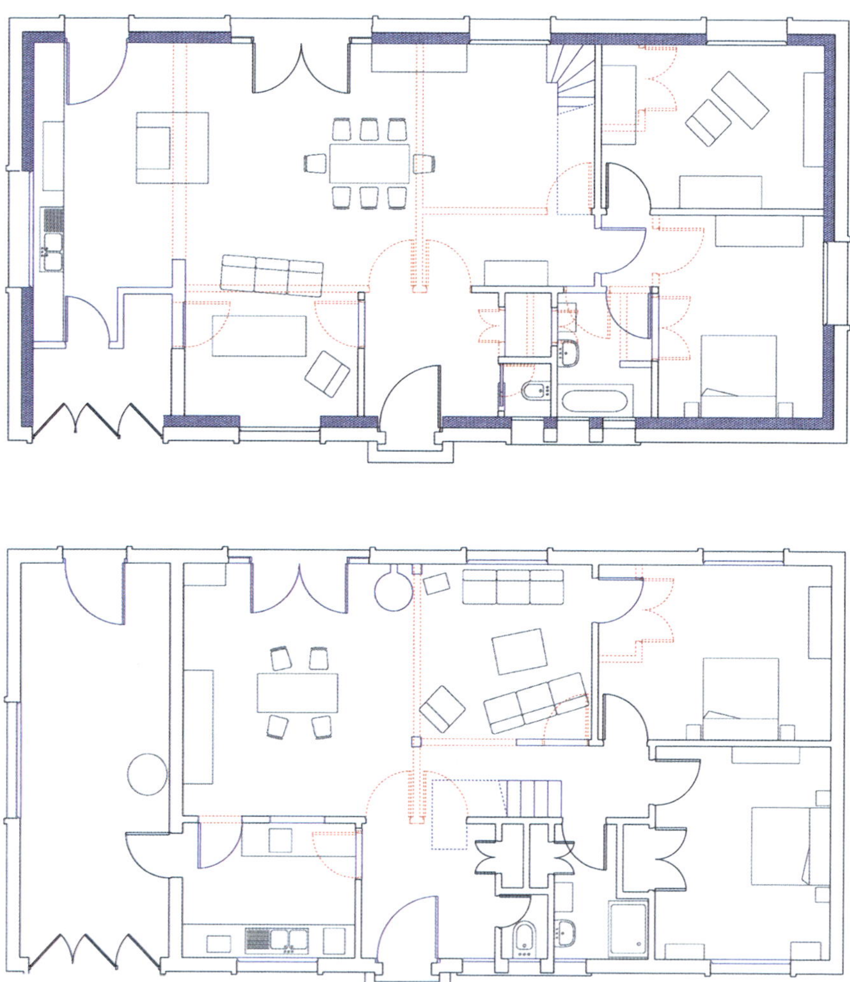

Fig. 5 — Plans of two transformation projects: black lines represent the existing original unit, red lines indicate removed sections, and blue lines show modified or added elements. Drawing by authors.

Fig. 6 — Room functions in nine transformed houses: kitchen (red), dining room (orange), living room (yellow), work space (green), closet (light green), lavatory (blue), bathroom (light blue), bedroom (purple), function pending (pink), pantry (beige), entrance (white), and garage (grey). Drawing by authors.

Fig. 7 — Examples of attic spaces and architectural features beneath the pitched roof. Photos by authors.

Home Adaptation Potential

Claire Cité's houses illustrate their immense adaptability to measure up to the challenges of energy efficiency. Several factors can shed light on this potential. Firstly, the built-up area is, overall, malleable. Visible electrical systems, accessible mechanical rooms, and simple spans between structural supports (masonry façades and load-bearing walls) facilitate work that needs to be done. Straightforward and traditional construction techniques make renovations easier. Concrete blocks, cast-iron radiators, and solid wood flooring are all durable, long-lasting, and easy to put in place and manufacture. The attic and original pantry also enable greater living areas to be achieved within the building envelope. In addition, the dimensions of structural elements were inflated from the onset to create the possibility of increasing living-space areas without the need for significant work. Examples of this include a load-bearing floor and concrete block partitions to relieve the floor load.

Another factor contributing to the houses's potential for adaptation is their qualitative architectural design. Where rooms are situated helps to know what interior transformations are possible. For example, lavatories grouped together within the house allow for greater freedom in renovation. The same also holds for bedrooms located adjacent to the living room, which makes scaling up the latter conceivable (and, to scale down, bedrooms can simply be closed off again). The house's compactness also facilitates the eventual work that will need to be carried out by keeping technical or accessibility challenges to a minimum. Moreover, the houses offer sought-after spatial characteristics because these characteristics are often nonexistent in new construction, such as high ceilings, an abundance of natural light, and spacious dimensions (including in high-traffic and storage areas). The façade articulations (decorative redan trim around windows and doors, brick molding around openings), as well as in the interior spaces (use of plaster ceiling), contribute to the production of an "old-world charm."

With regards to improving energy efficiency, very basic renovations, such as insulation or waterproofing, proved to significantly reduce energy usage, while demands for comfort continued to rise (namely in connection with indoor temperatures). Although the interior question of thermal comfort remains unaddressed by inhabitants, the houses ultimately present the potential to adapt to today's environmental concerns.

Towards Heritage Preservation

The late 1990s marked a new chapter in Claire Cité's history. The desire to preserve the urban and architectural characteristics of the neighborhood goes hand in hand with its changing demographic.[13] The goals and living tendencies of new occupants clash with their motivation to keep Claire Cité's identity intact. An alliance with Rezé City Hall was pivotal to setting in motion a gradual heritage preservation movement in Claire Cité. To best demonstrate this, the inhabitants published a white paper directed at the road network and related public spaces, and sent it to City Hall in 2013. That same year, one homeowner from the development tried to subdivide and sell a portion of his property, which is quite common in Rezé. Residents opposed this and the eventual construction of a 102nd home. This prompted municipal officials to take a stand.

From then on, starting in 2014, and as part of the Local Metropolitan Urban Planning Scheme (LMUPS), meetings have been organized involving residents, the municipality, and metropolitan urban planning services. A new road network and a public-space zoning scheme has since been devised, which was implemented from 2018 to 2020. As detailed in the LMUPS, Claire Cité belongs to a "heritage subsector" (UMd1p), and as such, is given its own set of regulatory measures.[14] This is not because Claire Cité sits within a Castor housing development. Claire Cité is protected not only because its materialization was made entirely possible by its inhabitants, but also because it embodies a present-day outlook enhanced by its proximity to Le Corbusier's Unité d'Habitation. Its garden city-inspired vegetation also reinforces its singular nature.

The regulatory measures, therefore, mirror the inhabitants' stance against adding to the neighborhood's built-up density, while allowing living areas to be expanded in each household. Residents hope to fully explore and exploit all the "nooks and crannies," both inside and out, and put an end to new construction within the subdivision. Even where exterior wall insulation is involved, the inhabitants are dedicated to preserving front façades by recreating their original decorative and functional

13. Figures provided by the inhabitants: 90 percent of Castors prior to 1995; less than 10 percent after 2015.

14. Version 4.1.1 of the Nantes LMUPS.

elements. Yet they prefer to decide themselves on the back façade. Not opposed to the neighborhood undergoing future transformations, the inhabitants simply ask that these not be visible from the street. To best accommodate such a request, for example, the LMUPS authorizes solar panels to be installed on hidden roof sections—even if their orientation dramatically compromises their output.

Ambiguity Between Energy Use Adaptation and Preservation

While there is consensus in Claire Cité on the importance of environmental qualities, there is dissensus about the preservation of its architectural heritage. For example, regardless of the importance of the front wooden doors, some occupants replaced them with a standard and cheaper alternative found in stores. Other inhabitants attempted to group the orders they placed with carpenters for the sake of homogenization, but their efforts ultimately gave way to cost. Others decided to rework the fences, repaint the bricks with more contemporary tones, add built-in rolling shutters, or change the color of the façade coating. In doing so, they modified the elements that give Claire Cité its recognizable charm.

That all said, there is one exception: vegetation maintenance and preservation. The abundant vegetation that has remained intact over the years at Claire Cité reinforces the "village within a city" feeling held dear by the Castors from the start. Outside difficulties tied to accessibility and parking, the human-scale, street network in the form of narrow thoroughfares, small squares, and alleys has not undergone any modifications. This offers inhabitants modifiable, green exteriors while ensuring privacy.

Conclusion: A Change in Scale to Scale Up Transformation?

Today, the renovated houses of Claire Cité have joined the ranks of comfort similar to more recent housing constructions on the outskirts of the city. The interior spaces have not only responded but also adapted to changes in living patterns; energy efficiency, in particular, has made tremendous strides thanks to envelope insulation, ventilation, sunlight, and thermal inertia. However, despite all efforts, many houses have reached their maximum capacity both in terms of space, as well as energy savings. They are now confronted with the limits of what the structures can tolerate to accommodate contemporary demands (multiple electrical installations, increasingly complex envelopes, etc.). The potential for transformation also grapples with heritage preservation, making exterior wall insulation, solar panel installation, energy-efficient window and door replacement, sun exposure protection, and the like, both costly and complex.

Adapting this type of construction cannot be avoided. Its future must follow perpetually changing lifestyles and the quest for energy savings. For this to happen, one solution would be to think on a collective level, perhaps in the form of renewable energy communities.[15] This would enable the inhabitants of Claire Cité and other preservation-minded ensembles to take back ownership of their neighborhoods through a joint endeavor. It would also be a way to reconnect with the cooperative mindset that exemplifies the Castors.

15. For more information, see: Grégory Lamotte, "Les communautés d'énergie ; comment en créer une ?," Comwatt, April 17, 2020.

Summer House Transformations: New Trends in How Families Enjoy the Mediterranean Landscape in Costa Blanca

Ester Gisbert Alemany

Introduction

The Costa Blanca is not a geographic area but a commercial name for a tourist destination. Coined in 1957 by the British aeronautical industry, it indicates the coastal areas of the southeastern Spanish provinces of Almería, Murcia, and Alicante. Presently, it functions as a tourist board covering the entire province of Alicante and its hinterland, revealing the pervasive influence of the tourist industry beyond the coast as well as its institutionalization. Compared to the French Côte d'Azur, the "White Coast" offered a budget-friendly alternative for clear blue skies, even during the winter.[1] What was historically a challenge for farmers, causing water scarcity for irrigating fields, turned into a boon for North European tour operators and their clients. The high-rise tourist towns, such as Benidorm, that hosted these operators and tourists, have been widely researched by urbanists and architects.[2] Yet tourism revenue was mostly made by selling travelers single-family second homes for longer stays. From 1969 to 2000, the real estate industry built 350,000 new tourist homes in the Province of Alicante alone.[3] [Fig. 1] Today, this residential sprawl has become more intricate, with older houses undergoing transformations made by subsequent generations of owners. Examples include a Norwegian professional retrofitting a house for remote work, local families adapting basements for hosting an increasing number of tourists, and retirees and young families moving between suburban homes and town centers based on their life stage. Five oral accounts are used here to illustrate broader trajectories of change influenced by wider social phenomena. These phenomena affect the housing stock, and in particular, they influence the evolving notion of leisure since the tourist boom. The study of what was or will

1. Valero Escandell, José Ramón, and María Dolores Fernández Poyatos, "El origen de la imagen turística de la Costa Blanca," *Canelobre: Revista del Instituto Alicantino de Cultura "Juan Gil-Albert"* 66 (2016): p. 17.

2. See Mario Gaviria, *Benidorm, ciudad nueva* (Madrid: Editora Nacional, 1977); José Miguel Iribas, "Benidorm. The Reasons for Success", in *What People Want*, (Basel: Birkhäuser, 2005), pp. 225–35; and MVRDV, Winy Maas, and Jacob van Rijs, *Costa Iberica* (Barcelona: ACTAR, 2000).

3. Alejandro Mantecón, *La experiencia del turismo* (Barcelona: Icaria Editorial, 2008), p. 95.

4. For more information on the *Consultorio de la Costa Blanca*, see the work of Drassana Architects, drassana.org.

5. For a summary of the methodologies used to work with the families, see Rodolfo Livingston, *Arquitectos de familia: El método arquitectos de la comunidad* (Buenos Aires: Nobuko, 2006); Selma Díaz, "El arquitecto de la comunidad en Cuba," *Vivienda popular* 11 (2002): pp. 33–42. For the implementation of the method as a government program in Cuba, see Arturo Valladares, "The Community Architect Program: Implementing participation-in-design to improve housing conditions in Cuba," *Habitat International* 38 (April 2013): pp. 18–24. For its development as a network of architects in Uruguay, see Alicia Berasategui et al., eds., *10 años Arquitectos de la Comunidad, Uruguay* (Montevideo: Sociedad de Arquitectos del Uruguay, 2010).

6. Carsten follows Lévi-Strauss's conceptualization of "house societies" in Janet Carsten and Stephen Hugh-Jones, *About the House: Lévi-Strauss and Beyond* (Cambridge: Cambridge University Press, 1995); and develops the importance of studying the biographies of houses together with families in Janet Carsten, *After Kinship* (Cambridge: Cambridge University Press, 2004); and Janet Carsten, "House-Lives as Ethnography/Biography," *Social Anthropology* 26, no. 1 (2018): pp. 103–16.

7. See Sergi Cuadrado-Ciuraneta, Antoni Durà-Guimerà, and Luca Salvati, "Not Only Tourism: Unravelling Suburbanization, Second-home Expansion and 'Rural' Sprawl in Catalonia, Spain," *Urban Geography* 38, no. 1 (2017): pp. 68–9; Chiara Merlini and Federico Zanfi, "The Family House and its Territories in Contemporary Italy: Present Conditions and Future Perspectives," *Journal of Urbanism: International Research on Placemaking and Urban Sustainability* 7, no. 3 (2014): pp. 223–4.

8. "Lifestyle migrants" is the term used by sociologists to name migrants who move looking for

become a second home provides a complementary perspective to the study of the single-family home, revealing how people utilize their houses to anchor their lives to a place and view building, updating, and maintaining as means to enjoy a landscape.

The oral accounts selected here are illustrated with ethnographic vignettes, pictures, drawings, and archive material, demonstrating how houses evolve alongside the changing needs and aspirations of the families inhabiting them. These materials were compiled in the *Consultorio de la Costa Blanca,* a practice inspired by the Argentinian architect Rodolfo Livingston and his proposal for an affordable architectural service for families.[4] Livingston's method has been implemented as a Community Architect Program in various countries.[5] In the *Consultorio de la Costa Blanca,* we have assisted over a hundred families of diverse nationalities. Houses endure beyond individual lifetimes, and milestones—such as childbirth, adolescence, marriage, divorce, and death—are materially expressed in the building, renovation, or extension of real estate assets of different social groups.[6] Accompanying families through significant shared life events has provided insight into how a plurality of subjects and cultures contribute to shaping a residential landscape, modifying it over time. Geographers and urban researchers have found that suburbanization processes in marginal Southern European regions share a specific suburban spatial organization where rural districts are rapidly transformed.[7] The *Consultorio* is a site of collective research on this phenomenon: engaging in the redesigning of houses offers a vantage point for a detailed exploration of the social and spatial process of suburbanization. This essay specifically delves into a commonly expressed desire, which is particularly shared by lifestyle migrants who have accelerated the urbanization of this landscape to foster outdoor dwelling patterns.[8]

The Transformation of the Mediterranean "Quiet Country"

"Better to show you our own home!" exclaims X., inviting us to the outskirts of Polop, Alicante. There stands the suburban home of T. and X., showcasing how they've organized the basement for tourist rentals on platforms like Airbnb. We are greeted by a group of old medlar and lemon trees that lead us to the pool, a cherished feature

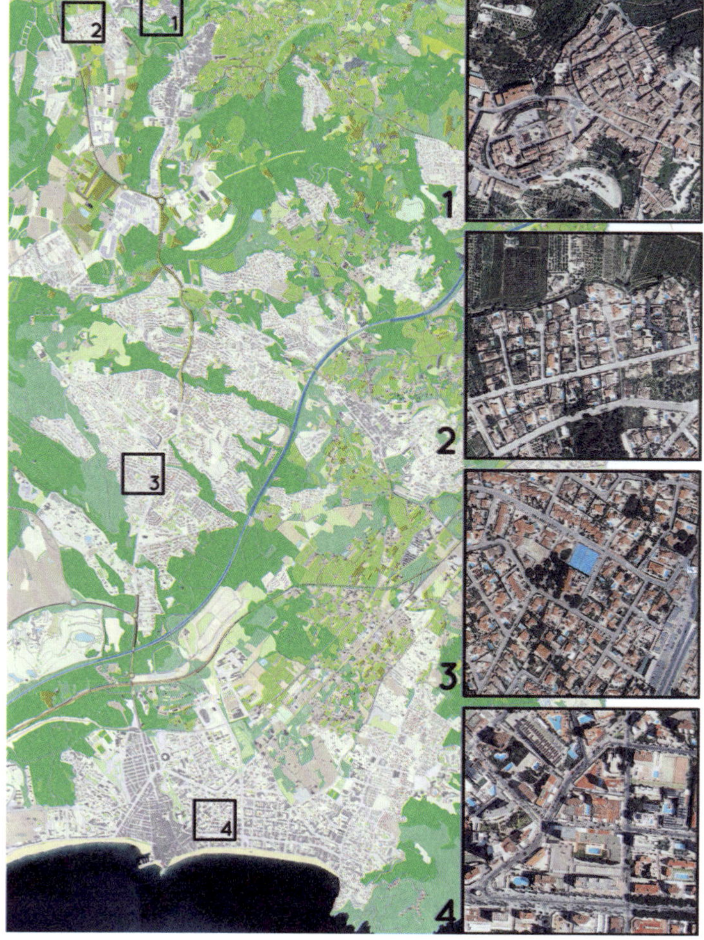

Fig. 1 — Map of Benidorm and its northern expansion toward the town of Polop, highlighting key locations in the story of T. and X. (1) The old town of Polop and the first apartments where T.'s family moved in the 60s; (2) T. and X.'s suburban house, built in the 1980s on what was once an agricultural farm, now surrounded by suburban development; (3) Completed suburban developments; (4) High-rise apartments in Benidorm, where T. and X. relocated for work (4).

Figures. 2, 3 — View of T. and X.'s garden pool and of the open performative kitchen in the basement in 2017. Project and photos by Drassana Architects.

a lifestyle change, to differentiate them from those who migrate for economic necessity; see Michaela Benson and Karen O'Reilly, *Lifestyle Migration: Expectations, Aspirations, and Experiences* (Abingdon: Routledge, 2016). The urban phenomenon is also called "residential tourism." For an overview of its development in the Costa Blanca and their expressed wishes, see Raquel Huete, *Turistas que llegan para quedarse: una explicación sociológica sobre la movilidad residencial.* (Alicante: Universidad de Alicante, 2009), pp. 192–200.

for their guests. Initially constructed separately for their toddlers, the pool is now something that they wish was more integrated. Walking us through the house, much like they would with guests, they showcase the recently added open kitchen. Pointing at the big oven where T. has been demonstrating the art of baking traditional pastries to their guests, she explains that tradition will be the theme for refurbishing her mother's house—the real reason for our visit. Located in the traditional town center, it will be transformed into a bed and breakfast, marking a shift from the rehearsal of vacation rentals in their suburban home to a more significant rural hospitality project. [Fig. 2, 3]

In our conversation, T. and X. share how tourism has influenced multiple generations of their family. They relocated from Polop, situated twenty kilometers from the coast, to an apartment in Benidorm due to job opportunities in the service industry. Eventually, they returned to the hinterland, building a detached house on family-owned agricultural land. Over three decades, their once-isolated house has found itself amidst residential tourist areas filled with single-family and semidetached housing. Polop was originally an agricultural settlement on a rocky promontory with both its terraced landscape and its town houses constructed from dry stone. T. and X. reminisce about Polop's earlier success with tourists, especially the French, who were drawn in by cool nights, water sports, and the rural landscape before the sun-and-beach tourism boom of the 1970s. T. once worked in one of the town's two hotels, experiencing such busy summers that tourists often lodged in locals' homes. This influx brought economic revival, with new apartment blocks being constructed for young families. T.'s family moved into one of these apartments, shifting from a life in the streets and orchards to a more confined indoor existence. Choosing a suburban home upon their return from Benidorm, T. and X. are now contemplating the social aspect of that shift. The B&B project at T.'s mother's house aims to recreate and share the collective experiences of townhouse living, where people gathered around fireplaces or took seats out on the streets, depending on the weather.

    T. and X.'s story highlights why researchers prefer the term "family house" over "single-family house" in Mediterranean suburban landscapes. This type of house often accommodates an extended family, forming a domestic welfare system.[9] This notion aligns with anthropological research on "house societies," a term coined by Claude Lévi-Strauss, which indicates an exploration of an intermediary social form between kinship and class-based societies.[10] In regions dominated by tourism, such as that of T. and X., house societies exhibit high mobility on both regional and international scales. Family houses extend not only in space but also across generations, with elders passing down properties and customs to keep the houses in shape.[11] T. and X. recognize that the success of their B&B relies on renewing a Mediterranean heritage landscape still discernible in Costa Blanca's interior. This landscape is often described as ecologically conscious and socially sustainable, akin to "arcadia" or Donna Haraway's "quiet country," which contrasts "flourishing and cared-for places" with "morph eroded and disowned no-places."[12] This paradox is common in all the stories related to summer houses in the *Consultorio*, as they are bought or built to enjoy a landscape that is appreciated and cared for. But at the same time, because of the new inhabitants' ways of life, it is necessarily transformed. Enjoyment, heritage, and mobility are the elements that make Haraway's approach so valuable to the study of suburban landscapes of leisure, and the way she poses the troubled paradox of contemporary landscapes remains pertinent. Is it possible that the blasted places of "the technological wild" ever come to be the "quiet country—the country in which all the care of generations of people is evident to those who know how to see it?"[13] The following accounts delve into how families preserve inherited landscapes in the context of residential tourism. The following four cases are situated approximately three to twelve kilometers from the coast in the sprawling area of the beach of Alicante that once was part of the *huerta* (irrigated fields) landscape.[14] [Fig. 4]

Trying to Make Ties with the Landscape

"Will it be repaid for when we sell the house?" inquires P., a Dutch business consultant who, together with his wife Y., is examining design sketches. For their home in Montnegre, ten kilometers from the beach of Alicante, they plan to add a kitchen in the basement near the new pool, a garage for their car, and a tool shed. The conversation revolves around how these new elements could be

9. Merlini and Zanfi, "The Family House and its Territories in Contemporary Italy": pp. 224–5.

10. Carsten, *After Kinship*, p. 42.

11. Judith Huggins Balfe, "Passing It on: The Inheritance of Summer Houses and Cultural Identity," *The American Sociologist* 26, no. 4 (1995): pp. 37–8.

12. Donna Haraway, "Speculative Fabulations for Technoculture's generations: Taking care of Unexpected Country," *Australian Humanities Review* 50, no. 5 (2011): p. 5.

13. Deborah Bird Rose, *Reports from a wild country: ethics for decolonisation*, (Sydney: UNSW Press, 2004), p. 4; quoted in Haraway.

14. The term *huerta* refers to a specific agricultural landscape and was included in the Dobris Report map for European Landscapes, based on the map in J. H. A Meeus, M. P. Wijermans, and M. J. Vroom, "Agricultural landscapes in Europe and their transformation," *Landscape and Urban Planning* 18, no. 3 (1990): pp. 289–352. For an extensive characterization of its evolution in several Spanish locations, see Pablo Martí and Clara García-Mayor, "The Huerta Agricultural Landscape in the Spanish Mediterranean Arc: One Landscape, Two Perspectives, Three Specific Huertas," *Land* 9, no. 11 (2020).

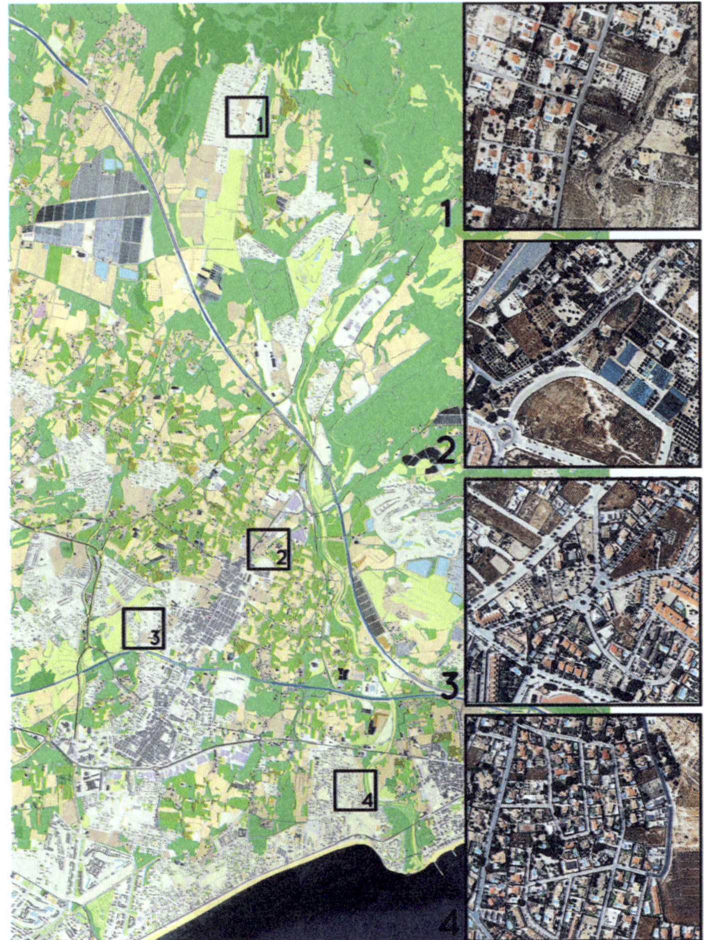

Fig. 4 — Map of the Huerta de Alicante, highlighting single-family house transformation. (1) P. and Y.'s house and the suburban development in Montnegre in 1990s; (2) N.'s house in a former agricultural area transformed into suburban developments; (3) K. and N.'s house in the suburban expansion of a traditional town; (4) G.'s house in a completed suburban development.

Figures 5, 6 — View of P. and Y.'s kitchen, pool, and other elements as they are placed in the landscape. Project and photos by Drassana Architects.

better integrated into the design. The designers, familiar with the area, explore ways to capitalize on the earth's movements to rebuild ancient terraces that once controlled scarce rainwater runoff. However, P.'s previous question inevitably concludes the discussion. This is a recurrent theme when proposing less conventional solutions, discovered through collective conversation, that clash with the compelling force of financial considerations. In the real estate market, the check list typically includes three bedrooms, a kitchen, a living room, at least two bathrooms, a pool, a shelter for the car, and some outdoor activity space, without concessions to the local landscape's features. [Fig. 5, 6, 7]

This case vividly illustrates how the single-family home has deviated from its idealized role as the stable abode of the nuclear family.[15] Instead, it is now part of a constellation of dwellings, people, and places interwoven across the landscape and spanning generations of time. This is evident in P. and Y.'s suburban house. Although they don't have children, they do not live alone. The house, in transforming to align with specific habits and desires, reveals that, in a way, it is shared with strangers. These so-called strangers are the potential future buyers who, even if unknown, influence every future alteration. When dealing with such hypothetical buyers, often represented by the real estate agents who are the designers' actual clients, detached encounters are likely.

The suburban house has long served as an economic instrument for governments, stabilizing banks and fostering employment.[16] Families, too, view it as an economic tool, calculating budgets for each milestone and projecting future returns. P. and Y., for example, emphasize that they chose their Costa Blanca house over buying a new car, intending to retire early and make it their primary residence. Their budget for upgrading the house is calculated with an eventual sale in mind. They aim for a return on their investment to fund a smaller apartment in a costal second-line town, closer to amenities and medical services, and later, perhaps, assisted living. Mobility, a key aspect of the American suburban experience, is also evident in Costa Blanca suburbia: the "daily commute" by car turns here into the "every-other-day journey to shop and relax," with an additional flight once or twice a month.[17] This heightened separation amplifies the tendency to cohabitate with these hypothetical

15. Avi Friedman, *Planning the New Suburbia: Flexibility by Design* (Vancouver: UBC Press, 2002), pp. 27–9, 174.

16. Keller Easterling and Richard Prelinger, *Call It Home: The House That Private Enterprise Built* (CreateSpace, 2013): section two, video.

17. Kenneth T. Jackson, *Crabgrass Frontier: The Suburbanization of the United States* (Oxford: Oxford University Press, 1987).

18. Robin M. Leichenko and William D. Solecki, "Suburban Landscapes and Lifestyles, Globalization and Exporting the American Dream," in *The Routledge Handbook of Urbanization and Global Environmental Change* (Abingdon: Routledge, 2015), pp. 242–3.

19. Haraway, "Speculative Fabulations for Technoculture's generations."

20. Leichenko and Solecki, "Suburban Landscapes and Lifestyles," p. 250.

future occupants—the ghostly harbingers of the future that appear every time one wants to change a socket or pull down a partition or paint a wall. The question invariably arises: will the buyers appreciate the new layout? The common response is affirmative if one opts for a more conventional, globalized solution. The linkage between suburbanization and the globalization of lifestyles and consumption, disseminated with the American Dream, is evident here.[18] In the Mediterranean version of this dream, the aggregate of these houses resembles a landscape tailored for the ghosts of the future: conservative investors who adhere to the market's lowest common denominator. P. and Y.'s house exemplifies how often the developer dictates design based on plot size, material costs, and profit goals. As a by-product of financing and consumerism, residential tourist landscapes join the category of "violently blasted places," labelled as "the wild" by Haraway, who provides spaces like "the mall, the highway, the lab, and the installation" as examples. As noted above, Haraway differentiates the wild from the quiet country in that one can *see* that these "violently blasted places" are not taken care of.[19] The knowledge of how a landscape is tended makes a significant difference. P. and Y. chose their house due to its expansive plot, which provides a sense of being surrounded by a landscape rather than by neighbors. They express an intention to spend much of their time on landscaping. While P. engages with local workers to repair a dry-stone wall—appreciating its color, soil quality, and local flora—new construction leans towards prefabricated elements that are "planted" on their land, rather than locally crafted ones that might connect with existing landscape patterns.

Their hesitancy in trusting local tradesmen stems from a contradictory relationship. While these tradesmen provide insight into local customs, P. and Y. fear that collaboration may lead to a loss of control over their budget. Suburbia has been characterized as a space where middle and high-income residents distance themselves from local environmental and social issues. Suburbanization, much like globalization, enables consumers to separate themselves from the consequences of their actions.[20] P. and Y., like many suburban dwellers, try to commit to a landscape, but the prospect of moving among several properties as life stages progress impedes a deep commitment. Their retirement plans remain feasible as long as they can control short-term investment budgets and remain attentive to long-term revenues. In dealing with this housing stock, home-owners not only plan and design their family's future, but also the future of the landscapes. Returning to Haraway's question: the "technological wild" of suburban landscapes, which blasts through the work of many generations, emerges not solely due to immense economic forces, but also through the fantasies of a distanced, unbound future harbored in each family's imagination.

An Emerging Landscape of Enjoyment

G., a Norwegian digital worker, commutes to his home country every two weeks to manage his business, embodying a new residential tourism trend in the province of Alicante.[21] The region sells nearly 50 percent of its housing stock to foreigners.[22] To establish himself in Alicante, G. acquired a family house built during the construction boom of the 1970s near the beach. The surroundings, once typical of a *huerta* with orchards, almond trees, and vineyards, have transformed, much like P. and Y.'s plot. Today, it is surrounded by other houses. In the refurbishment, the kitchen was opened to the outdoor pool and garden. G. and his family kept the plot's distinctive features, including old trees and porches, recognizing their contribution to the home's personality. Recently, the *Consultorio* has assisted many families, akin to G. or P. and Y., who value the landscape and are committed to sustainability. For instance, G. opted to enhance the house's energy efficiency and use only ecologically responsible materials, including sustainably sourced wood and chemical-free paint. [Figure 8, 9] Like P. and Y.'s plans, G.'s family viewed their investment as temporary. Eventually they moved, selling the upgraded house with improved energy efficiency at a higher price than they originally paid. Housing mobility shifts homeowners' localized concerns for ecological issues and landscape sustainability into a quest for globally standardized, conventional solutions. Often, the homeowners bring technical specifications to the *Consultorio*, from certified wood sources to more efficient window solutions, passing by prefabricated pools or garage sheds that come with solar panels. In doing so, the homeowners demonstrate a commitment to the planet on a global, abstract scale. However, the detachment inherent in housing market logic makes it challenging for them

21. Pablo Torres et al., "Alicante: Destino de teletrabajo y nómadas digitales" (workshop, September 26, 2022, Alicante, Universidad de Alicante).

22. Sonneil Research, "Los extranjeros compran más casas que nunca en Alicante: el 43% del total en el tercer trimester," *Alicante Plaza*, December 21, 2022.

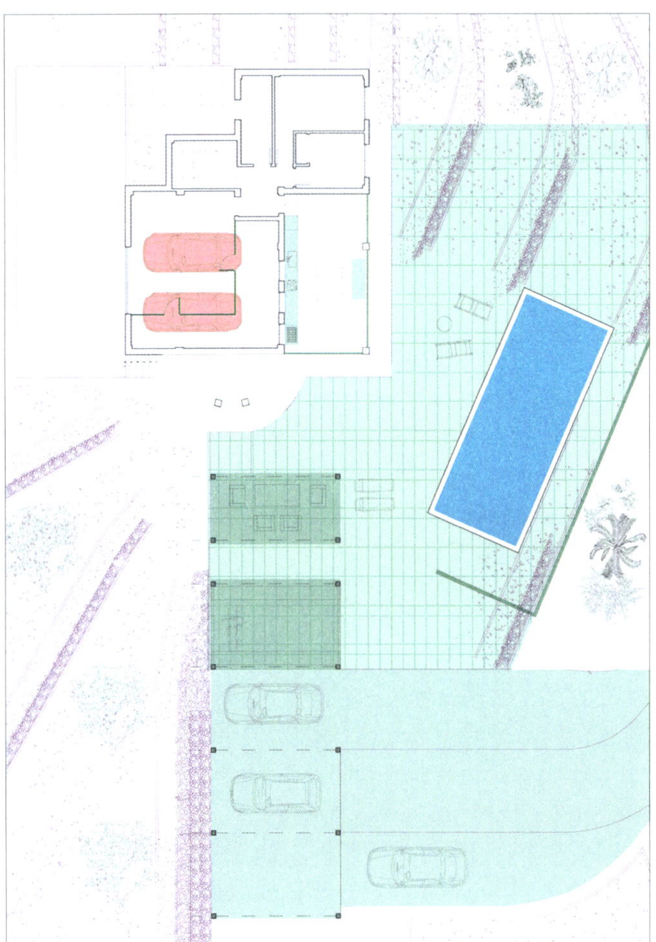

Fig. 7 — Plan of P. and Y.'s house, 2021, highlighting demolished elements (red), new additions (blue), and the old terraces (purple) that could not be recovered. Project and drawing by Drassana Architects, *Consultorio de la Costa Blanca*.

Fig. 8 — View of G's family house, 2014. The intervention increased the opening towards the garden while keeping the existing porches and trees. Project and photos by Cor&Asociados and *Consultorio de la Costa Blanca*.

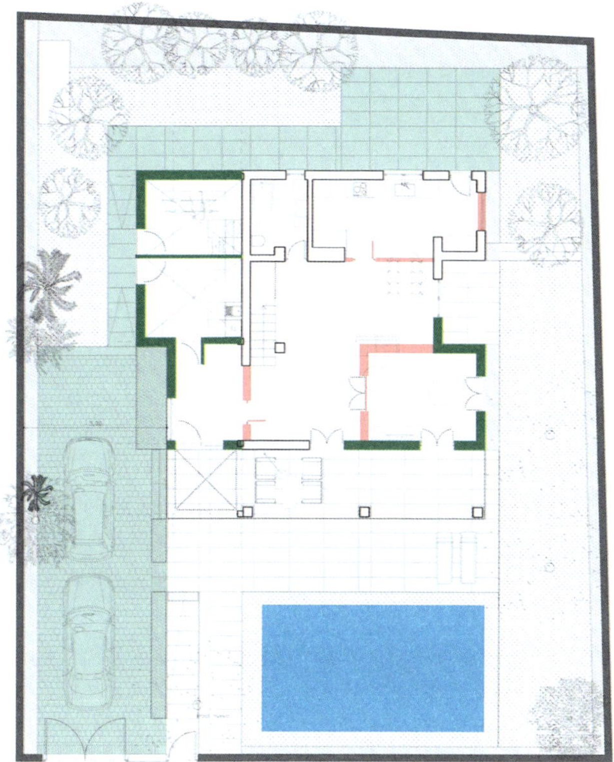

Fig. 9 — Plan of G's family house, 2014. The plan shows demolished elements (red) and new additions (green and blue). Project by Cor&Asociados and *Consultorio de la Costa Blanca*.

Fig. 10 — K. and N.'s wedding invitation, 2020. Photo by Fernando Gosalbez.

Fig. 11 — Debris infill found in the excavation of urbanized suburban development in Mutxamel, Alicante, 2018. Photo by Drassana Architects and *Consultorio de la Costa Blanca*.

Fig. 12 — The last remaining plowed lands around K. and N.'s house, 2023. Photo by Drassana Architects and *Consultorio de la Costa Blanca*.

23. Pier Vittorio Aureli and Martino Tattara, "Platforms: Architecture and the Use of the Ground," *Conditions* (e-flux Architecture and Sharjah Architecture Triennial, 2019).

to see themselves as responsible for the features of the concrete landscape that they are transforming.

We have seen that, even if P. and Y. appreciated stories about managing the arid landscape with dry-stone terraces, they feel safer controlling the budget with prefabricated elements designed for generic, flat plots that require few adaptations to the existing topography. These components do not fit the landscape, much like the housing development they are part of, which lacks meaning for committed locals attuned to the landscape's patterns. However, there is a potential for this to change in the current trend favoring more sustainable materials and dwelling patterns. The two oral accounts presented next were chosen because they raised such questions in a more radical manner. They revolve around two of the most distinctive features of the outdoor, detached summer house: the pool and the land itself.

Attempts at Reconnecting with the Ground

"After two children, three houses, and two countries, we are marrying!" So reads the wedding invitation from K. and N., received after we accompanied them in the refurbishment of their detached house. What surprises us is the image included on the card: a quarter of the family photo is dedicated to a gabion wall filled with debris resulting from construction. The walls form terraces around a garage basement that, now open with windows, has been transformed into a living and guest room. In the 1970s, the house was built as a summer house with two floors, less insulated partitions and walls, and smaller rooms. This meant that the house's seventy-square-meter (750-square-foot) footprint could not meet the family's current needs. Making the basement habitable for people, instead of cars and clutter, has made a significant difference and has shifted the discussion toward the uses of the garden. [Fig. 10]

Platforms elevating houses seem as ancient as the first semipermanent domestic spaces, the consolidation of which as "an enclosed permanent space was paralleled by the levelling of the dwelling's interior (and its) elevation."[23] This elevated platform differentiated areas for reproductive activities and allowed for the ritualization of domestic life. In this case, the former owner informed K. and N. that the basement was built to elevate the house and protect it from rainwater runoffs, as the area tended to flood under heavy seasonal rains. This phenomenon occurs in many suburban areas in Costa Blanca, as urbanization has modified the existing topography of agricultural land.[24] Recently, there has been a growing concern about this issue, gaining centrality in the planning that occurs with the assistance of geographic information software.[25] In the *huerta* area of K. and N.'s house, water streams are precious and their runoffs have been designed and managed through centuries. Rapid urbanization changed this, sealing off the ground with asphalt and concrete, impeding water filtration, and altering the levelling of runoff. Urbanized streets are often higher than the fields that were formerly there, and sometimes plots are elevated with landfills after the urbanization is incorporated. These artificial grounds may not be resistant enough for foundations. [Fig. 11] Thus, it is typically advised to raise the house from the ground and bring the ground floor some steps higher than the street. This also forms crawl spaces under the ground floor, or sometimes even complete basements. Contemporary designers of new single-family houses in Costa Blanca are reinterpreting this pattern, separating the house from the ground with pole structures that transform the land as little as possible, emphasizing the ancestral "contrast between the interior and the uneven topography of the outside landscape."[26]

With residents increasingly embracing an outdoor lifestyle, the domestication that begins within the interior extends to the exterior. This transition involves the proliferation of flat surfaces and the platforms supporting them, ultimately encompassing the entire plot. In the house that K. and N. bought, the plot had not yet been levelled, and it was one of the few that still retained part of the structure of the landscape of the irrigated fields around. [Fig. 12] They realized that these land patterns were valuable and wanted to preserve them. This was achieved through a different kind of domestication that aimed to embrace the legacy of farming with a series of terraced vegetable gardens. During the excavation, the conversation in the *Consultorio* revolved around the importance of the land, the problem of landfills with construction debris, and the risks of flooding. This rich conversation encouraged the clients to accept the proposal to build the walls with debris. At the start, they were reluctant to share the garden with what seemed like rubbish. Now, they are so proud that they get pictured together

24. Antonio M. Rico Amorós, Jorge Olcina Cantos, and Antonio Gil Olcina, eds., *Aguaceros, aguaduchos e inundaciones en áreas urbanas alicantinas* (Alicante: Servicio de Publicaciones Univesitat d'Alacant, 2004).

25. Jorge Olcina Cantos, "Riesgo de inundaciones y ordenación del territorio en la escala local: El papel del planeamiento urbano municipal," *Boletín de la Asociación de Geógrafos Españoles* 37 (2004): pp. 49–84; Jorge Olcina Cantos and Andrés Díez-Herrero, "Cartografía de inundaciones en España," *Estudios Geográficos* 78, no. 282 (2017).

26. Aureli and Tattara, "Platforms." For examples, see Antonio Abellán Alarcón and Javier Esquiva López, "Casa de la Mota del Rio," *Pasajes de arquitectura y crítica* 139 (2016): pp. 32–6; Andrés Jaque and Miguel Mesa del Castillo Clavel, "Rambla-Climate-House, Molina de Segura, Murcia (España)," *AV: Monografías* 247 (2022): pp. 66–71.

Fig. 13 — Views of K. and N.'s house, 2020. Project and photos by Drassana Architects and *Consultorio de la Costa Blanca*.

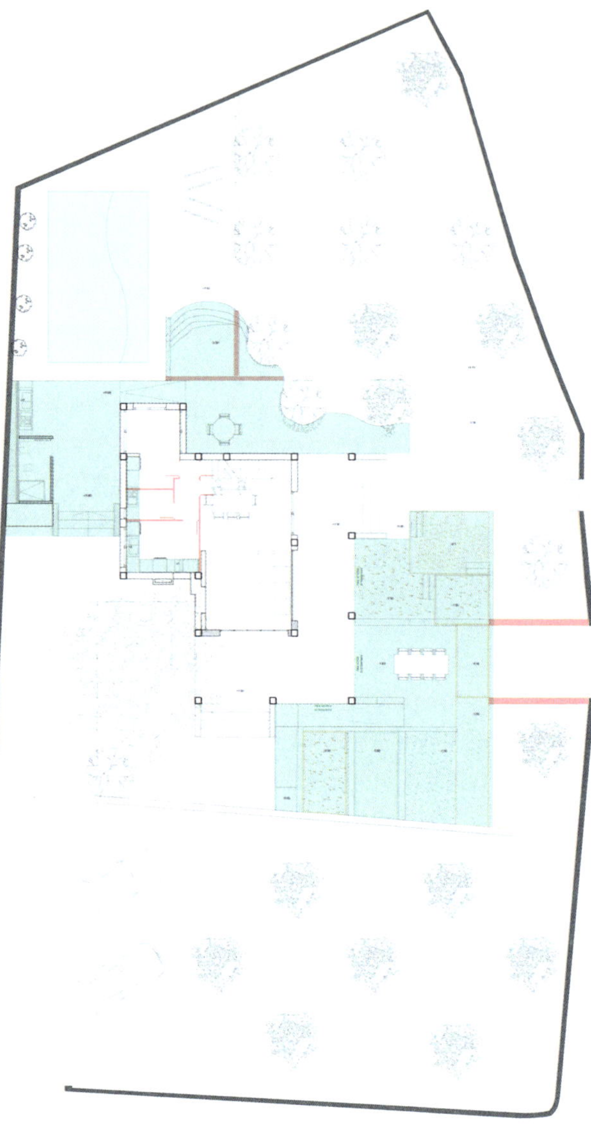

Fig. 14 — Plan of K. and N.'s house, 2020. The plan shows the demolished elements (pink) and the new additions (green and blue). Project by Drassana Architects and *Consultorio de la Costa Blanca*.

Fig. 15 — View of the natural pool at K. and N.'s house during a period of imbalance in the water ecosystem, 2017. Photo by Drassana Architects and *Consultorio de la Costa Blanca*.

Fig. 16 — View of N.'s house, 2017. Photo by Drassana Architects and *Consultorio de la Costa Blanca*.

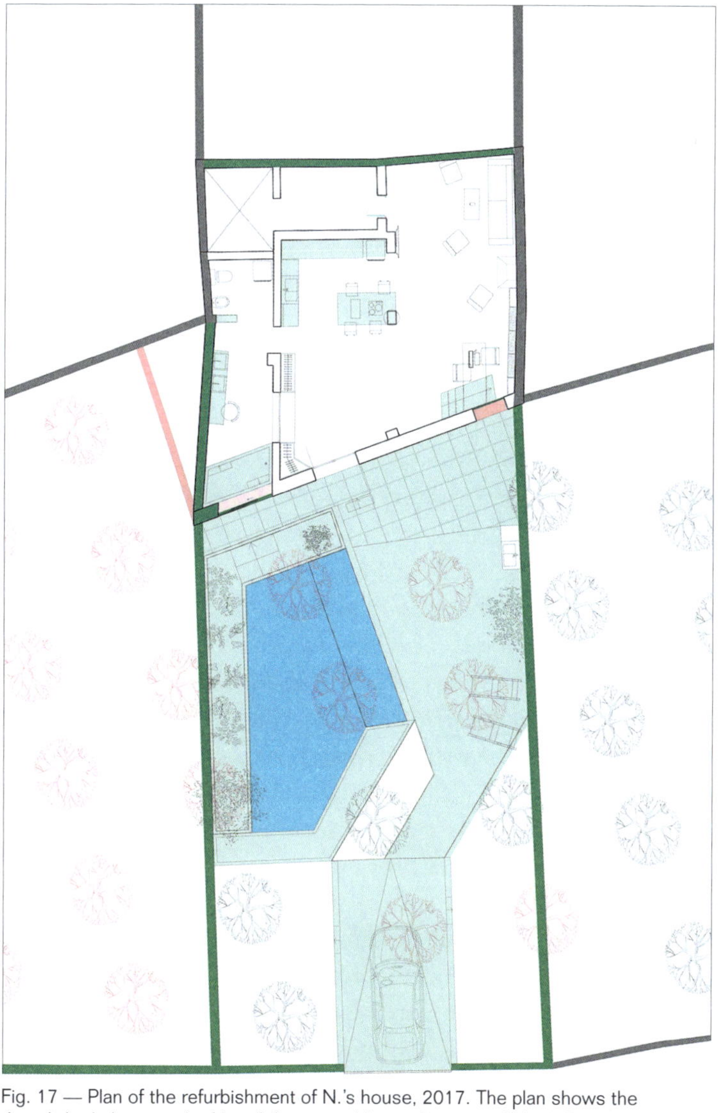

Fig. 17 — Plan of the refurbishment of N.'s house, 2017. The plan shows the demolished elements (pink) and the new additions (green and blue). Project by Drassana Architects and *Consultorio de la Costa Blanca*.

27. Tim Ingold, "Ground," in *The Life of Lines* (Abingdon: Routledge, 2015), p. 43.

28. Donna Haraway, "Anthropocene, Capitalocene, Plantationocene, Chthulucene: Making Kin," in *Environmental Humanities* 6, no. 1, (2015), pp. 159–65.

with it as a member of their family. This story demonstrates that the suburban house has the potential to reconnect people with the ground, if its platforms are understood as "standing between" earth and sky, and not merely set up on the ground.[27] For that to happen, the domestic rituals that it hosts will have to change. As Haraway might say: make suburban dwellers composters again.[28] We add: even if it is with the debris of the construction boom. [Fig 13, 14]

Attempts at Enlivening Pools

"I cannot take care of it anymore!" N. says. These words are filled with sadness, as it means adding chlorine to the pool, thereby disrupting the entire ecosystem that relied on her meticulous attention to maintain a delicate balance between plants, fish, and her care. This shift came about because her immediate family had expanded, demanding significantly more attention: first, a dog; then, a husband and two babies. Her desire for a natural pool ended with an algae outburst that transformed the pool into a conventional, chlorine one. [Fig. 15]

All the projects featured in this essay involve a transformation of the kitchen, which gains prominence on the ground floor and becomes a focal point in discussions about its integration with the garden. In the imaginations of suburban dwellers, at least in residential tourist areas, the kitchen is often tied to the pool. The scenario of an informal outdoor dinner by the pool emerged in conversations across all five accounts, clearly revealing its significance. This last case is a new pool that was constructed adjacent to the house. While cooking on the kitchen island, one can gaze directly at the running cascade that oxygenates the pool's water, and the plants that digest organic matter to maintain healthy enough water for bathing. The connection is not only optic but also haptic, with merely a sliding window-door separating the built-in bathtub in the bathroom from the pool's water. N.'s vision of an outdoor lifestyle blending with the landscape's features is shared by many single-family homeowners, although she has taken it to the extreme by bringing it so close to nature and utilizing a maintenance system without chemicals. Her surrender to chlorine speaks volumes about how hard is to keep up the "quiet country" that Haraway envisions.

Local geographers, urbanists, and ecologists have underscored that water is the Achilles' heel of the tourist development of Costa Blanca, which experiences either insufficient or excessive rainfall, as well as frequent drought episodes.[29] Yet incorporating a pool is one of the most common albeit controversial modifications in detached houses. Pools are just part of the problem, alongside plants with high water demands, large-scale features like golf courses, or extensive ground sealing. N.'s case represents an attempt to engage with water differently, highlighting that new water and landscaping practices can also be developed on a smaller scale, and asserting that suburban dwellers can influence future arrangements. However, as Haraway notes, "To care is wet, emotional, messy, and demanding of the best thinking one has ever done."[30] [Fig. 16, 17]

Conclusion: How Do We (Enjoy What We) Inherit?

In her study of residential tourism in the Costa Blanca, sociologist Raquel Huete has referred to lifestyle migrants as "house bound."[31] We find that this characterization is also applicable to locals. The family home binds individuals to past and future generations, and those who renovate a house are perpetuating a narrative that extends beyond their own lifetimes. Through the detached house, homeowners also become bound to a landscape, even when the choice of suburban living was intended to distance them from local issues. Not only because the suburban house is part of a constellation of dwellings spread throughout a territory, but because it affords residents direct contact with earth, water, and other elements that constitute the outdoors of suburban living. Studying the transformation of family houses enables us to comprehend new trends in people's relationships with the landscape. The experiences of the *Consultorio* align with findings from suburban dwellers: they share a desire to enjoy the outdoors, manifested in the retrofitting of houses to open and connect them to garden areas and the pool. This is especially apparent with the kitchen.

In this essay, the desire to enjoy the outdoors is linked with another less tangible trend: the appreciation of traditional Mediterranean landscapes that have been replaced by the houses where families are choosing to settle. This essay has considered the outdoor lifestyle as it is associated with the existing family

29. See María Hernández Hernández and Alfredo Morales Gil, "Los aprovechamientos tradicionales de las aguas de turbias en los piedemontes del Sureste de la Península Ibérica: estado actual en tierras alicantinas," *Boletín de la Asociación de Geógrafos Españoles* 63 (2013): pp, 105–24; Francisco Calvo García-Tornel, "Sureste español: Regadio, tecnologías hidráulicas y cambios territoriales," *Scripta Nova: Revista electrónica de geografía y ciencias sociales* 10 (2006).

30. Donna Haraway, "Speculative Fabulations for Technoculture's generations": p. 12.

31. Raquel Huete, *Looking for Paradise: Images of the Spanish Lifestyle* (Brighton: University of Brighton, 2005), p. 2.

32. Haraway, "Speculative Fabulations for Technoculture's generations": p. 16.

33. Pier Vittorio Aureli and Martino Tattara, "The Home at Work: Una Genealogía de la Vivienda para las Clases Trabajadoras," *El Croquis* 208 (2021): p. 21.

34. See Henri Lefebvre, *Toward an Architecture of Enjoyment* (Minneapolis: University of Minnesota Press, 2014).

house in relation to a broader heritage. For this purpose, Donna Haraway's concepts of the "quiet country" and "technological wild" have proven invaluable. Contrasting with their expressed dreams about Mediterranean landscapes, families often lack the knowledge to connect with the specific features of the landscapes that they inherit with the houses they buy. Nevertheless, the plot of land surrounding the detached house imparts a sense of attachment and continuity to families who feel they are part of something worth preserving over time. This sense of preservation is not motivated by nostalgia, but by a profound engagement with the enjoyment of the landscape.

K. and N.'s wedding invitation opened the possibility to consider Haraway's proposal to make kin in unexpected landscapes of the technological wild as a path toward transforming these landscapes into the "quiet country." According to her, this would establish a "generational obligation of and capacity for responsive attentiveness." She encapsulates her argument with a simple question: "*how* to inherit, *how* to face the living—and killing—past?"[32] To respond to Haraway's question regarding the technological wild of suburbia, we require valuable knowledge about how families are envisioning the enjoyment of their summer houses today. They are not only investing their budgets, but also rolling up their sleeves to materialize their visions.

Pier Vittorio Aureli and Martino Tattara have explained that "(a) fundamental misconception about the essence of home is that once we enter it, we leave behind the world of work."[33] The summer house epitomizes this contradiction, as its function is supposedly to provide rest from work. However, owners of detached summer houses demonstrate that enjoyment lies in an active engagement with shaping the landscape that surrounds the house.[34] Specifically, it lies in the yearning for the outdoors that opens kitchens, basements, and living rooms up to nature. Within the pleasure derived from active landscaping lies the detached family house's potential to reduce the distance that suburbia imposes between a dweller and their social and ecological local environment.

PERSPECTIVES

Overcoming the Minimum Lot Size Ordinance in Single-Family Suburbs

Gabriel Cuéllar and Athar Mufreh

Cities are composed of individual pieces of land called parcels. Just as atoms dictate the properties of matter, parcels dictate the size, shape, and placement of the built infrastructure of which cities are composed. Changes in technology and economic conditions cannot induce fundamental changes to this built infrastructure without changes to parcel boundaries. Thus, the long-run evolution of cities—and the economic growth and innovation they generate—depends upon the ease of modifying parcel boundaries.[1]
—Leah Brooks and Bryon Lutz

Imagine a city where official blundering had resulted in making it impossible to buy flour or sugar or any other staple in parcels of either less or more than a hundred pounds, or cloth or textile fabrics of any width except in pieces of ten yards' length, and one will be able to form some idea of the absurdity of the [property] system at present prevailing...[2]
—Edward Tuckerman Potter

Mom and dad's house, and suburban life in the United States in general, is an outcome of spatial values prescribed by governmental regulations and real estate specifications. This essay explores how such prescriptions, especially those related to the minimum size of lots, might be overcome to address a variety of social, ecological, and economic issues produced by the spatial order of real property in American suburbs. As much as mom and dad's house constitutes a physical dwelling, it is also representative of a spatial infrastructure consisting of predesigned increments, legal instruments, and socioeconomic norms. Before earthworks begin and the flurry of contractors arrive to erect houses, suburban territories are established through the creation of regularized lots marketable to prospective homebuyers. In this subdivision of land, no spatial prescription plays a more governing role than what is known since the early twentieth

1. Leah Brooks and Byron Lutz, "From Today's City to Tomorrow's City: An Empirical Investigation of Urban Land Assembly," *American Economic Journal* 8 (2016): pp. 3, 69.

2. Edward Tuckerman Potter, "Urban Housing—I: The Influence of the Size of City Lots," in *The American Architect and Building News*, March 16, 1878.

3. David M. Becker, "The Police Power and Minimum Lot Size Zoning Part I: A Method of Analysis," *Washington University Law Review* 263 (1969), p. 283.

4. Professionals were discussing the topic even as early suburbs were being constructed: the American Society of Planning Officials issued a report on minimum lot and building sizes in 1952, and the Urban Land Institute published a bulletin on large residential lots in 1958. More recently, legal theorist Robert Ellickson identified large-lot zoning as one of the key metrics in exclusionary zoning. See Robert Ellickson, "Zoning and the Cost of Housing: Evidence from Silicon Valley, Greater New Haven, and Greater Austin," *Cardozo Law Review* 42 (2021): pp. 1611–92. Architect and property scholar Sara Bronin has also analyzed the impact of minimum lot-sizes from the perspective of spatial inequity. See Sara Bronin, "Zoning by a Thousand Cuts," *Pepperdine Law Review* 50 (2023): pp. 719–84.

5. See Joseph Gyourko, Jonathan Hartley, and Jacob Krimmel, "The Local Residential Land Use Regulatory Environment Across US Housing Markets: Evidence from A New Wharton Index," *National Bureau of Economic Research* (December 2019).

6. See Marc Weiss's book on the emergence of the suburban real estate industry, *The Rise of the Community Builders: The American Real Estate Industry and Urban Land Planning* (Philadelphia: Beard Books, 2002).

7. Ellen Dunham-Jones and June Williamson, *Retrofitting Suburbia: Urban Design Solutions for Redesigning Suburbs* (Hoboken: Wiley, 2011).

century as the "minimum lot size": a zoning regulation that prevents the creation of any lot smaller than a given area.

Across the United States, minimum lot sizes commonly range from 0.1 to 1 acre (0.05 to 0.5 hectares) and are legally enforced in local government regulations. These comparatively coarse lot increments constitute an "immutable mold."[3] This mold, on the one hand, makes landholding the privilege of those who can afford to buy land in large quantities, and on the other, limits a territory's carrying capacity while exacerbating environmental change. Since at least the 1950s, those concerned with the social and ecological impacts of oversized lot dimensions have argued for reform. Increasingly, legal and public scholars, community groups, city councilors, and others are also organizing to demand change in how lot sizes are regulated.[4] Yet, in 2020, 94 percent of suburban communities in the United States enforce a minimum lot size.[5] Given the prevalence of lot size prescriptions and their role in suburbanization, it is important to consider how such dimensions have shaped mom and dad's house and what assumptions this practice carries. Therefore, this essay traces the recent history of minimum lot subdivisions, discusses their spatial implications, and presents a series of design scenarios proposing new suburban dynamics.

Land subdivision and the broader processes of suburbanization have been largely directed by commercial real estate developers and town planning authorities.[6] As a result, suburban communities and individual residents typically have had little agency when it comes to changing the lot fabric that undergirds their neighborhoods. Other contributions in this volume demonstrate the strategic and vital activities of suburban communities to refashion their homes, yards, and broader environments. The property infrastructure of suburbs, however, is part of an entrenched regulatory system that is systemic and less flexible. Accordingly, it is primarily commercial developers who wield the capital-heavy tools of subdivision and suburban development. Indeed, even the most important publications to conceptualize and chart out strategies of suburban transformation, such as *Retrofitting Suburbia* by Ellen Dunham-Jones and June Williamson, still rely substantially on case studies centered on the large-scale investments of commercial developers.[7] What might a resident-driven retrofitting of the suburban property system then look like? Social movements in the US demonstrate the potential that resident activists have to reimagine and recast how land could be organized beyond the concentrated investment projects of real estate developers. For example, the Minneapolis-based Neighbors for More Neighbors has played a crucial role in shaping the revised zoning ordinances for the city, allowing a wider variety of houses, uses, and lot sizes. Similar groups across the US are working to change zoning ordinances, and the minimum lot size almost always comes into play.[8] Thus, if the initial subdivision and expansion of suburbs represented the influence of commercial developers and burgeoning munici-palities, the transformation of suburbs in the near future may be driven by a smaller and more flexible form of spatial agency, one that designers can help articulate.

The Lot in US History

While the premise of land subdivision has ancient roots, the more recent precedent to US suburbs is the settler-colonial town of the nineteenth century.[9] As Native sovereignty dimin-ished through the process of "original acquisition," a national real estate market emerged in territories conquered for Euro-American settlement.[10] The federal government and private land speculators structured this new land economy through a parcelization scheme known as the "townsite plat." Prepared well in advance of settlers setting foot on the ground, townsite plats subdivided land into a field of urban lots and streets envi-sioned for a given urban center.[11] This spatial instrument is the town-scale manifestation of the better-known Jeffersonian Grid, and facilitated the territorialization of now well established American cities such as Denver, Minneapolis, Phoenix, Seattle, and virtually every other western city.

Cities inaugurated this way were characterized by two morphological features. First, every lot was identical in size and aggregated to create continuous street frontage. This pretence of equality resulted in blocks of back-to-back lots, and is perhaps a reflection of the traffic that is conducive for urban commerce and the desire to simplify right-of-way infrastructure. The typical plat thus supplied an efficient, undifferentiated product to the masses of white, male pioneers. Second, the standard parcel width set forth in townsite plats was calibrated to match prevail-ing single-span construction methods of the time, usually twenty

8. See community-based organiza-tions, such as A Better Cambridge, East Bay Yimby, and Desegregate Connecticut.

9. For the historical roots of land subdivision schemes and associated spatial politics, see Pier Vittorio Aureli, "Appropriation, Subdivision, Abstraction: A Political History of the Urban Grid," *Log* 44 (Fall 2018): pp. 139–67.

10. On the role of townsites and speculative real estate syndicates in displacing Natives on the ground, see for example chapters 8 and 10 of John W. Reps, *Town Planning in Urban America* (Columbia: University of Missouri Press, 1980). Reps was admittedly not interested in legitimizing indigenous land relations, but his frequent mention of Natives in the context of frontier town development highlights the scale of their dispossession. Legal scholar Joseph William Singer considers this period in US history to be the source of "fundamental defect," because all land titles rest upon the unjust conquest of indigenous territories. See Joseph William Singer, "Original Acquisition of Property: From Conquest & Possession to Democracy & Equal Opportunity," *Indiana Law Journal* 86, no. 3 (2011): pp. 763–778. Tribal law scholar and practitioner Lindsay G. Robertson, in *Conquest by Law: How the Discovery of America Dispossessed Indigenous Peoples of Their Lands* (Oxford: Oxford University Press, 2005), describes how settlement, townsites, and real estate speculation were instrumentalized in the contested US supreme court decision that formalized settler-colonial land grabs. Barbara Barton discusses how early settler towns and their associated civil engineering infrastructure also devastated the ecological conditions that Natives depended on, see Barbara Barton, *Manoomin: The Story of Wild Rice in Michigan* (East Lansing: Michigan State University Press, 2018).

11. John Reps's books on early American settlement and bird's eye lithographs capture the townsite era. Keller Easterling's *American Town Plans* (Princeton: Princeton Architectural Press, 1996) suggests property as the basis of urbanism in the US.

to twenty-five feet (6 to 7.5 meters). In effect, architectural form dictated parcel geometry, because a parcel was only as wide as the possible footprint of a building. When any peripheral land beyond the initial plat was to be developed, its subdivision would be attached to the original town plat as an addendum following pre-existing increments. In this process, each lot was conceived of as a site for future construction, rather than a landed estate. Adhering to these two spatial characteristics, and with zoning ordinances still unheard of, townsite plats facilitated the circulation of a regular parcel that prefigured the suburban territories of the following century. [Fig. 1]

Contemporary Suburban Subdivision

The contemporary US suburb carries forward the premise of the town plat in an expanded and more codified form. Virtually every suburban government regulates subdivision through ordinances for minimum lot sizes, which shape individual houses and the broader territory alike. Like cities based on the townsite plat, the residential zones of US suburbs generally consist of a single, repeated parcel type.

One of the defining characteristics of mom and dad's house is that it stands alone. The American and French terms for suburban houses, "detached dwelling" and *pavillonnaire*, capture the architectural implications of lot size prescriptions: every house is a pavilion set in its own garden. This is achieved through legislated spatial offsets and a maximum footprint that situates buildings at a distance from the parcel boundary and adjoining street. The ubiquitous ordinance that permits only one principal dwelling per lot works in tandem with the maximum lot coverage value—another regulated parameter— to virtually predesign the territory. Under such circumstances, the urban form is fixed in advance, such that developers only need to fill in the legally allowable building area. While this may seem self-evident, the coupling of a single, self-standing house to a given lot is part of the suburb's innovation. With buildings coordinated so rigidly with their underlying lots, any transformation to the built form must therefore be imagined in concert with a shift in legal geography.

The lot module is also significant when considering the demographic and environmental conditions that suburban single-family housing produces. Subdivision developers seldomly create lots larger than the zoning minimum, because they aim to maximize the quantity of lots they bring to the market. Accordingly, once a locality is fully subdivided—which is often the case in suburbs from mom and dad's era—its carrying capacity, or ability to sustain a given population, is all but capped because the land is already reduced to its smallest legally permissible increment.[12] Consider that within 160 acres (sixty-five hectares)—a typical area of land development—a minimum lot size of 0.25 acres (0.1 hectares) yields around 500 units, while a one-acre (0.4-hectare) minimum would hold less than 130. The lot size minima also have an impact on landscape ecology. For example, as lot size increases, so does the length of public roads and utility infrastructure needed to service them. Furthermore, the conventional suburban lawn does not provide much of a habitat, and demands extensive watering depending on the climate. As larger lots cumulatively occupy much more land than smaller ones, urbanization in these large increments exaggerates the already outsized environmental footprint of fossil-fuel dependent suburban lifestyles.

The Spatial Politics of Lot Fabrics

While minimum lot size ordinances limit architectural possibilities and consume land for a sparse form of inhabitation, they also shape the spatial politics of suburbs and broader areas. The suburban lot accordingly can be understood as an entity embedded in political relations that transcend legal boundaries.

According to early critical legal theorists of property, minimum lot sizing must be understood within a broader social context and metropolitan real estate economy.[13] This means that whatever benefits suburbs purport to enjoy from maintaining large lots come at the expense of housing costs in other locations. For example, by effectively preventing densification in broad swaths of a city, suburbs limit the quantity of new housing units that can be created. As a result, the overall existing stock is scarcer and more expensive. Furthermore, as large lots occupy much land on their own, any new suburban housing must be sited in localities even further afield.[14] As areas with minimum lot sizes cannot readily densify, US cities either extend outward or redevelop internally through lot consolidations and

12. The co-author notes that, returning to the suburb of his mom and dad's first house after twenty years, the population of the jurisdiction was virtually unchanged despite the metropolitan population having increased by around 20 percent.

13. See David S. Schoenbrod, "Large Lot Zoning," *Yale Law Journal* 78 (1969): p. 1418; American Planning Association, *Information Report 37: Minimum Requirements for Lot and Building Size* (1952).

14. See Paul Boudreaux's spatial-legal analysis of lot-size zoning, in which its metropolitan impacts are articulated in four spatial terms: uneven development, spillover, segregation, and sprawl. "Lotting Large: The Phenomenon of Minimum Lot Size Laws," *Maine Law Review* 68 (2016): pp. 1–43.

Fig. 1 — Aerial image of a US suburb with superimposed lot lines. Drawing by authors.

gentrification. Minimum lot sizing, which is often included in policies termed "exclusionary zoning," also aggravates inequity in racial and ethnic terms, as land and housing are less affordable when they are only available in large increments.[15]

Architectural theorists have drawn parallel conclusions. While approaching property from different perspectives and contexts, their conclusions are consistent: a fine-grained, diverse, and variable lot fabric produces spatial agency and architectural richness. In contrast, when a fabric is dominated by fewer, oversized landholdings, urban society is disadvantaged. George Baird's observations on contemporary Tokyo and Toronto, for example, shed light on US standards.[16] Baird, in fact, identified a correlation between parcel geometry and political agency: Tokyo's "highly differentiated pattern of ownership of land" precipitates a myriad of architectural responses to land division and city life, while the expansive commercially owned suburban centers in Toronto yield slowly changing, less vital environments.[17] In a similar observation of central Paris from the seventeenth century onward, Michel Jean Bertrand documented how the variegated property boundaries of urban blocks were the result of, at once, building techniques, social conventions, shared infrastructure, commerce, luxury, and efficiency.[18] Bertrand's drawings of Parisian blocks, overlaid with lot lines over time, reveal a dynamic property market that traded in parcels of diverse shapes and sizes occupied by various social groups. Bertrand shows how the subdivision and redivision of land provides an expandable supply of ever smaller, variously configurable lots. And Los Angeles arguably gains its urban character from the innumerable small-scale interactions that occur between neighbors of varying land uses.[19] For these architectural theorists, lot lines reflect the nature and the actors of spatial transformation, encoding political and economic values into urban space. Lot lines are therefore a useful lens for analyzing and speculating on the politics of land division.

The fine-grained, flexible urban lot fabrics mentioned above are commonly found in history, but recently established cities have been influenced by the regularity of zoning and, by extension, limitations imposed by modern legal principles. In the US, the subdivision of property has been limited by the concept of numerus clausus (Latin for "a closed number") present in the American legal tradition.[20] This concept is

15. Critiques of minimum lot-sizing have been made even by the US government. See Cecilia Rouse, Jared Bernstein, Helen Knudsen, and Jeffery Zhang, "Exclusionary Zoning: Its Effect on Racial Discrimination in the Housing Market," The White House, blog, June 17, 2021.

16. George Baird, "Thoughts on Agency, Utopia, and Property in Contemporary Architectural and Urban Theory," in *Writings on Architecture and the City* (London: Artifice Books on Architecture, 2015).

17. George Baird, "Thoughts on Agency, Utopia, and Property," p. 120.

18. See Michel Jean Bertrand, *Casa, Barrio, Ciudad: Arquitectura del hábitat urbano* (Barcelona: Editores Gustavo Gili, 1984), p. 31.

19. See Roger Sherman, *L.A. Under the Influence: The Hidden Logic of Urban Property* (Minneapolis: University of Minnesota Press, 2009).

20. See Thomas Merrill and Henry Smith, "Optimal Standardization in the Law of Property: The Numerus Clausus Principle," *The Yale Law Journal* 110, no. 1 (2000): p. 170.

recognized to prevent the creation of any property that would be deemed worthless or useless by a given society. In the US, numerus clausus precludes the creation of parcels deemed value-less due to their small area. Perhaps for many Americans, a parcel of 0.05 acres would not be socially useful or worth the invest-ment, hence the rarity of such a lot. In alignment with the tra-ditional reasoning that zoning ordinances maintain the health, welfare, and property values of a community, the minimum lot size can be understood as an expression of the numerus clausus principle. In effect, the principle prevents small land units. In territories governed by minimum lot sizes, housing and land quickly become scarce, and ever fewer residents benefit from the belonging that property promises to provide. At the social and environmental turning point of today, the numerus clausus, and the social norms around real property, may need readjustment.

If mom and dad's house in the suburbs has been shaped by prescribed values, especially spatial dimensions such as the minimum lot size, it should be noted that these have remained largely unchanged for decades. While many jurisdictions have reduced their minima ordinances over the years, those changes are typically applied to peripheral areas undeveloped at the time, rather than existing areas. Consequently, and with lot sizes sometimes even written into land title deeds, suburban neighborhoods are withdrawn from the urban metabolism and indisposed to future change. Therefore, while suburbs tend toward exclusivity and consumption, they also lack malleability, virtually fixed in time and format. Like many products of mo-dernity, mom and dad's house does not readily metabolize. For this reason, suburbs might benefit most from opening to new contingencies and relationships.

The cases described above offer several lessons that can serve as starting points in identifying the potential paths of transformation for suburbs. First, suburbs based on a singular parcel type, especially one requiring a large size and street front-age, are prone to become spatially, culturally, and economically inflexible. Second, where open space is too precious to subdi-vide, homeowners mustn't necessarily be owners of land. Third, suburbs must account for changing urban dynamics within a metropolitan scale and outlook. Lastly, the norms of numerus clausus and the very concept of ownership must be reopened for debate. How, then, to transform rigid subdivisions into spatially responsive fabrics? Or, using Brenda Case Scheer's terms, how to make a "static tissue" "elastic"?[21]

Property Ecologies

The following proposal speculates on the potential for transforming mom and dad's house—and the single-family housing model in general—vis-à-vis the adaptation of its land system. The set of design strategies described here are a way of addressing the minimum lot size ordinances of suburban territories. The term "property ecology" captures how these strategies might generate new relationships, contingencies, and variability beyond a single solution.

The proposed strategies address three central urgencies in the typical US suburb. Firstly, residents and individual landholders have little agency in shaping their city because they must contend with commercial developers and the inflexible zoning system. The first objective is thus to facilitate smaller scales of spatial agency by expanding the range of revisions that residents can make to lot fabrics. Next, affordable and diverse models of housing and living are largely inaccessible in US cities, in part for the reasons described above. Housing variety and accessibility could be advanced by making smaller, more varied units of land and dwelling available. Lastly, the suburban territorial model is ecologically unsustainable. Thus, increasing the carrying capacity of already built-up areas— rather than extending further into the frontier—could reduce the environmental impact of new housing.

The property ecologies are designed to operate within existing suburbs and draw, in part, from urban planning tools typically applied to new subdivisions. While there are various lot morphologies in American suburbs, the scenarios here focus on grid-based, single-family housing zones that make up most of the fabric within the legal limits of many American cities.[22] Miami, Dallas, Minneapolis, Phoenix, Seattle, and Denver, for example, are typically suburban in their form. These cities are governed by lot size minima and therefore near the limit of their regulated carrying capacity.

While the participation of governmental planning authorities is a prerequisite, once activated, the ecologies could continue to unfold through residents' neighborly activity.

21. See Brenda Case Scheer, "The Anatomy of Sprawl," *Places Journal* 14, no. 2 (2001): pp. 28–37.

22. Scheer, "The Anatomy of Sprawl," p. 33.

23. See Nolan Gray and Adam A. Millsap, "How Houston Achieved Lot Size Reform," *Planetizen*, July 22, 2020.

Furthermore, following the example of Houston in the universal reduction of its lot size minimum, every lot would be eligible to participate.[23] Any disinterested landholders can formally refuse participation without obstructing the broader transformation. While conditions vary from city to city, aspects such as existing building lot coverage, proximity, land value, and the kind of neighborly relationships that are present could provide helpful criteria in navigating the applicability of the ecologies in each area. Each ecology is demonstrated in connection to pertinent sociospatial conditions, representative of the US context.

Ghosting

Ghosting, or a ghost plat, applies a series of incremental subdivisions, producing an increasingly fine property grain. Usually applied to large rural estates that are expected to densify in the future, ghost plats apply a latent subdivision scheme that facilitates redivision in some future context. In the context of the US, large yards are common, yet zoning regulations largely prevent landholders from building there. Minimum lot size ordinances prevent yards from being subdivided into separate lots, but doing so would create the conditions for a more varied land market, social proximities, and smaller environmental footprints. For example, in a city where land values are increasing and where corresponding property taxes put landholders in a tough economic situation, ghosting would offer an opportunity to reduce the tax burden by selling the rear half of a lot. Ghosting would also allow small lots and small houses for families and friends eager to live close to each other, or for elderly residents seeking companions. Places such as Minneapolis or the state of Oregon, which have recently opened single-family zones to more dense dwellings, are also candidates for this strategy, which makes better use of existing urban land for new housing. [Fig. 2]

The ghost plat could be geometrically designed to not only add smaller, more affordable parcels over time, but to also guide the construction of an altered urban form. At first, the ghost plat slices each parcel into two lots. The original landholder holds both resulting parcels, but could sell one, reducing the property tax. Sometime later, the interior lot is then split again, creating new parcels along the block alley that then takes on the character of a new street. This lot is split again, creating

Fig. 2 — *Ghosting*. This strategy applies a series of incremental subdivisions, producing an increasingly fine property grain. Drawing by authors.

Fig. 3 — *Averaging*. This strategy expands the range of lot sizes by making the minimum lot size ordinance a collective stipulation. Drawing by authors.

even more affordable units of land along the inner street. Along the way, smaller parcels are purchased by private households or collectives, and in cases where multiple, adjacent divided lots are available, a commercial developer may buy and assemble them. As the smaller parcels change hands and use, the original detached dwellings are resituated among new streets, open spaces, and accessible apartment dwellings.

Averaging

Averaging expands the range of lot sizes by making the minimum lot size ordinance a collective stipulation. As a rule, the minimum lot size ordinance applies to each individual lot. This reflects the townsite conception of territory as the mere aggregation of discrete parcels. Lot averaging is now used to assist developers in navigating boundary constraints, such as protected habitats. Averaging allows for smaller lots, provided the average size of all lots combined is not below the minimum. Employed as a tool for suburban transformation, however, averaging could be used to create some flexibility in a more conservative suburb that would otherwise refuse to modify its minimum lot size. For example, some metropolitan planning commissions distribute forecasted housing needs across their respective jurisdictions, which means suburbs are legally required to contribute a certain quantity of housing units. Such suburbs could identify areas where lot size minima could be collectively calculated and gradually add affordable housing in a way that avoids large-scale projects that often face resident opposition. [Fig. 3]

Averaging might also be applicable in older subdivisions where gentrification is now occurring. In such areas, developers tend to consolidate multiple parcels and build luxury apartments. In the process, they substantially increase the average lot size of a district and usually the range of neighborhood prices as well. In response to such change, ordinary landholders could offset that increase by splitting parcels into smaller lots that would be suitable for solidarity-oriented housing organizations, such as community land trusts, which have limited operating funds. With this kind of neighborhood-led subdivision, existing residents would pay less property tax, benefit economically from the land sale, and contribute to the accessible housing stock. As developers continue to build in an area, the lot averaging mechanism provides existing residents with more flexibility in organizing the social, spatial, and financial parameters of their neighborhood.

Multiplying

Multiplying activates the seldom occupied spaces of existing houses for the provision of new dwellings. While publicly backed mortgages are available for dwellings as small as 400 square feet (37 square meters), suburban jurisdictions have historically required dwelling and building sizes three or four times that size.[24] At the same time, while the number of persons living in each home has markedly decreased, the US still grows today by one million households a year.[25] Oversized and near the end of its material lifespan and energy code conformance, the suburban house needs to realign with these new social realities. For example, for a couple whose children have now moved out of the house, multiplying is a way to maintain neighborly social life and share the burden of rising energy costs. Conversely, rather than simply becoming rentier landlords, by legally subdividing their home, such landholders could pass on their equity to their children who are likely to be priced out of homeownership. In another case, a group of friends or colleagues might pool their resources and buy a single large house through a collective mortgage that may be unobtainable on an individual basis. [Fig. 4]

Following declarations of the housing stock as a public good, the minimum dwelling size ordinance could also be reduced for landholders who agree to renovate their houses into multiple units.[26] Mom and dad's rarely used rooms could be restyled as dwellings purchased with "micromortgages," reducing the original debt. Such a program could be supported by local governments who benefit from housing appreciation and the meeting of climate goals. As with nineteenth century mansions that are converted into multiple apartment units, a deep energy retrofit of mom and dad's house could create a studio in the dining room or living room, a one-bedroom in the garage, or a shared flat on the second floor. The multiplication of dwellings within a single house can be reflected in the surrounding yard, offering a small garden to each one.

Decoupling

Decoupling creates a collectively managed landscape structured by individual houses, the footprints of which are separately

24. American Planning Association, *Information Report* 37, pp. 13–19.

25. Justin Fox, "US Household Size, at a Record Low, May Finally Be Bottoming Out," *Bloomberg News*, February 10, 2020.

26. See, for example, the City of Minneapolis's 2040 Comprehensive Plan and the Right to the City discourse: https://www.right2city.org/.

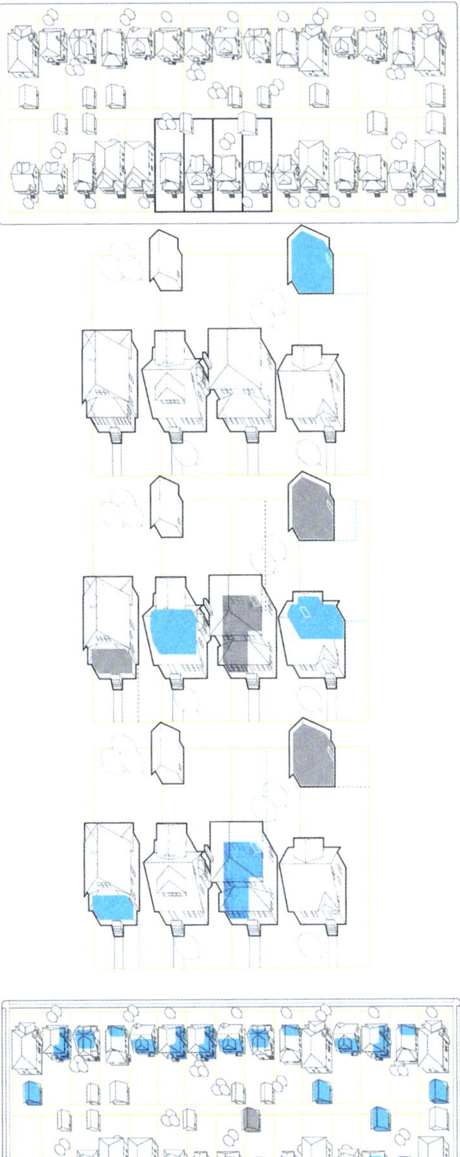

Fig. 4 — *Multiplying*. This strategy activates seldom occupied spaces within existing houses for new dwellings. Drawing by authors.

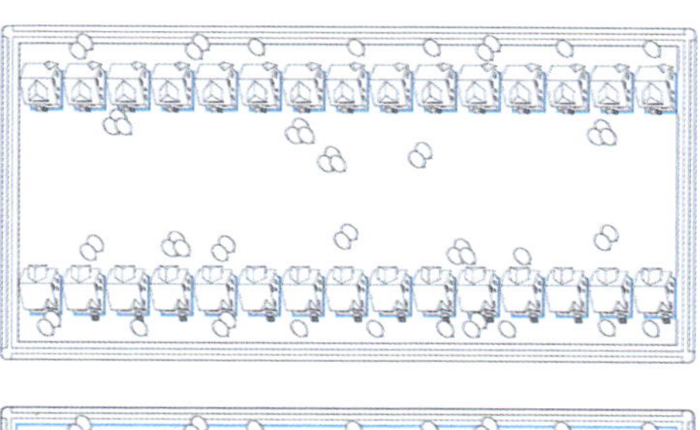

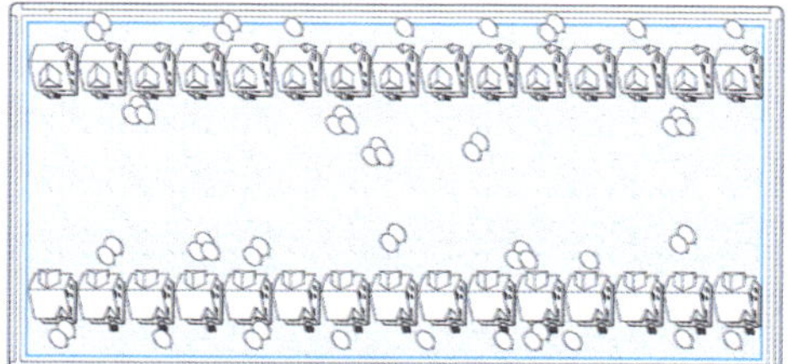

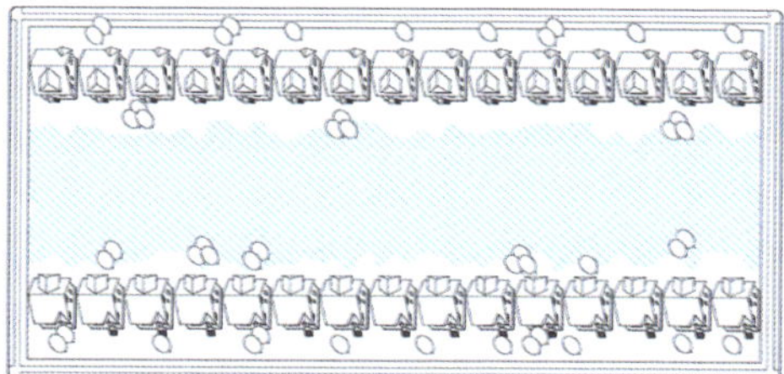

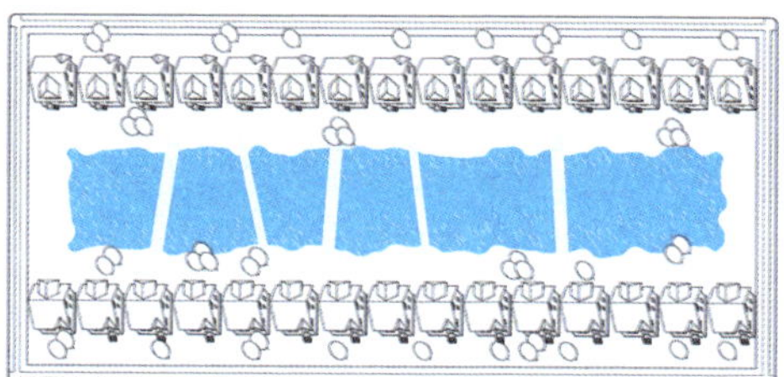

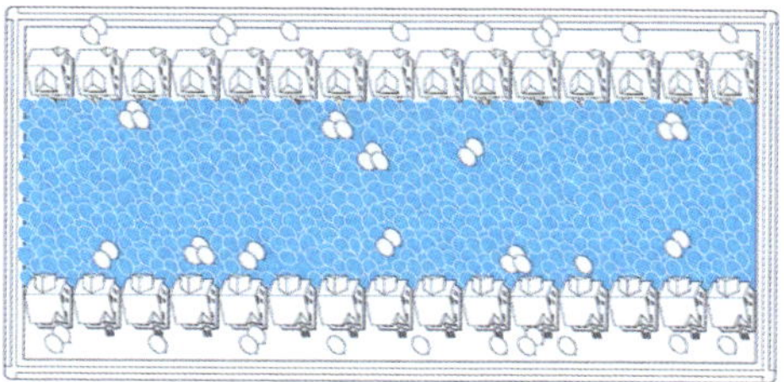

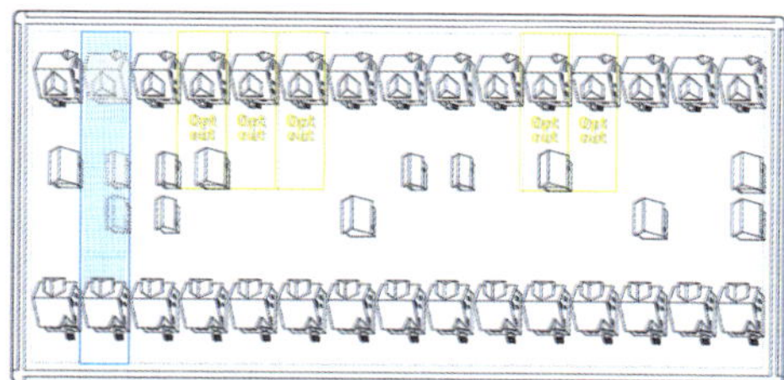

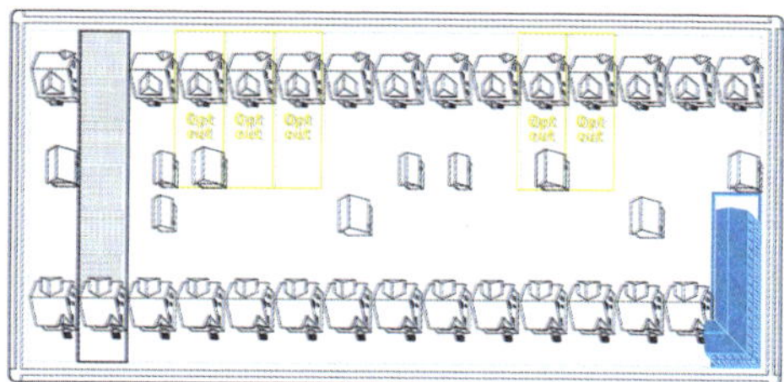

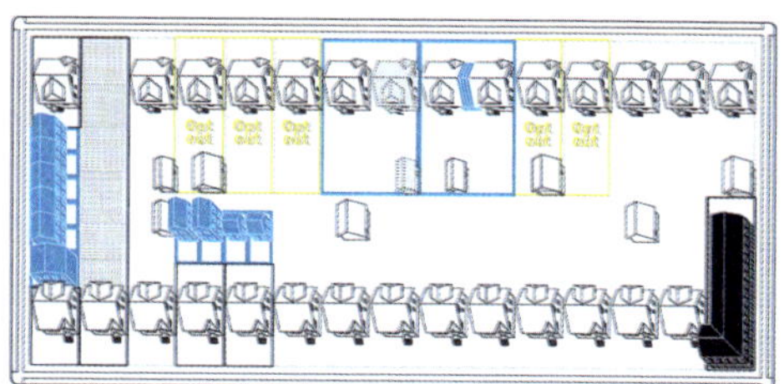

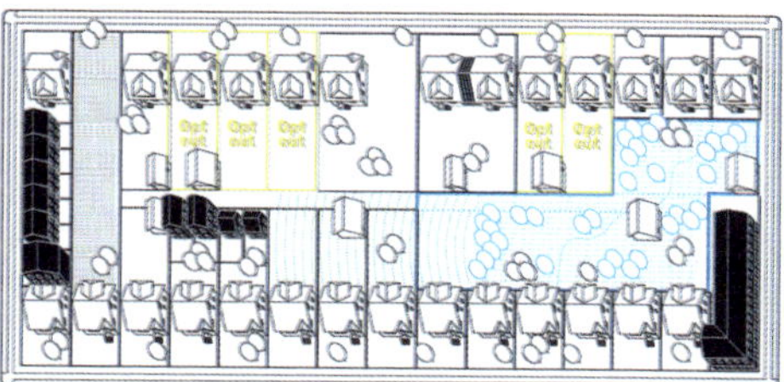

Fig. 5 — *Decoupling*. This strategy creates a collectively managed landscape structured by the footprints of individual houses, which are separately held. Drawing by authors.

Fig. 6 — *Readjusting*. This strategy asks the residents of a block to dissolve, negotiate, and redraw their property relations. Drawing by authors.

27. The distinction of the land directly below a building from the land that surrounds it is also seen in condominium developments that typically have legally binding agreements about the use and maintenance of collective yards.

held. The term "homeowner" does not capture the fact that, in suburbs, possessing a house also involves presiding over a substantial amount of open land. The coincidence of a building and its underlying lot is so commonplace that the two are almost indistinguishable. Beyond the dwelling that the house provides, the territorial and ecological role of the yard should not be underestimated. This cadastral intervention appropriates a mechanism already used in Texas, whereby the footprints of rural houses are decoupled as separate parcels, because "improved" land is taxed higher than unbuilt land.[27] Decoupling would facilitate the collaborative use of large suburban yards for specific environmental purposes. In suburbs of the American South and West, for example, flooding and wildfires are now commonplace. If pooled thoughtfully, the expansive yards of these suburbs could provide some spatial insurance against these disasters. In such cases, the individual assets of each landholder are protected through spatial coordination, which in the process could prompt broader collectivity around other environmental matters. [Fig. 5]

In this scenario, subdivision homeowners who opt for the decoupling process would hold the land directly under their house, but would contribute their yards to a continuous, collectively organized landscape. The vast acres cleared by minima ordinances could give way to a remediating and recreational landscape where single-family houses are one element of a broader territory. In the context of a "managed retreat," merged yards could be cultivated in ways that reduce environmental risk and alleviate urban heat-islands. For example, in California or in Washington state, the large middle of the collective landscape could serve as a firebreak against wildfires, and in Florida or Texas, as a rainwater retention basin that reduces the impact of flooding.

Readjusting

Readjusting asks the residents of a block to dissolve, negotiate, and redraw their property relations. Historically, lot lines in US suburbs do not change once platted. While further subdivision could be beneficial, strategies that only produce smaller land parcels largely leave the nature of real property unchanged. Therefore, the United Nation's land readjustment tool might allow new social and extra-legal arrangements beyond simple subdivision.[28] While traditionally used to homogenize and regularize vernacular property fabrics and municipal infrastructure, this tool could introduce variety and flexibility in American suburbs.[29] Going beyond the property ecologies described above, readjusting can make more substantial transformations, provided that the potential rewards are sufficient to entice landholders to participate. Readjusting, which requires the support of local government and property lawyers, would be worthwhile where a combination of economic, spatial, social, and/or environmental pressures impact most of an entire urban block, or where neighborly coordination is already high. [Fig. 6]

In this scenario, the residents of a block agree to reorganize their property lines. Some may prefer to expand their yards, others might like to have less or combine with neighbors for urban agriculture, and some leftover land might be made available for new neighbors. Variations of the block could also be harnessed: a high-traffic corner lot might be cooperatively owned and rented as commercial space; a well shaded area could be designated as a public space; or a low-lying stretch could retain stormwater. Regularly implemented, readjustments could introduce new cross-boundary relationships and possibilities of use and access that are otherwise precluded by minimum lot sizes.

Conclusion

The suburban house is rooted in a spatial order that contradicts the characteristics found by architectural and legal theorists to represent adaptability and an equitable distribution of spatial agency. Alongside its concerning contribution to environmental change, the minimum lot size tends to stiffen any territory under its rule. Where such ordinances are in effect, the narrow repertoire of urban action is reserved for commercial developers whose land subdivision and consolidation activities produce socioeconomic disparities on metropolitan scales.

Against this backdrop, this essay has outlined design scenarios that aim to metabolize suburban territories and their respective houses for present urgencies and future eventualities. In the process, it suggests that residents can participate in in situ, fine grained transformations to reconfigure lot lines and property dynamics. This approach complements, and contrasts

28. Land readjustment is part of a broader set of spatial tenure strategies called the UN Global Land Tools, which are typically applied in the Global South. See Global Land Tool Network, https://gltn.net/.

29. UN Habitat, "Global Experiences in Land Readjustment," *Urban Legal Case Studies* 7 (2018).

with, the spatial agency articulated by Dunham-Jones and
Williamson in *Retrofitting Suburbia*. Indeed, its authors remark
that, for residential areas such as those highlighted in this paper,
"any new development ... must come from redevelopment."[30]
Rather than enlisting major real estate projects to remediate
suburbs, this essay has explored the small-scale agency made
possible by a sufficiently articulated property system. Instead of
prescriptively zoning a limited range of outcomes, the design
approach proposed here reconditions the very foundation of the
suburb with new property dynamics.

While lot lines may seem distant from the traditional
objects of design disciplines, codified as they are in legal documents, spatial creativity *can* engage with property. Designing
with such legal constructs is a shortcut to imagining how
suburbs can sidestep the homogenizing logic of zoning, make
new forms of accessible urban life possible, and account for their
role in environmental change.

Slack Spaces: Informal Transformation in Melbourne's Single-Family Housing

Rory Hyde

Introduction

The suburbs do not feature in the Australian national anthem, nor in our great artworks, but this vast terrain between the city centers and the rural fringe is undeniably the dominant landscape of Australians' daily lives. Of the 89 percent of the country living in metropolitan regions, 86 percent (some nineteen million people) live in areas considered suburban or exurban.[1] Australia is the suburbs and the suburbs are Australia. The experience captured by these raw statistics varies greatly, from the grand streets of Toorak, one of Melbourne's most expensive postcodes, to the cul-de-sacs of Tregear, one of Sydney's most affordable. Some suburbs are spacious, while others are compressed; some are leafy, while others are cleared of nature; some are well-served by public transport, others entirely car dependent. What unites them is a pattern of development that is so ubiquitous as to be invisible: private blocks of land, contained by fences, each with a freestanding single-family house, with its own front door, strung together along a roadway.

The suburbanization of Australia happened rapidly and recently. In 1945, Melbourne's population was only 1.1 million, and concentrated around the inner suburbs. With the end of World War II, returning servicemen and servicewomen—and the associated baby boom—created a huge demand for housing. The city would open up, spreading into the surrounding farmland to lay out the new subdivisions of Glen Iris, Coburg, Greensborough, Moorabin, and Altona. Divided into quarter-acre (500-square-meter) suburban lots, these cleared rectangles of land would offer the promise of the suburban dream to young families, placed within reach thanks to rising car ownership and war service bank loans.[2] This process of suburban development has continued almost unabated for 80 years, with the population of Melbourne now exceeding 5 million. Almost all of

1. David Gordon, "Is Australia a Suburban Nation?," *Alexandrine Press*, June 30, 2016.

2. Rory Hyde, "Utopia Weekly: Robin Boyd and the Small Homes Service," *RMIT Design Archives Journal* 9, no. 2, (2019): pp. 8–17.

3. Robin Boyd, "The Neighbourhood," in *Living and Partly Living: Housing in Australia*, ed. Ian McKay (Melbourne: Thomas Nelson, 1972), p. 8.

4. Tim Ross, "Designing a Legacy," ABC TV, 2023

5. Stephen Lacey, "The Triumph of Ugliness," *Sydney Morning Herald*, March 22, 2008.

6. Danielle Cahil, "What does Australia's ideal house look like?," *realestate.com.au*, April 16, 2016.

this growth has been accommodated by the construction of single-family houses on the ever-expanding suburban fringe. What started as a project driven by generosity—every home their own roof, own garage, own garden—has now become a trap. Houses have become larger, while blocks have become smaller, eroding the generosity that once defined suburban living. As the city expands, long commutes, choking traffic, and a lack of public services—such as schools, hospitals, and transport—mean the new suburbs are no longer as desirable as they once were.

Architects have not held back their critiques of this mode of city-making. Robin Boyd famously railed against the stifling limitations of life in a single-family house, asking "Is it just that the Australian public clings to its depressing little boxes because it knows no better, has seen no better design?"[3] Gabriel Poole has said, "The suburbs we're putting up are just bloody inhuman, how people live in them I just don't know."[4] And according to Australia's only Pritzker Prize winner, Glenn Murcutt, "It's appalling housing, it's appalling spatially, it's not architecture, it's merchandise."[5] And yet these houses continue to be popular. Analysis of real estate website searches shows that the ideal house in Australia is a freestanding, four bedroom, two bathroom house with a two-car garage on a large block.[6] What could explain the continued popularity of this housing type, when a conveniently located apartment would arguably be more suitable? Americans will tell you it's " freedom," and in Australia we still refer to the "Great Australian Dream" of homeownership. Both are ideological and cultural concepts, grounded in grand ideas of autonomy, independence, and aspiration. But perhaps it's even simpler than that. [Fig. 1]

"Slack Space" in Suburbia

This essay argues that it is the "slack space"—garages, spare rooms, sheds, gardens—of the single-family house that explains the desirability of suburban homes. Contrary to the way these homes are marketed, and simplistic public perceptions, the single-family house can be used and misused for many functions beyond living. From starting a small business to home childcare, from restaurants to nail salons, the single-family house holds the potential for great complexity, experimentation, and entrepreneurialism. "Slack space" is defined by Jeremy Till as "space that

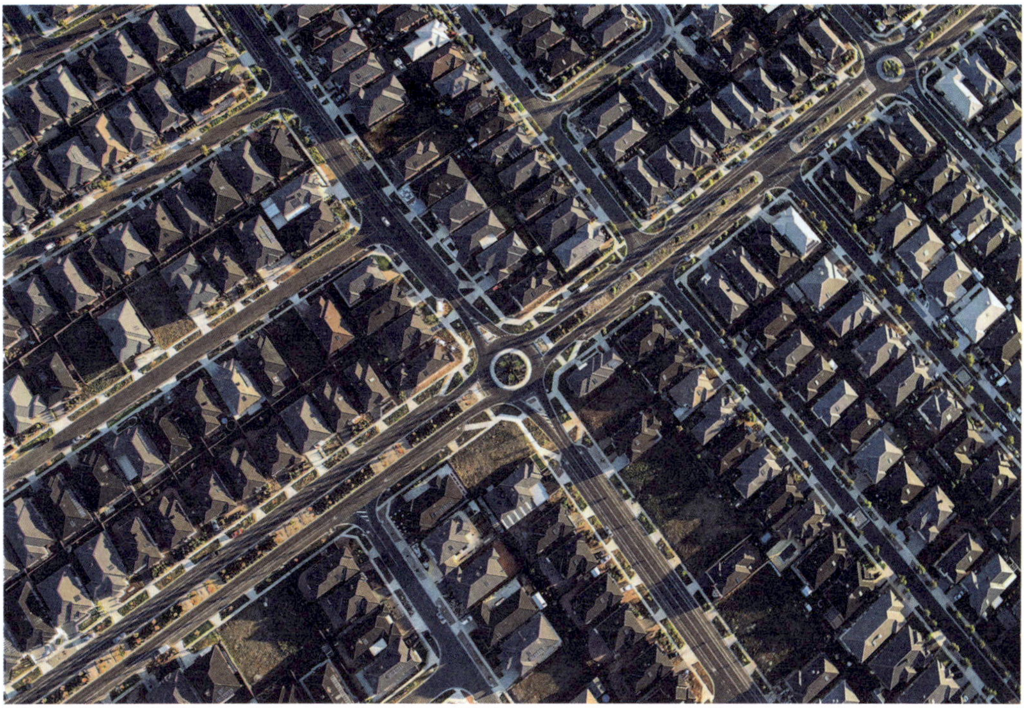

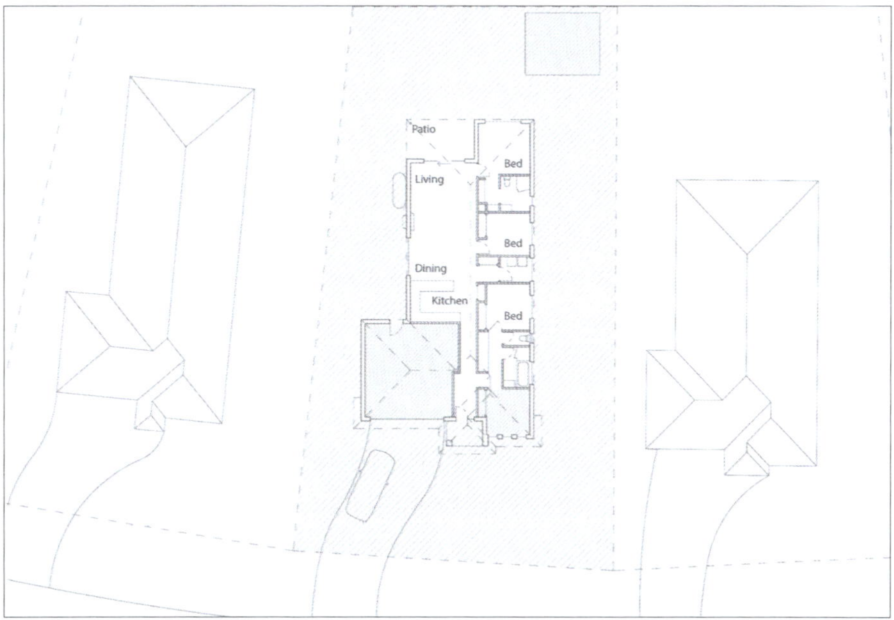

Fig. 1 — Aerial view of new single-family houses built in the growth area of Altona, outer suburban fringe of Melbourne, Australia. Photo by John Gollings.

Fig. 2 — Floor plan of a typical contemporary single-family house in Melbourne, Australia. "Slack spaces" (garage, garden, spare bedroom, shed) are shown hatched. Drawing by author.

7. Jeremy Till, *Architecture Depends* (Boston: MIT Press, 2013), p. 133.

8. Kristina Sälgvik, "Peter Barber interview: housing's architectural evangelist," *The Architects' Journal* (September 2021).

9. Cristina Diáz Moreno and Efrén García Grinda, "A Conversation with Anne Lacaton and Jean Philippe Vassal," *El Croquis* 177–178 (2015): p. 11.

10. "Are there 1 million empty homes and 13 million unused bedrooms?," AHURI (Australian Housing and Urban Research Institute), September 13, 2022.

something will happen in, but exactly what that something might be is not determinedly programmed."[7] It's one of those ideas that seems self-evident, and yet at the same time is hard to pin down. Till points to the political theorist William E. Connolly who uses the word "slack" to declare the need for ambiguity in everyday life. In architecture, though, Till cites Peter Barber who uses the term in relation to his housing design, where a shared courtyard could be occupied in an unstructured way by residents introducing their own planting and furniture.[8] Barber in turn credits Cedric Price as the originator of the general concept—think of the flexible ambiguity of the Fun Palace, for instance—although it's unclear whether he used the specific phrase.

Slack space in the private dwelling can be found in the work of Lacaton and Vassal, specifically the extended sun rooms in the Bois le Pretre Tower in Paris, for example. As the architects explain, these unprogrammed spaces are about creating possibilities. "The space should not impose a particular way of life. You don't have to conceive of everything; you just must give him or her the potential space to be used and appropriated. If you give enough qualities and a range of capacity, then you provide maximum opportunities for everybody."[9] In the suburban single-family house, this slack space is ever-present and yet rarely remarked upon. A recent report estimated there are 13 million spare rooms in Australian homes, as older residents hold on to their "empty nests" with little incentive to downsize. 76 percent of homes have more bedrooms than are required for sleeping arrangements.[10] Add to these figures the countless garages and second living spaces, and there is an enormous surplus of unprogrammed space hidden in plain sight in Australia's suburbs. These spaces are often dismissed as "excess"—garages with plastic tubs piled high, not sparking joy. And yet, slack space is arguably the core asset of suburbia. Recognizing that this space is what makes suburbia desirable is a useful starting point for how architects might begin to develop new typologies that at once recognize the issues of the suburban house, while also celebrating the benefits. [Fig. 2]

Case Studies in Suburban Slack Space

Starting a business in your own home is perhaps the lowest rung on the ladder of entrepreneurship. In Victoria, many businesses do not require any additional licenses or permits to operate out of a home.[11] Whether you own or rent, it requires very little additional overhead. And many businesses can be done in parallel with other unpaid responsibilities, like parenting or caring for dependent family. Conducting business on the kitchen table while the kids are watching TV after school is a key way that we work today. The following three case studies of home-based businesses illustrate the critical role of the home in supporting entrepreneurship and experimentation. [Fig. 3]

Helly Raichura, Chef
One of Melbourne's most in-vogue restaurants is not in the inner city, but in the outer suburb of Box Hill. Located in the kitchen of a 1950s brick-veneer house, the restaurant is named with the instructions given to diners as they arrive: "Enter Via Laundry." It's the home of Helly Raichura, a chef combining flavors from her home region of Gujarat, India with native ingredients of Australia. The restaurant was started as a side project, an experiment, with few additional overheads. It does not promote itself on the street and bookings are by reservation only. Instead of entering through the front door, diners make their way down the driveway to a secondary door at the rear of the house. From here, they make their way through the service part of the house, through the kitchen, and into a small dining room. Diners are seated together around a single table, accomodating only six people. The existing residential kitchen is Raichura's domain—a modest space, made to work hard to produce restaurant-quality food. You are very much a guest in her home, albeit one who has paid. It is an ambiguous space, neither one nor the other, rarely encountered in life. Here the suburban home, typically considered a monofunctional private domain, is reimagined as a public restaurant. The building itself remains the same, and yet the threshold between public and private is redefined, by inviting others in.

After being featured on the popular cooking show MasterChef, Raichura's website was overwhelmed with bookings that stretched to an eighteen-month wait. This success enabled Raichura to expand her business, relocating her restaurant from her home to new premises in the inner-city neighborhood of Carlton North.[12] The suburbs are where the vast majority of migrants to Australia settle, and where they find

11. "Licences and registrations," Business Victoria, accessed August 10, 2022. https://business. vic.gov.au/business-information/ start-a-business/choose-a-location-and-set-up-premises/ start-a-home-based-business.

12. Melissa Woodley, "Challenging Indian cuisine stereotypes with Gujarati chef Helly Raichura," *SBS Food*, September 29, 2021.

Fig. 3 — Evidence of the use of domestic slack space in the Melbourne suburb of Sunbury, Australia. Photo by author.

Fig. 4 — Plan of the restaurant "Enter via Laundry" in Box Hill, Melbourne, Australia (1. street, 2. driveway, 3. entry, 4. laundry, 5. kitchen, 6. dining). Drawing by author.

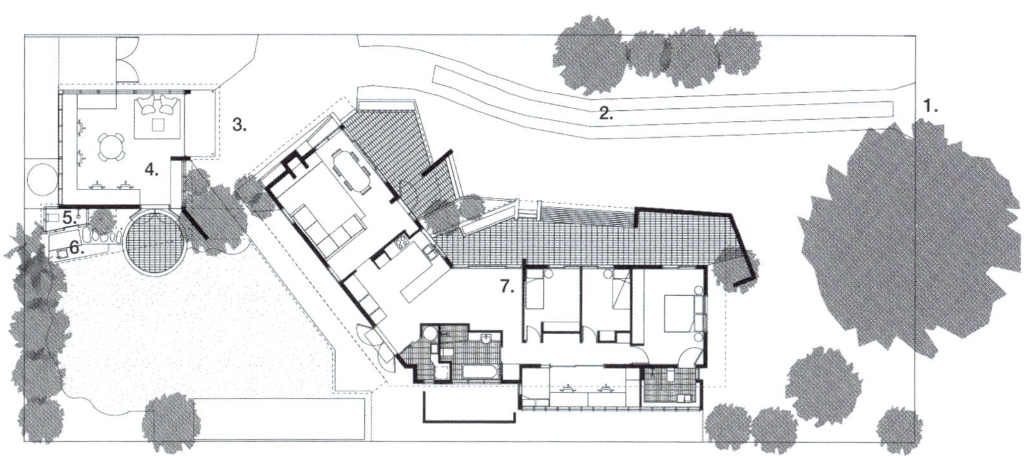

Fig. 5 — a. Channel Street Studio, designed by architect Anna O'Gorman. The studio was created out of an open car port, located at the rear of her own home, and where she founded her practice. Photo by Anna O'Gorman Architects; b. Plan (1. street, 2. driveway, 3. entry, 4. studio, 5. bathroom, 6. kitchenette, 7. main house). Drawing by Anna O'Gorman Architects.

13. Anna O'Gorman, interview by author, June 29, 2022.

a critical foothold. As this example illustrates, it is arguably the slack space of these houses that allows new ideas and opportunities to emerge. [Fig. 4]

Anna O'Gorman, Architect

The slack spaces of the suburban home have also incubated numerous architectural practices through the first years required to build up a reputation and client base. Architect Anna O'Gorman founded her practice in the garage of her suburban house in Brisbane to allow her the flexibility to look after her young children. She had been commuting an hour each way to work for a practice in the city when, as she says, "it was just crazy, it was way too hard, and I thought there must be an easier way."[13] Relocating her work to her home allowed Anna to continue her career as well as look after her family. "With little kids, it made sense to keep everything really close together. So having work and daycare and school and everything in a five to ten kilometer radius just meant I could manage it better."

Anna took over the garage that had been used by her husband to store tools and fishing equipment, making incremental changes over a number of years to make it comfortable as a workspace. She enclosed the garage, insulated it from the hot sun, sealed the concrete slab, and eventually added a kitchenette and bathroom so that her staff didn't have to use the facilities in the main house. "It was very important for me to have a separate space," she explains. The office is one space, square in plan. Custom desks are built-in to two sides, with a meeting table in the center of the space and lounge chairs scattered throughout. Entry is via a single garage door that remains open all day in the warm climate of Queensland. Highlight louvres around the perimeter provide natural daylight, as well as a shelf for small objects and art. Being so close to home allowed Anna to multitask, combining her work for her business with her work for the home. "When I was working in the studio, if I was on the phone to someone, I'd quite often put my headphones on, just walk into the house, and hang up the washing." After six years, Anna's practice outgrew the garage, and she has moved to commercial space nearby. In a two-car garage, they had managed to squeeze in five workstations and a meeting table. But as Anna explains, "if we had a meeting, we could at any one point have up to ten people in the garage, which isn't a very big space."

Relocating the practice was the plan from the outset. "I always knew as the kids got older and needed me less, and as I could grow the business, that I would have to move. It was always in the back of my mind. It did serve a really good purpose." She does miss the old space though. "We had lots of natural light, no air conditioning, a casual atmosphere, not uptight. We could go and sit in the garden, a connection to nature, the sound of birds, the neighboring kids would come home after school and play in the backyard. And so you just become familiar with those suburban noises and smells that we don't have here in the new office." The garage is now entering its third use in less than ten years. As the children become teenagers, Anna is considering transforming it into another living space. This case study shows how the slack space of the single-family house can adapt to changing businesses and family needs. [Fig. 5]

Janusz Kania, Powerlifting Coach
Janusz Kania runs a powerlifting club out of his garage in Sunshine, an outer western suburb of Melbourne. He jokes by saying it is "less of a club and more of a garage that I trick people into lifting weights in."[14] Kania was working in a hotel in Peru when Covid-19 hit, and he had to return to Melbourne. He set up the gym in his garage "to avoid going stir crazy" during lockdown, but unable to find steady work, he decided to get back into coaching and open it up for others to use. He has about fifteen clients total, with about half coming to the gym a couple times a week, and half whom he trains online. People find out about his work via word of mouth in the powerlifting community. It's proper high-level stuff. Kania coaches the junior world champion for the "120 kilograms plus" category, and a lot of nationally competitive lifters as well.

There's no sign, just a garage door onto the street. Inside, the garage is designed for a single car. "It's really, really tight," Kania tells me, "I couldn't lose a millimeter of space here." This dictates the kind of equipment he has—combo racks that can be taken apart and moved around to completely transform the space depending on what coaching he's doing. Like Enter Via Laundry, Kania has no signage on the street. "Do the neighbors mind?" I ask. "Not really, I think if there were a lot of extra cars parked in the street they might complain, but I only ever have a

14. Janusz Kania, interview by author, June 30, 2022.

15. Jennifer Baxter and Diana Warren, "Two thirds of Australians are now working from home," Australian Government, Australian Institute of Family Studies, June 2021.

16. Dolores Hayden, *Redesigning the American Dream: Gender, Housing, and Family Life*, (New York: W. W. Norton & Company, 2022); Dolores Hayden, *The Grand Domestic Revolution: A History of Feminist Designs for American Homes, Neighbourhoods, and Cities*, (Cambridge: MIT Press, 1988).

couple of people at any one time," he says. The space is organized sparely. It is dominated by two weightlifting machines—red steel structures able to be adjusted and customized. A separate heavy-duty rack holds the various plates. Along one of the side walls is a simple shelf for bags and jackets, and a row of seats for rest and recovery between lifts. There is a wall clock, a pinboard with graphs relating to training, and a magnetic whiteboard with a schedule marked out. It is quite separate from the house proper.

The reason for setting up the gym in the garage was the low overheadsand low risk. He explored setting up a bigger club in a dedicated space. However, he says "it was just impossible, the running costs of rent on a commercial property, it just didn't math out. The rent on the whole house, including the garage, is $380 a week—very affordable for Melbourne, and keeping it this size gives me a lot of freedom." The revenue generated from the training easily covers his rent, and allows him the time to focus on his next step in life. Kania is planning to study medicine, and will continue coaching out of his garage as a way to support himself through university. In Kania's hands, with his particular expertise and reputation, this tiny surplus space is transformed into an unlikely space of entrepreneurship—a story that is certainly happening in any number of homes in any given street. [Fig. 6]

These are just three of the countless creative and entre-preneurial success stories originating in Australia's suburbs. It challenges the easy stereotypes of the suburbs as stifling and conservative, revealing them to be the source of genuine invention and craft, cultural collision, and imagination. These examples also show the importance of slack space in the single-family house as a place for businesses to begin. This importance has only grown since Covid-19, which has upended job opportunities for many, particularly in the hospitality and cultural sectors. Covid-19 has led to many more of us to work from home (a rise from 42 percent to 67 percent) and relocate from the city centers to the suburbs, seeking out more space, a greater connection to nature, and to be closer to family.[15]

This restructuring of our relationship to the home and neighborhood as a consequence of the pandemic has parallels with historical experiments in living and working, as examined by feminist historian Dolores Hayden.[16] I asked her how she saw

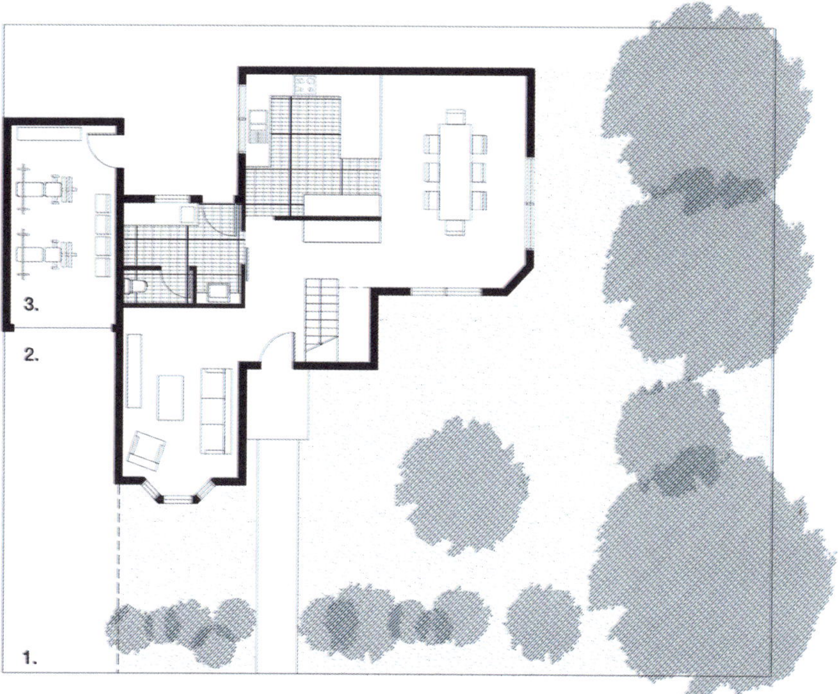

Fig. 6 — a. Janusz Kania in front of his gym in the Melbourne suburb of Sunshine. The powerlifting gym was created in the single-car garage of a suburban house. Photo by the author; b. Plan (1. street, 2. driveway, 3. garage gym). Drawing by author.

17. Linda Cheng, "Car Free Apartments Prevail," *Architecture, AU*, February 8, 2017.

these changes recasting the social and gendered relationships of the home. "Lockdown brought us to a moment when we had to say, 'we see caring labor is essential. Let's treat nurturing as valuable, necessary work, whether unpaid or paid.' And then let's think about how space could be reorganised to make it fairer," she told me. In this way, slack space is not only a prerequisite for entrepreneurialism, but could also be space required for the renegotiation of and recognition of other forms of home labour, such as caring.

The "Missing Middle" is Missing the Point

And yet, the development of typologies in Australia seems to be going in the opposite direction, by eliminating any slack space. The new focus in residential development, and a proposed "answer" to suburban sprawl, is the so-called "missing middle" housing projects—medium-density apartment buildings, between five and ten stories tall, located in the middle-suburbs, and close to public transport. The "middle" that these projects purport to address is the gap between the single-family-house and the high-rise apartment tower. Apart from some notable exceptions, Melbourne has very little medium-density housing. These new projects seek to occupy this middle ground, inspired by European examples in Vienna or Barcelona. These projects claim to be the answer to suburban sprawl by offering a generosity of space in higher density footprints than single-family houses. They also promise community through shared facilities, and are generally located close to transport connections. All of this is great, but can these projects really be a substitute for the suburbs? Without the slack space that is so critical to the value of the suburban single-family-house, they are merely apartment buildings for suburban sites. While "missing middle" housing addresses the pressing need for greater density, it overlooks what makes the suburbs attractive in the first place.

The Commons by Breathe Architects contains twenty-four apartments with a shared rooftop terrace. The units are compact, with little opportunity for nonresidential use, and the units don't have garages. This was the focus of much discussion, as the architects argued that the project should be exempt from local council parking requirements due to its proximity to a train station.[17] Instead of a parking garage, the ground floor is given over to retail tenancies, artists studios, and a substantial bike parking area. [Fig. 7]

The Terrace House by Austin Maynard Architects is, as the name suggests, explicitly seeking to provide a denser alternative to the urban terrace type, conceived as a series of terrace houses stacked up four per floor. This may be a great option for families, and certainly the residents whom I met there loved the building. But are the apartments meaningfully different from regular ones? The terrace house type in Melbourne, largely built in the 1880s and 1890s, will typically have a back lane, with space for a shed and a garden. This is the slack space that allows for different forms of living like a granny flat, or a studio in the garage. In this contemporary reinterpretation, residents have a place to store bikes and a small storage cage, but nowhere to start a business. There are retail tenancies on the ground floor, but these are subject to commercial leasing. [Fig. 8]

The project Freespace by emerging practice Lian was a winning entry in the Victorian State Government's Future Homes competition, and will begin construction in 2024. The project aims to be a model for replacing single-family houses with a medium-density apartment building in a suburban setting. To achieve this, the project required large setbacks to avoid overshadowing neighboring homes. These setbacks are used for shared spaces including parking, garden beds, bike parking, and water tanks. But, again, there's little to no slack space; nowhere to start a business, and nowhere to expand if your family situation changes. [Fig. 9]

It's tricky to criticize these projects, because in many ways they're the best things coming out of Melbourne at the moment. Medium-density, sustainable, good design, and connections to public transport are all beneficial elements of "missing middle" housing. They are also often more affordable than comparable apartments, and vastly more affordable than single-family houses in these middle-ring suburbs. They are largely architect-led, and put pressure on commercial developers to diversity their products. This is certainly the kind of housing that this city needs more of. But, without slack space, can these models be sufficiently adaptable for the residents' changing needs? Do they miss the opportunity to encourage entrepreneurship? If they are to meaningfully substitute the single-family house, it would be by including space for "nothing."

Fig. 7 — View of the multi-unit resident building
The Commons by Breathe Architects in Brunswick
Australia, 2014. Photo by Tom Ross.

Fig. 8 — View of Terrace House by Austin Maynard Architects in Brunswick
Australia, 2021. Photo by Derek Swalwell.

Fig. 9 — View of the affordable housing block Freespace by Lian Architects
in suburban Melbourne, project ongoing. Render by Lian Architects.

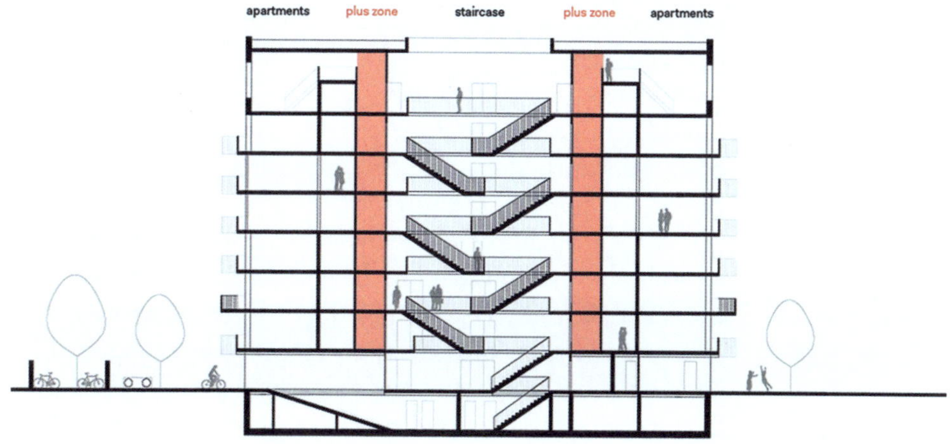

Fig. 10 — Section diagram of residential building Neu Leopoldau by Feld 72, Vienna, Austria, 2019.

Fig. 11 — "Reconfiguring Suburbia" master thesis project by Jamal Tompkinson, University of Melbourne, 2021.

Precedents for a "Slack Suburbia"

There are various precedents for housing that embrace this polyvalence of use and activity. Hayden's *Redesigning the American Dream* is a catalog of such alternative approaches. One example is Tynggarden, a 1970s Danish cohousing project by architects Vankunsten, where "each family gave up 10 percent of its allocated interior square footage to create a shared neighborhood center for ten to fifteen families," including space for childcare, classes, and political meetings.[18]

Despite being of considerably higher density than the typical suburban subdivision, the project Neu Leopoldau by the Austrian studio Feld 72 introduces the useful concept of a "plus zone," which "provides space for yet to be defined self-realisation and connects the private with the (semi-)public areas." In concrete terms, the "plus zone" is a room at the threshold to each apartment, between the stairwell and the private dwellings. These rooms extend up throughout the building, on every level, with suggested uses including a start-up room, exhibition space, and tattoo studio. As the architects write, the inclusion of this space aims to "inspire the imagination of the residents." Presumably the availability of a space like this invites its own uses, allowing the residents space for creative experimentation, or a side project.[19] It is easy to imagine such a space being introduced to lower-density housing typologies. [Fig. 10]

Finally, the project Reconfiguring Suburbia by Jamal Tompkinson, a Masters student whom I supervised in 2021, explores how these ideas might be applied in a post-Covid suburban Melbourne. Six existing single-family houses are adapted to accommodate a variety of uses and family types, from elderly coliving and shared childcare to a coworking cluster. By taking the fences down, these adaptations come together to form a new semipublic realm in the space once occupied by private backyards; a new community of diverse occupants and uses. [Fig. 11]

Conclusion: The Suburbs on Its Own Terms

This essay argues something very simple: one must approach designing for the suburbs on its own terms. To recognize what is desirable about the suburban house, and to take this seriously, rather than assuming that those who choose to live there are

18. Dolores Hayden, *Redesigning the American Dream*, p. 177.

19. "Neu Leopoldau," Feld72, accessed August 14, 2024, https://www.feld72.at/en/neu-leopoldau/

ill-informed and wrong. By criticizing the single-family house
in this way, and in proposing to wipe it away to be replaced by a
denser model, we architects and urbanists have misunderstood
the lessons that are in front of us. What makes the single-family house valuable to those who live in it is the slack space
that enables experimentation. This is the space that has been
designed out in the translation to higher density alternatives,
stripping away the potential of the suburban home to act as an
engine of entrepreneurship and opportunity.

A new alternative to low-density car-dependent suburbia
is surely needed, for reasons of sustainability, sociability, and
much else. But instead of simply stacking up the living and
sleeping areas into a denser configuration, we ought to—par-
adoxically—start with the suburban space that appears to be
least valuable: the slack space of the spare room or garage. In
starting here, and placing it at the center of this new model, we
recognize the critical role this space plays in generating vitality,
diversity, and local economies. And hopefully by recognizing
this, we architects can begin to fully recognize the people who
live there too.

Upgrading Architectural Components in Single-Family Houses to Meet New Needs and Aspirations: Envisioning Conversions in Northern Italy

Fabio Lepratto

Feeling at Home

Every home comes into being, first and foremost, through an act of election: a series of gestures through which we select a disparate and relatively incompatible set of objects, people, and walls and change it into a privileged place in our world.
—Emanuele Coccia[1]

Numerous reasons may encourage an individual, a couple, or a family to move into a single-family house (whether bought or inherited) in the suburbs, leaving behind the urban center where they may have been born or where they moved to for study or work.[2] But perhaps above all, these include the constant growth in housing prices compared to the average wage. In many global contexts, living in or close to the city center—the source of one's income—often involves paying rent that is disproportionate to that very income. Buying a house, conversely, requires an investment that is likely to turn into a life-long burden. Taking the Northern Italian context, as an example, and more precisely, the urban region of Milan, the average cost per square meter of an apartment in a semi-central area is four times that of a single-family house in the suburbs.[3] For those who might also need additional work space, the option of relocating one's domestic and work lives to a single building, even if located a few kilometers from the urban center, can be highly advantageous. This is even more so in the wake of the pandemic, which has multiplied remote working opportunities and reduced the need for daily commuting.

However, the existing stock of single-family houses—a legacy of widespread urbanization process in the twentieth

1. Emanuele Coccia, *Filosofia della casa* (Torino: Einaudi, 2021), p. 17. Translation by author.

2. CECODHAS European Social Housing Observatory, "Housing affordability in the European Union. Current situation and recent trends," *CECODHAS Housing Europe's Observatory RESEARCH BRIEFING* 5, no. 1 (January 2012).

3. Direzione Regionale Lombardia, "Statistice Regionali. Il mercato immobiliare residenziale. Lombardia," *Osservatorio del Mercato Immobiliare*, June 2023.

4. Frances Holliss, *Beyond Live/Work* (London: Routledge, 2015).

5. John S. Allen, *Home: How Habitat Made Us Human* (New York: Basic Books, 2015).

6. Francis Rambert et al., *Un bâtiment, combien de vies? La transformation comme acte de création* (Cinisello Balsamo: Silvana Editoriale, 2015).

7. Fabio Lepratto, "Housing Bricolage. Tools for Manipulating Post-War Collective Housing," in *From dwelling to dwelling: radical housing transformation,* ed. Dick van Gameren et al. (Rotterdam: nai010 uitgevers, 2018), pp. 14–31.

8. Vittorio Gregotti, "Modificazione," *Casabella* 498–9 (1984): pp. 2–7.

9. The reflection underlying this chapter developed during research aiming to investigate the potential of single-family houses in Italy held at Politecnico di Milano with the scientific coordination of Federico Zanfi and Martino Tattara, to whom I am indebted for the background knowledge. The potential of architectural makeover was also explored when supervising the Master's Thesis *"Oltre il domestico. La trasformazione della casa unifamiliare nella città diffusa,"* written by Agata Bandini and Federica Fazio (Politecnico di Milano, 2023).

century's—is often outdated and far removed from contemporary needs and aspirations. Addressing this requires rethinking the functional, spatial, technological, and aesthetic aspects of their design. It is also important to take into consideration sociodemographic changes that affect both domestic and work spheres, such as an aging population, falling birth rate, migration, new ways of cohabitating, modern working lives, post-pandemic habits, etc.[4] In taking over a second-hand single-family house, it is essential to establish a sense of belonging. To "feel at home" is more than just a manner of saying it; it expresses the existential need to have a place of one's own.[5] Turning someone else's house into one's own home requires both superficial and deep changes that go beyond tailoring the space to one's momentary needs. In this context, architectural design has the potential not just to meet practical needs, but also fulfill desires, resolve concerns, and achieve happiness. With a small budget, which often prompts the decision to leave the city, it is not possible to build a new house from scratch. But it may be possible to afford minor alterations to take possession of what already exists. These creative actions can lead to reading, interpreting, and giving a different role and meaning to the same old house. They are low-intensity, but radical modifications.

In recent decades, the discipline of architecture—at least in Western contexts—has shifted its attention to issues of reuse, rehabilitation, renovation, and regeneration. It has applied a creative attitude towards existing buildings, with the aim of adapting them to the demands of present-day and future society.[6] When it comes to housing, research has largely prioritized the renovation of large housing estates.[7] Much still needs to be investigated in rethinking single-family housing models, which cover large swaths of peri-urban districts. How does the approach to modification—which has thus far been applied to a collective, dense, homogeneous housing stock—adapt to this individual, diffuse, wide-ranging built environment?[8] What is the architect's role in responding to the demands of a changing society, within the context of a housing affordability crisis, as well as a transforming relationship between work and home? The essay that follows outlines a partial response, highlighting the possibility of interpreting renovations to single-family houses not through a building-based approached, but through an element-based one.[9]

Building-Based Transformations vs. Element-Based Upgrades

Architecture is a strange mixture of persistence and flux, a collage of some elements that have been unchanged for over 5,000 years and others that were (re)-invented yesterday.
—Rem Koolhaas[10]

Single-family houses in Northern Italy all look different from each other. Their size, volume, color, composition of windows and balconies, finishing materials, and decor all enhance the particularity of each house. Extremely customized outcomes are influenced by a fragmented construction sector. This distinguishes the Italian case from contexts such as North America or Australia, where construction processes are largely managed by real-estate developers and result in formal repetition. Despite this difference, there is only a narrow range of typologies, spatial characteristics, and building components used in single-family housing in Northern Italy. In the Brianza area, for instance, located between Milano and Como, the housing stock can be categorized into two main types: small single-story houses built with a limited budget on a small plot in the 1950s; and more spacious structures built on larger plots in the 1970s and 1980s, reflecting the wealthier society of the time.[11] In both, however, fundamental elements are repeated, such as fencing that separates the house from the street, a raised ground floor above the natural level, distance maintained from front and side boundaries, and pitched rooves. Standard components, such as doors, windows, shutters, gates, and metal fencing, also repeat, which contribute to determining the houses' architectural identity.

When considering renovating, there are two approaches that can be taken. One is holistic, and looks at the building in its singular entirety. We might define this approach as "building-based." The other is fragmentary, and separates the building into distinct recurrent parts. We could refer to this approach as "element-based." The former is based on inventing a unique solution for a specific building, while the latter simply impacts and alters the original condition. Building-based renovations might change the house into something radically different, by relocating partition walls or staircases, updating plumbing or electrical plans, increasing or reducing volumes, or designing a

10. Rem Koolhaas, *Elements of Architecture* (Köln: Taschen 2018), p. 193.

11. For an in-depth exploration of the single-family house in Italy, see: Stefano Boeri, Arturo Lanzani, Edoardo Marini, *Il territorio che cambia: ambienti, paesaggi e immagini della regione milanese* (Milano: Segesta 1993); Chiara Merlini and Federico Zanfi, "The family house and its territories in contemporary Italy: present conditions and future perspective," *Journal of Urbanism* 7, no. 3 (2014): pp. 221–44; Federico Zanfi, Chiara Merlini, Viviana Giavarini. et al. "A portrait of Italian 'Family houses': diversified heritage in a redefined territorial and demographic context," *City Territory Architecture* 7, no. 20 (2020).

12. Rem Koolhaas, *Elements of Architecture*, p. 45.

new façade. All of these alterations are expensive, and might fall outside of a new tenant's limited budget. These costs might also discourage intervention, considering the ratio between refurbishment costs and an increase in property value. Conversely, an element-based approach might limit changes to a series of less costly operations that can be implemented incrementally over time, and even in part by the occupants themselves.

An element-based approach recalls the 14th International Architecture Exhibition at the 2014 Venice Architecture Biennale, "Fundamentals," curated by Rem Koolhaas. The exhibition titled "Elements of Architecture" identified a set of fifteen essential elements of architecture: floor, wall, ceiling, roof, door, window, façade, balcony, corridor, fireplace, toilet, stair, escalator, elevator, and ramp.[12] An element-based approach to renovating single-family houses does not need to address all fifteen of Koolhaas's elements to significantly affect its quality. For the purposes of this investigation here, we will look at: front fences, side setback strips, raised ground levels, windows, and pitched roofs. Using ready-made, standard components, with some degree of customization, can impact spatial and symbolic qualities, overwriting new meanings, and triggering a sense of belonging.

The architect's role in these changes needs to be redefined. Architects could participate in the renovation process, supporting the owners. They could also be called upon to perform a purely technical service, given the need for authorizations required to implement certain changes like altering a building's external appearance, or simply the size and design of a window, which requires checks on ventilation and lighting ratios. In some renovations, one might not even need an architect. Architects might also consider designing and prototyping standard building components, in an activity more akin to furniture design.

The essay explores the potential for changing five elements of the typical single-family house—the front fence, windows and doors, ground elevation, pitched roof, and side setback—to prove the point that altering ordinary architectural components can produce surprising effects on the quality of a space. At a certain point, however, there is a complementarity between building-based and element-based approaches. This often emerges when people inherit or buy a second-hand house, like with bathroom renovations, a new layout for the kitchen (which is often opened into the dining room), or a technical upgrade to the wiring, heating, and air conditioning systems. This work requires a sequence of interventions whose impact, however significant, will not interfere with the original structure and is therefore compatible with an element-based approach.

The Potential for Change in Five Fundamental Elements

A Dynamic Front Fence

Let's imagine that new residents of a house want to open businesses that cater to the public from their ground floor. The existence of a fence around the house's perimeter might suggest an impervious boundary and deter potential customers. A hairdresser, a personal trainer, an architect, a psychologist, a private kindergarten, a baker, or a home restaurateur would probably benefit from access that is more permeable and evocative. They could do so by creating a forecourt that opens onto the street; a place where customers can look out, sit, or chain their bicycle. At the same time, the newcomers would probably need to ensure privacy and security for themselves, especially at night. Hence, they might not feel like giving up the physical boundary between the street and their private property. This means that a compromise is needed: something that opens to the public while offering protection from intruders and onlookers at different times of the day. This would allow homeowners to enjoy their garden as a safe place for children and pets without worrying about prying eyes.

We are used to thinking about fences as static boundaries designed with a range of materials and styles, such as customized wrought iron with decorative elements or minimalist design. But they are simply made of standard welded or assembled parts: a modular precast concrete palisade; a system of ready-assembled metal bars, rods, or hexagonal netting secured to a row of mounting posts; or a combination of these materials. They are often aligned with an evergreen hedge, defining a static, impervious, and outward-facing boundary.

A less static fence design could enhance the relationship between the single-family house and its surroundings, and help introduce different uses within the urban context and streetscape. An impermeable boundary would thus become a dynamic,

permeable membrane. As a modular structure, a fixed set of
elements anchored to the ground might gradually accommodate
prefabricated fixed, sliding, folding, transparent, or opaque
components. This could also include expanded metal panels,
fixed or swinging on hinged frames, wrought-iron sliding gates,
wire mesh with plants, and linear curtains designed to increase
privacy. This would allow for a continuous and changeable
configuration according to daily needs: open (physical and
visual permeability), intermediate (visual permeability only),
and closed. The fence would therefore be a three-dimensional
structure with its own symbolic quality that provides a new
public image for the entire building. [Fig. 1]

A Fitted-Out Side Setback Strip
Reclaiming abandoned spaces and giving them new meaning is
an integral part of the process through which one builds one's
own habitat within an initially alien context. The recovery and
fitting out of currently underused or underestimated interstices
can particularly increase the habitability of small buildings. The
needs of residents for extra room, for work or hobbies, can be
fulfilled through the use of discarded, secondary portions of the
lot, such as side setback strips.

The placement of a single-family house within a private
lot is commonly subject to urban planning regulations to
ensure compliance with certain minimum quality conditions.
In particular, the definition of a side setback strip (a minimum
legal distance between buildings) regulates the delicate relationship between private properties and buildings. Their aim is
to prevent the shading of nearby properties, to allow adequate
light into the interior, and to guarantee a minimum of privacy.
The outcome of these regulations is to leave linear strips about
three to five meters wide between boundary walls and building fronts. The spatial characteristics of these strips—long
and narrow—often leave them underused. This is the case for
both larger plots, which can benefit from a more pleasant and
enjoyable front yard and backyard, and for smaller plots, which
have no additional open spaces and should make good use of
these strips.

The transition from a wasted space to a quality space
requires imagining different uses and designs, and thus grasping
its intrinsic possibilities. This can be achieved through modular

prefabricated microstructures, leaning against the line of the side wall to define the plot boundary. Applying the principle of modular furniture—a plug-in support to which modular elements can be attached and which change over time—the side wall and the side strip can be fitted out to serve different purposes. For instance, the side wall and side strip can be used to arrange plant pots for ornamental greenery, to grow an herb garden, or to cultivate a vertical vegetable garden. All different kinds of accessories can also be installed, including space for pets, outdoor workstations, work-tops, storage for DIY equipment, or gym equipment like benches or bars. The modular structure may even include a mobile roof system, like a roll-up shade that protects the small outdoor strip from rain or sun and transforms it into a winter garden that is connected to the indoors. [Fig. 2]

The deck as a space connecting the interior and exterior
As the demand for outdoor living continues to grow, the relationship between a house and its garden is crucial. For various typological and construction reasons, a relationship that might seem obvious is often poorly considered. Indeed, in Northern Italy, the ground levels of single-family houses are often raised by a few steps. This choice can help minimize the costs of ground excavation to achieve a flat surface. Moreover, incorporating a raised level enables the creation of an aerated crawl space beneath the floor, which offers notable advantages in terms of thermal insulation as well as the prevention of moisture seepage. Nevertheless, this elevation hinders the connection between the house's interior and exterior, effectively preventing a seamless indoor-outdoor experience.

In response to this specific condition, the installation of decks adjacent to the built volume and positioned at floor level extends the house's surface into the garden, shifting the threshold. This can be further achieved through the addition of French windows that connect the deck with the indoors. The envisioned concept involves the installation of a frame raised on adjustable, vertical legs to match the height of a house's raised ground floor, fitted with metal and wooden modules that can be placed side by side. The platform would then be completed with a metal structure, raised to the height of the floor, and fitted with fixed and sliding curtains, lighting, plants, and other

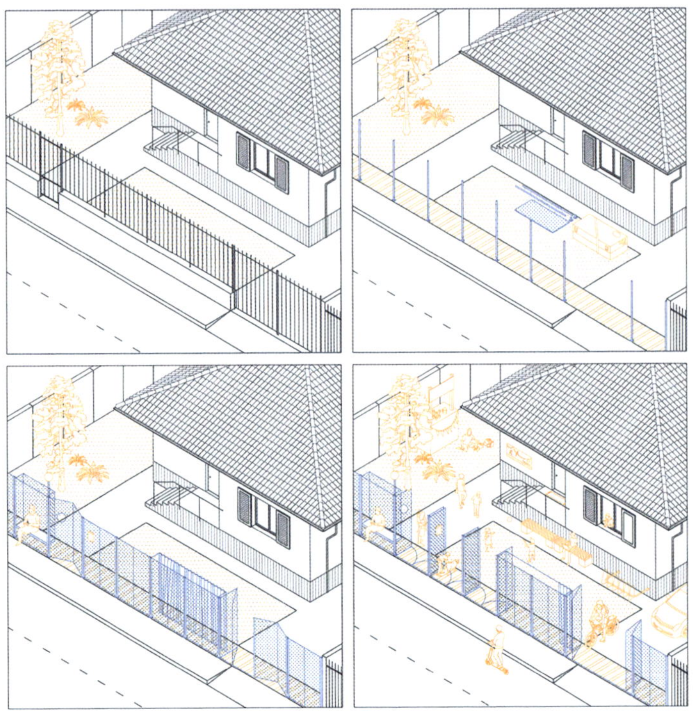

Fig. 1 — Transforming the relationship between the house and the street through a dynamic front fence (starting, intermediate, and final stages). Drawing by author.

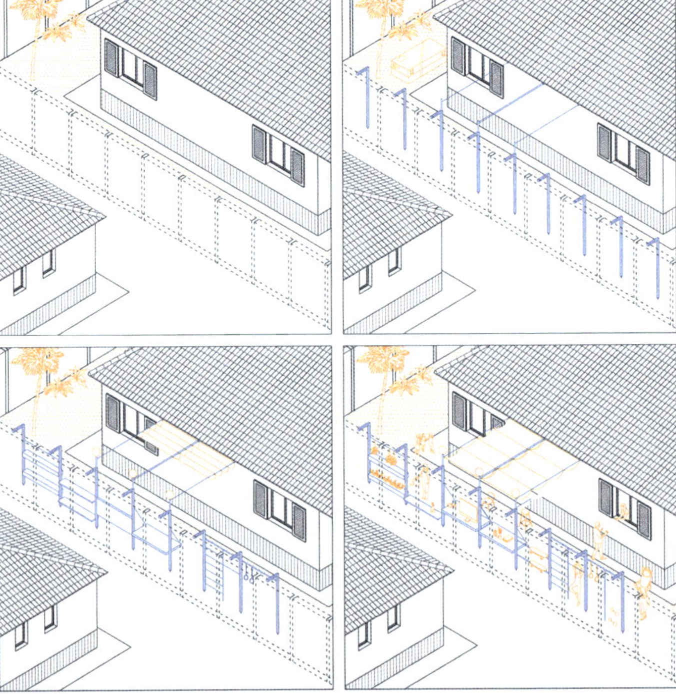

Fig. 2 — Transforming often neglected open spaces around a single-family house into a functional, fitted-out side setback strip (starting, intermediate, and final stages). Drawing by author.

Fig. 3 — Developing a new deck on the back of a single-family house, connecting interior and exterior spaces (starting, intermediate, and final stages). Drawing by author.

Fig. 4 — Enlarging existing openings of a single-family house to create larger "inhabitable windows" (starting, intermediate, and final stages). Drawing by author.

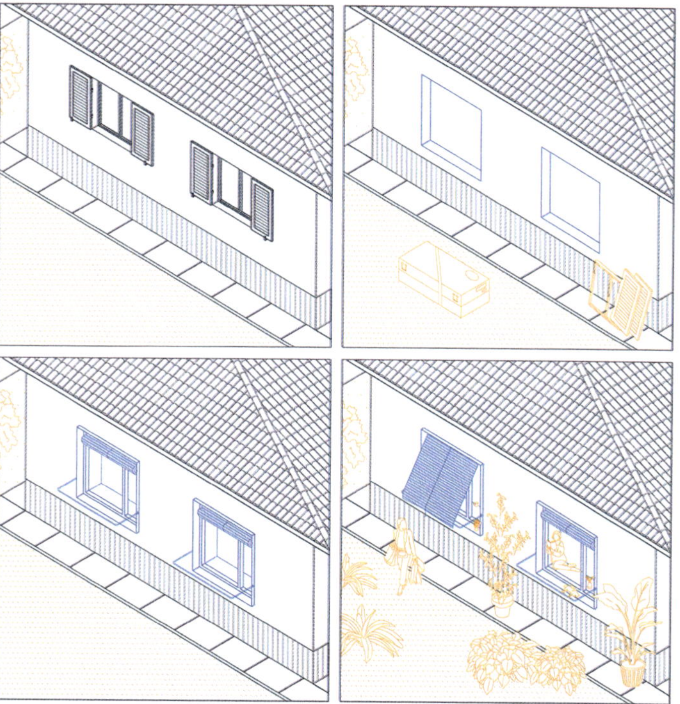

elements to create a comfortable outdoor living space. A staircase would then connect the platform to the garden.

This structure, spanning the entire front, would significantly upgrade the building's overall identity and character, while simultaneously enriching the living space. The platform could be entirely self-constructed. Indeed, the installation does not involve any particular risk, nor does it require a special building permit as it is a removable element. Furthermore, in addition to connecting the building and the yard, this type of intervention could be integrated with others that aim to renaturalize the open spaces, like removing paving from the ground or introducing new greenery. This would not only enhance the domestic microclimate but also foster biodiversity, making a small contribution to the challenges posed by climate change. [Fig. 3]

A Larger, Inhabitable Window

Something as simple as modifying a door or enlarging a window can transform a house's space and image. Over the centuries, windows have been an essential component of any building. They provide lighting and ventilation, and establish visual connections with the outdoors. During the industrial revolution, windows were increasingly conceived of as a standard, technological, independent component. In parallel, the advent of modern architecture elevated windows to a primary element of design. Experimentation with new solutions (frame design, materials, finishes, opening mechanisms, width, and thickness) led to striking results, enhancing the quality of indoor spaces (as in the case of Gio Ponti's "furnished window"). However, this has never gone beyond a limited number of works and has not been incorporated into general construction practices, nor does it influence ordinary products available on the market. Today, if we look at windows that are available in catalogs, they all look the same, whether they are made of wood, aluminum, or PVC. They are selected primarily for their ability to meet energy efficiency requirements, not their spatial impact. Similarly, in most single-family houses, windows are small, impersonal fixtures placed in thin walls, about a meter from the floor and complemented by external swings or roller shutters.

Changing a window is a localized micro-action that can make a domestic environment more welcoming while also enhancing its environmental comfort. Making it bigger requires altering the surrounding masonry, which means hiring specialist artisans and applying for relevant building permits. The proposed modifications include lowering the windowsill to a suitable height for sitting (approximately fifty centimeters) and increasing the side jamb or internal sill. These adjustments aim to create a small niche suitable for sitting or displaying objects or plants. The increased thickness can also extend outward, transforming existing openings into small bay windows that project along the building façade. These window units can improve the regulation of natural light and heat gain by incorporating filtering and shading systems, like curtains and shutters that allow air to enter while blocking the sun. The modification of one or more windows in the perimeter wall can enrich the interior space and enhance the connection with the surrounding landscape. This, in turn, makes a positive impact on the building's appearance, as it changes the architectural composition of the entire façade. [Fig. 4]

An Altana *Over the Pitched Roof*

Many single-family houses in Milan's suburbs that were built during the early 1950s stand on a minimum-sized plot and lack any outdoor space. Considering these conditions, it is worth examining roofs to see if extra open-air space can be created, despite the challenges posed by their pitch. The pitched roof is an architectural trope in Northern Italy. Their sloping surface allows rain to easily slide off, while the cavity underneath offers attic space that can be used for storage. However, the attic is often converted to enlarge the house's livable area through the installation of dormer windows or skylights. The outer surface, which is here generally covered with a layer of clay tiles, is increasingly used to capture solar energy through photovoltaic panels.

The addition of an *altana*—an Italian term describing a terrace built by raising a platform on the roof over the building—could be a relevant option for offsetting the lack of private gardens with a large enough space to hold deck chairs, a table, a sunshade, and flowerpots. Unlike a cut-away roof terrace, the *altana* does not require drastic or expensive work to be installed, apart from establishing some load-bearing points. Indeed, it is designed as an entirely external element, attached to the main

Fig. 5 — Increasing potential sun exposure by constructing a light altana over the pitched roof of the single-family house (starting, intermediate, and final stages. Drawing by author.

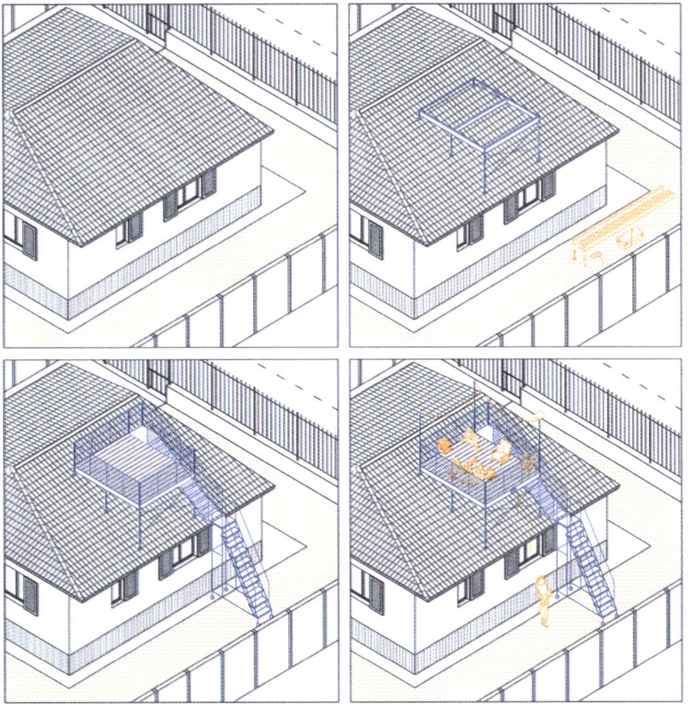

Fig. 6 — Diagram of Farnsworth House compared with its hypothetical prefabricated version as imagined by Druot, Lacaton, and Vassal (2007). Drawing by author.

roof frame. Envisioned as a standard product, the modular platform should be supported by adjustable feet to achieve a flat surface that compensates for the pitch of different roof's slopes.

As in the case of the deck platform mentioned above, this would require a simple assembly of steel, aluminum, and timber components. However, in this case, preliminary work would be necessary to identify attachment points to the roof structure, and it is likely that the assistance of a technician or artisan would be needed. Furthermore, as assembly would be conducted at a height, it would be difficult for residents to do this themselves. Weight can be kept down by combining a metal framework with wooden planks or metal grids for the railings and floor surface. In both cases, there should be enough room for water to fall back on the roof underneath to avoid bearing extra load. Access to this rooftop loggia can be either directly from the attic—adding a few steps at a dormer window—or from the outside, with a staircase set against the building with metal steps rising along the tiles to reach the new space. [Fig. 5]

A Diverse Notion of Luxury

Mille regrets Madame Farnsworth.[13]
—Frédéric Druot, Anne Lacaton, and Jean-Philippe Vassal
[Fig. 6]

Breaking down the single-family house typology into fundamental elements and standard components allows for a variety of new-design and precast components to positively impact the quality of living, even with a limited budget. As IKEA has done in the past, these components can be ordered with a little customization, delivered to one's home, and in low-risk situations (like the deck platform), assembled by residents. Upgrading of the single-family housing stock could strengthen residents' sense of belonging. However, these affordable interventions using modular furnishings and building components are not currently on the market. The research conducted here intends to expose an unexplored demand and push relevant industries towards the development of a new range of products.

In the furniture industry, many manufacturers like IKEA have raised the bar by distributing standardized modular furniture at scale. This type of furniture combines aesthetic

13. Frédéric Druot, Anne Lacaton, Jean-Philippe Vassal, *Plus* (Barcelona: Editorial Gustavo Gili, 2007), p. 49.

14. David Cheshire, *The Handbook to Building a Circular Economy* (Newcastle-upon-Tyne: RIBA Publishing, 2021).

15. Druot, Lacaton, Vassal, *Plus*, pp. 41–43.

qualities, standardization, and partial customization. Regarding interior fittings, affordable, high-quality solutions have become the norm, strengthening market appeal without sacrificing the economy of mass production. Kitchens, bookshelves, and wardrobes are suitable to incorporate a range of modular elements chosen from a catalog into a fixed support, adopting a "plug-in" approach. Picturing how a similar set of building components could upgrade single-family houses, we could assume that they would belong to a verified low-carbon production chain and share a reversible dry-assembly construction technique, allowing for future reuse.[14]

This quantum leap in standardized elements could play a key role in the "light" recovery of the residential stock, partially recalling the work that Druot, Lacaton, and Vassal have done in the rehabilitation of postwar collective housing. By provocatively reimagining Ludwig Mies van der Rohe's Farnsworth House built out of cheap, precast building components—making it into little more than a container—the French architects implicitly highlight the risks of mass production and downward standardization. Conversely, in their renovation projects, they refer to the concept of luxury, which they interpret unconventionally and see as preferable to the more generic concept of "quality" when speaking of domestic spaces. Anne Lacaton argues:

> The notion of luxury implies offering a plus when tackling a concrete situation. That is to say revealing the unexpected and letting it be implemented, a plus that is scarcely imaginable for other people and not at all for ourselves. It is not a static idea. It enables the modification of a given circumstance to be addressed.[15]

In the challenging process of taking over a second-hand house, the search for luxury matches the idea of intervening into the elements of a house. A sense of domestic well-being can be cultivated from elements such as: a welcoming, furnished window where one can sit and read a book; a fence that can open or close to the neighborhood; a rooftop loggia with a view for taking a break; a multipurpose open-air strip; or a furnished deck that extends the living room into the garden where one can sit with friends and family, work, or relax.

APPENDICES

Michela Bassanelli is an Assistant Professor in Interior Architecture and Exhibition Design at Politecnico di Milano. Her research focuses on domestic interiors, museography, and practices for sharing collective memory through multidisciplinary approaches. Recently, her work has examined the impact of the COVID-19 pandemic on contemporary living and working spaces. Her recent publications include *Gli spazi delle donne. Casa, lavoro, società* (co-authored with Imma Forino, DeriveApprodi, 2024), *Abitare oltre la casa. Metamorfosi del domestico* (DeriveApprodi, 2022), and "In Praise of Fabric: Italian Interior Design and Its Women 1923–1957," *RADDAR* 2 (2020).

Rebecca Carrai is a Postdoctoral Researcher at the Kunsthistorisches Institut in Florenz – Max Planck and co-chair of the EAHN Interest Group "Building Word Image." She holds a PhD in Architectural History from KU Leuven's Faculty of Architecture, where she examined global domestic interiors through the lens of IKEA, the world's largest furnishing corporation. Her research explores the intersection of capitalism and architecture, covering interior design, material culture, media studies, philosophy, and anthropology. Her recent works include "Normalizing the Home. A Synchronic Comparison Between the Ikea Catalogue and God Bostad," *Studies in History and Theory of Architecture* 9, (2021), and "The Materialisation of Bauhaus in IKEA's Democratic Design," in *Bauhaus × IKEA: Legacies of Modernism*, eds. Thea Brejzek, Rochus Urban Hinkel, and Lawrence Wallen (Uro Publications, 2022).

Céline Drozd is a Researcher at the Graduate School of Architecture of Nantes, specializing in the sensory qualities of inhabited spaces, with a particular focus on the energy transition process. Drawing on her experience in teaching architecture, her recent work also focuses on how to teach the design of housing interiors and environmental conditions. She currently coordinates a research project aimed at developing educational tools for teaching lighting design through innovative digital technologies. She recently published "Pédagogie des ambiances dans la formation architecturale: la référence comme support de connaissances," *Platéia* 4 (2024).

Gabriel Cuéllar is an Assistant Professor of Architecture at the University of Michigan. His work focuses on the role of architecture in land politics, contemporary environmental challenges, and struggles for spatial and housing justice. Together with Athar Mufreh, Gabriel directs Cadaster, a design practice concerned with supporting organizations driving systemic change. He has recently published "Virtues of Proximity: The Spatial Coordination of Community Land Trusts," *Footprint* 29 (2022), and "Property as Practice: The Collective Landholding Patterns of Black Churches," in *Urban Space Unsettled: Routines, Temporalities, and Contestations*, eds. Tihomir Viderman, Sabine Knierbein, Elina Kränzle, Sybille Frank, Nikolai Roskamm, and Ed Wall, (Routledge, 2022).

Lawrence Davis is an Associate Professor in Architecture at Syracuse University, where he is a past Undergraduate Chair and coordinator of Architecture for SU Florence, and currently directs Lawrence Davis Architects. His research, design and teaching gravitate around the study of the exurban built environment and the underlying social, cultural, and technical circumstances. His writings include the book *Rewriting Exurbia: New People in Aging Sprawl* (List Lab, 2024), the chapter "Philip Johnson's Crystal Cathedral and the Rhetoric of its Free-Form Polyhedron Structure," in *Beyond the Cube: The Architecture of Space Frames and Polyhedra*, ed. J. Francois Gabriel (John Wiley & Sons, Inc., 1997), and articles in blogs, journals, and newspapers such as *Architecture Player, Architects Bulletin, Foglio, Journal of Architectural Education, Architext, Architettura,* and the *Syracuse Post-Standard*.

Ester Gisbert Alemany is a Research Fellow in Architectural Design at the University of Alicante. Her current research focuses on the evolution of coastal landscapes in the Mediterranean area and the urbanization processes derived from tourism. Her writings include "From Land Ownership to Caring for Water: Some Lessons from a Flooded Costa Blanca," in *Urban Liquefaction: Rethinking the Relationship between Land and Sea*, eds. Cristián Simonetti, Michel Lussault, and Tim Ingold (Punctum Books, 2025), and "Towards an Architecture in-gens: Learning, 'Tejiendo la Calle', new tools for participation in architectural projects" (co-authored with Enrique Nieto Fernández and Marina Fernández Ramos), *RITA* 19 (2023).

Hilde Heynen is a Professor of Architectural theory at the Department of Architecture, KU Leuven. Her research focuses on issues of modernity, modernism, and gender in architecture. In *Architecture and Modernity. A Critique* (MIT Press, 1999), she investigated the relationship between architecture, modernity and dwelling, arguing that critical theories such as those of Walter Benjamin and Theodor Adorno offer crucial insights when revisiting the Modern Movement. She also engaged with the intersection between architecture and gender studies, resulting, among other publications, in the volume *Negotiating Domesticity. Spatial productions of gender in modern architecture* (co-edited with Gulsum Baydar, Routledge, 2005). Her intellectual biography of Sibyl Moholy-Nagy, *Sibyl Moholy-Nagy. Architecture, Modernism and its Discontent* has been published by Bloomsbury (2019).

Rory Hyde is an Associate Professor of Architecture (curatorial design and practice) at the University of Melbourne. His work is focused on new forms of design practice for the public good and redefining the role of the architect today. His writing on architecture and the future of design practice has been featured in various newspapers and journals including *The Economist, The Guardian, Harvard Design Magazine, Domus*, and *Icon*. He is the author of *Future Practice: Conversations from the Edge of Architecture* (Routledge, 2012), co-editor of *Architects After Architecture: Alternative Pathways for Practice* (with Roberta Marcaccio and Harriet Harriss, Routledge, 2021), and has recently guest-edited an issue of *Architecture Australia* on the theme of the suburbs.

Fabio Lepratto is an Assistant Professor in Architectural Design at Politecnico di Milano. His research and design activity focuses on housing retrofitting, the production of affordable housing, and the regeneration of post-WWII residential compounds. His writings include *Ground Level-scape. Mass-Housing Adaptive Design Strategies in Italy* (co-authored with Lavinia Dondi, Elena Fontanella and Michele Morganti, Listlab, 2022), *Trasformare Case e Quartieri. Temi progetti e strumenti per la rigenerazione della residenza collettiva* (Maggioli, 2021), and "Housing Bricolage: Tools for Manipulating Post-War Collective Housing," *DASH* 14 (2018).

Kateryna Malaia is an Assistant Professor of Architecture at the University of Utah. She studies the evolution of quotidian architecture in times of change through the lenses of cultural practices and material culture, particularly in relation to the collapse of the USSR. As part of her interest in change, she also examines architectural transformations brought forth by housing insecurity in the United States. Malaia's articles have appeared in *East/West, PLATFORM, Architectural Histories*, and the *Journal of the Society of Architectural Historians*. She is the author of two books: *Taking the Soviet Union Apart Room by Room* (NIUP/Cornell UP, 2023) and *Mass Housing in Ukraine* (co-authored with Philipp Meuser, DOM Publishers, 2024).

Athar Mufreh is a Lecturer in Architecture and Urban Design at the University of Michigan. Her pedagogy and research engage with spatial adaptation, cooperative practices, and heritage preservation. Prior to pursuing an academic career, Athar worked as a designer and researcher at the Storefront for Art and Architecture, the New York City Landmarks Preservation Commission, the United Nations Relief and Works Agency for Palestinian Refugees, Decolonizing Architecture Art Residency, and the Bethlehem Center for Cultural Heritage Preservation. Together with Gabriel Cuéllar, she directs Cadaster, a design practice concerned with supporting organizations driving systemic change. Among their recent work is a project to revitalize agricultural commons and kinship relationships in Palestinian villages. Athar's publications include, "Private Citizenship: Real Estate Practices in Palestine," *Humanities* 6, no. 3 (2017).

Daniel Siret is a Senior Researcher at the Graduate School of Architecture of Nantes, France. His research focuses on the integration of sensitive dimensions in the design of the built environment, with a particular emphasis on the architectural and urban expressions of climate. His recent publications include "Microscale Thermal Variations in a Walkable Urban Area During Hot Days: Analysis Through Mobile Measurements and Day PET Signatures" (co-authored with Ignacio Requena-Ruiz and Thomas Leduc), *Building and Environment* 267 (2025), "Designing Thermal-Sensitive Public Spaces: An Analysis Through Urban Design Media" (co-authored with Ignacio Requena-Ruiz, Xenia Stavropulos-Laffaille, and Thomas Leduc), *Journal of Urban Design* 28, no. 1 (2022), *Experiential Walks for Urban Design. Revealing, Representing, and Activating the Sensory Environment* (co-edited with Barbara E. A. Piga and Jean-Paul Thibaud, Springer Nature, 2021).

Martino Tattara is a Professor at the Technische Universität Darmstadt, where he leads the Institute of Design and Housing. His research and teaching explore the transformation of domestic space in response to contemporary socio-economic challenges. Before joining TU Darmstadt, he taught at the Faculty of Architecture at KU Leuven. In addition to his academic role, Tattara co-directs Dogma, a Brussels-based architectural practice. His publications include *Living and Working* (co-authored with Pier Vittorio Aureli, MIT Press, 2022), and *Loveless* (co-authored with Pier Vittorio Aureli, Black Square 2020). Most recently, he co-edited *Contested Legacies* (with Andrea Migotto, Leuven University Press, 2023), a volume addressing the transformation of post-war large-scale housing estates.

Federico Zanfi is an Associate Professor in Urban Planning at Politecnico di Milano. His research and design activity gravitates around the transformation of contemporary cities and territories with a focus on the adaption of the residential heritage facing social change and transition issues. His publications include "The città abusiva in Contemporary Southern Italy," *Urban Studies* 50, no. 16 (2013), "The Family House and its Territories in Contemporary Italy: Present Conditions and Future Perspectives" (co-authored with Chiara Merlini), *Journal of Urbanism* 7, no. 3 (2014), *Post-War Middle-Class Housing. Models, Construction and Change* (co-edited with Gaia Caramellino, Peter Lang, 2015), "A Portrait of Italian 'Family houses': Diversified Heritage in a Redefined Territorial and Demographic Context" (co-authored with Chiara Merlini, Viviana Giavarini, and Fabio Manfredini), *City, Territory and Architecture*, 7, no. 20 (2020).

Redesigning the Single-Family House: A Critical Look Back, and a Glance Forward

1. Courtesy of Dennis R. Holloway, University of Minnesota
2. Courtesy of Paola Viganò and Chiara Cavalieri
3. Courtesy of OpenScope Studio
4. Courtesy of ReHousing, University of Toronto tuf lab, and LGA Architectural Partners
5. © VG Bild-Kunst, Bonn
6. Courtesy of Lars Lerup
7. a. Courtesy of Guthrie + Buresh Architects. b.-c. Courtesy of Guthrie + Buresh Architects and Tom Bonner Photography.
8. From Peter Katz, *The New Urbanism: Towards an Architecture of Community* (New York: McGraw-Hill, 1994), pp. 135 and 140.
9. From Galina Tachieva, *Sprawl Repair Manual* (Washington: Island Press, 2010), pp. 80.
10. a.-b. Courtesy of MOS Architects. c.-d. Courtesy of WORKac Architects.
11. From Dolores Hayden, "What Would a Non-Sexist City Be Like? Speculations on Housing, Urban Design, and Human Work," *Signs* 5, no. 3 (1980): pp. 184–85.
12. Courtesy of Cadaster.

The Single-Family Home in Flanders: The Emergence and Decline of a Popular Housing Type

1. © KADOC Documentatie- en Onderzoekscentrum voor Religie, Cultuur en Samenleving (Belgium).
2. © KADOC Documentatie- en Onderzoekscentrum voor Religie, Cultuur en Samenleving (Belgium).
3. Courtesy of Martino Tattara.
4. Creative Commons Attribution 4.0 International license.
5. Courtesy of Martino Tattara.

Domestic Spaces, Family Models, and Gender Roles: Investigating the Imaginary of the Villetta Housing Type in Italy

1. a. From *Villette moderne. Esempi di architettura di ville con studi, progetti, realizzazioni* (Milan: Görlich, 1967). b. From Mario Ravegnani Morosini, *La casa individuale in Italia* (Milan: Görlich, 1957). c. From *Ville—Casette al mare, al lago, in collina, in montagna* (Milan: Görlich, 1971).
2. a. From *House Beautiful*, no. 7 (1955): pp. 93. b. From House Beautiful, no. 7 (1955): pp. 89.
3. © Archivio Storico Fondazione Fiera Milano.
4. From *Grazia*, no. 947 (1959): cover.
5. From *Grazia* no. 947 (1959): pp. 65 and 74.
6. © Archivio Storico Fondazione Fiera Milano.
7. © Fondazione La Triennale di Milano, Triennale di Milano – Archivi.
8. From *Grazia* no. 896 (1958): pp. 94.
9. From *Annabella* no. 15 (1961).
10. From *A. Attualità Architettura Abitazione Arte* no. 1, 4, 5, 7 (1946).

The IKEA Suburb: A Cataloged Imagery of Single-Family Housing

1. © The Museum of Modern Art, New York and Scala, Florence.
2.–6. © Inter IKEA Systems B. V.
8.–9. © Inter IKEA Systems B. V.

Mixing Metabolisms: New People in Aging North American Sprawl

1. © William Cooper Center for Public Service, University of Virginia, Charlottesville.
3. Courtesy of Chenhao Luo and Zhi Zheng.
4. © Zillow Group, Inc.
6. Courtesy of Chenhao Luo and Zhi Zheng.
7. Courtesy of Chenhao Luo and Zhi Zheng.
9. Courtesy of Bridgecreek, Real Estate Agency.
10. Courtesy of Chenhao Luo and Xinyu Tang.
11. Courtesy of Clay Larsen.
12. Courtesy of Chenhao Luo and Zhi Zheng.
13. Courtesy of James Rojas.
14. Courtesy of Chenhao Luo and Xinyu Tang.
15. Courtesy of Chenhao Luo and Xinyu Tang.
16. Courtesy of Estudio Teddy Cruz and Fonna Forman.

Balancing Energy Challenge Adaptation and Heritage Preservation: The Evolution of Single-family Homes in 1950s Residential France

2. © Google Maps 2023.
3. © Léon Péneau Architect.

Summer House Transformations: New Trends in How Families Enjoy the Mediterranean Landscape in Costa Blanca

1. © Institut Cartogràfic Valencià (gva.es).
2.–3. Courtesy of Drassana Architects.
4. © Institut Cartogràfic Valencià (gva.es).
5.–7. Courtesy of Drassana Architects.
8.–10. Courtesy of Cor&Asociados.
11. Courtesy of Fernando Gosalbez.
12–20. Courtesy of Drassana Architects.

Slack Spaces: Informal Transformation in Melbourne's Single-Family Housing

1. Courtesy of John Gollings.
5. Courtesy of Anna O'Gorman Architects.
7. Courtesy of Tom Ross.
8. Courtesy of Derek Swalwell.
9. Courtesy of Lian Architects.
10. Courtesy of Feld 72.
11. Courtesy of Jamal Tompkinson.

What's Next for Mom and Dad's House?

Vol. 1
Essays on the Single-Family Housing
Type and Its Future

Edited by
Martino Tattara and Federico Zanfi

Editorial assistance
Robert Stürzl, Anne König

Graphic design
Filippo Nostri

Translation
Krista Schmidtke (chapter by Céline Drozd
and Daniel Siret)

Copyediting
Nick Axel, Victoria Nebolsin

Proofreading
Anne König

Printing
Druckhaus Sportflieger, Berlin

The publication has been peer-reviewed

Published by
Spector Books Verlagsgesellschaft mbH
Harkortstraße 10
04107 Leipzig
www.spectorbooks.com

Distribution
Germany, Austria: GVA, Gemeinsame Verlagsauslieferung
Göttingen GmbH&Co. KG, www.gva-verlage.de
Switzerland: AVA Verlagsauslieferung AG, www.ava.ch
France, Belgium: Interart Paris, www.interart.fr
UK: Central Books Ltd, www.centralbooks.com
USA, Canada, Central and South America, Africa:
ARTBOOK/ D.A.P., www.artbook.com
South Korea: The Book Society, www.thebooksociety.org
Japan: twelvebooks, www.twelve-books.com
Australia, New Zealand: Perimeter Distribution,
www.perimeterdistribution.com

© 2024, for all texts the authors and editors, for all images
the photographers, Spector Books, Leipzig
First edition: 2024
Printed in Germany

ISBN 978-3-95905-816-2